The Competent Cook

INCLUDES 150+ NEW BASICS FOR TODAY'S KITCHEN!

ESSENTIAL TOOLS, TECHNIQUES, AND RECIPES FOR THE MODERN AT-HOME COOK

Lauren Braun Costello

Chef, Culinary Instructor, Food Writer

Adamsmedia

Avon, Massachusetts

Published by
Adams Media, a division of F+W Media, Inc.
57 Littlefield Street, Avon, MA 02322. U.S.A.
www.adamsmedia.com

ISBN 10: 1-60550-145-X
ISBN 13: 978-1-60550-145-1

Printed in the United States of America.

J I H G F E D C B A

Library of Congress Cataloging-in-Publication Data
available from the publisher.

This publication is designed to provide accurate and authoritative information with
regard to the subject matter covered. It is sold with the understanding that the publisher is not engaged in rendering legal, accounting, or other professional advice. If
legal advice or other expert assistance is required, the services of a competent professional person should be sought.
— From a *Declaration of Principles* jointly adopted by a Committee of the
American Bar Association and a Committee of Publishers and Associations

Many of the designations used by manufacturers and sellers to distinguish their product are claimed as trademarks. Where those designations appear in this book and
Adams Media was aware of a trademark claim, the designations have been printed
with initial capital letters.

Interior art by Eric Andrews.

*This book is available at quantity discounts for bulk purchases.
For information, please call 1-800-289-0963.*

Dedication

For my father, competence personified.

competent \com·pe·tent\

adjective: having requisite or adequate abilities

[as in *competent* cook]; specifically having the capacity to be:

organized: plan ahead, appreciate the structured process

clean: hold a high standard of sanitation

neat: abhor clutter, know where things are

thrifty: avoid wasting food and resources

efficient: take time to save time, group like tasks

informed: seek information on tools, techniques, and recipes

joyful: understand that cooking is about giving and receiving pleasure

Acknowledgments

The Competent Cook has been a work in progress for many years. I could not have written it without the support and encouragement of many people. I offer my sincerest gratitude and heartfelt thanks to:

Molly Lyons, my agent and friend, for your abiding belief in this project. There would be no book without your brilliant ideas, unfailing encouragement, and steady persistence.

Noel Volpe, for your devoted friendship, magnificent generosity, and two quiet, comfortable places to work. I literally could not have done this without you.

Russell Reich, for your devoted friendship, skilled editing, and undying support to the finish line. Your encouragement and insights have impacted every page.

Meredith O'Hayre, Laura Daly, and everyone at Adams Media, for all your efforts on behalf of the book, especially your enthusiasm.

Brent and Valerie Whitmore of CDKitchen.com for first publishing my food column, "The Competent Cook," which became the inspiration for this book.

All my teachers and colleagues who helped make me a competent cook: Barbara Braun, Grandpa Ted, Aunt Candy, Nana, Chef Henri, Chef Sixto, Chef Roger, Chef Michel Nischan, Maggie Odell, Liliana Scali, Ashley O'Neal, Kim Pistone, Rian Smolik, Tim Shaw, Julie Negrin, and Irene Yager.

My many students who have influenced and inspired this book, in particular, the Borenstein Family, Judy Goodman, Anne Grossman, Nicole Putzel, and Ellen Schwarzman.

Very special thanks to Dorothy Cann Hamilton and Penelope Pate Greene for believing in me.

To my family and friends, I am indebted to you for carrying me through all the hard work with support and love:

Ken and Hara Braun, Alexandra Bruskoff, Yolanda M. Chendak, Marcia S. Cohen, Nicole and Lucas Carrasco, Dana B. Davis, Paula Dolson, Betsy Feinstein, Charlotte and Bernard Feinstein, Limor Geller, Lara Glazier, Kathy Goldstein, Timothy P. Graf, Carol

Leibenson, Tamara McKenna, Maureen Bennett O'Connor, Joan S. Richter, Zibby Right, Lindsay Smithen, Rachel L. Spector, and Paula E. Vayas.

To my husband, Sean: thank you not only for supporting my dream in every way possible, but for awakening it in me. Without you, there never would have been a "Chef Lauren." I will love you always.

To my son, Jonathan: thank you for being such a delicious boy! Feeding you is my greatest pleasure. But you feed me even more with your affection, wonder, and unabashed joy. I love you more than you could ever know.

To my father, Ken: thank you for making me a better writer, for all your loving and supportive guidance, and for coming up with the very clever title, *The Competent Cook*.

To my sister, Nicole: thank you for your love and support (and the beautiful photo!).

To Fanny Lopez and Lili Sandoval: thank you for taking such good care of Jonathan with love and devotion, being so flexible, and making it possible for me to work on this book without worry.

Contents

Part 2 ✳ Essential Recipes..........105

Introduction

AS A COOK, you likely crave the essential cooking knowledge that will lead to competence in the kitchen. You're probably wondering: What do I need to have? What do I need to know? What do I need to do?

Cooking is such a personal pursuit. Only *you* fully understand your tastes, comfort, skills, environment, routine, and budget. Yet in a marketplace that has every conceivable gadget, on a culinary information superhighway of encyclopedic proportions, and with a bottomless global print and web recipe database, it's hard to recognize what is essential.

The Competent Cook identifies what you must have, what you should know, and what you ought to do to be considered a competent cook. Yes, you can find a wide variety of resources that cover every conceivable aspect of cooking. They are both useful and worthwhile. Bigger is not better, though, and more is not always more helpful. This book only concerns itself with the *essential* elements of cooking in two component parts: tools and techniques, and recipes. It is designed to answer: "What do you *really* need to know?"

As a chef and caterer, I have come to realize that with all the tools accessible to me, I rely on very few items to execute virtually every cooking task I encounter. As a cooking instructor, when eager students ask me what equipment they need, or what knives I recommend, my answers always go back to what I actually use day in and day out, both professionally and personally. These answers are the foundation of *The Competent Cook*.

Sure, I have my preferred pots and pans (I love my All-Clad stainless steel 10-inch sauté pan and my Le Creuset enameled cast iron Dutch oven), and favorite knives (my Kyocera 5-inch white ceramic chef's knife is so sharp, and beautiful, too). But what is best for me in my kitchen with my needs might not be ideal for you. For that reason, I do not usually recommend brands. I think it's best for you to learn what is required, understand the attributes of those items, and then do your own choosing, taking your unique tastes and newly acquired knowledge into consideration.

This book provides a thorough explanation of the fundamentals. If you obtain the basics listed here, and achieve proficiency with these methods and recipes, you will experience many of the countless pleasures of cooking: the confidence, enjoyment, and sense of accomplishment that only true *competence* can unleash.

Part 1

Essential Tools and Techniques

A CUPBOARD OF COUNTLESS POTS AND PANS. Drawers bursting with gadgets. Counters cluttered with appliances. This is not the picture of an efficient kitchen. Having the right tools and knowing what to do with them is the best way to prepare for any cooking task. "How much" is not the question, and "more" certainly is not the answer. Ask instead, "what is essential?"

Thankfully, quantity is not the end game in cooking well. The kinds of tools you use and your mastery of essential techniques (paired with the best ingredients, of course) determines the quality of the food you cook. Very little is actually needed in your cupboards and drawers. Depending on your personal affinity, only a few appliances are required to execute virtually any recipe you wish to prepare. The essential pieces are the universal baseline for *any* cook. Your skill in using those tools with your chosen ingredients is what defines your mastery of technique.

Technique is important, too. The manipulation of heat to transform food is what cooking is all about—not assembling prepackaged goods to make a meal. Your influence—your *competence*—is your unique gift that makes the food you cook "one of a kind." You might not employ equally all the essential techniques outlined in the pages that follow. Perhaps you sauté and broil more frequently than you braise or bake. Knowing how to do it all, or at least understanding the basic principles of each method, however, makes you an authentically competent cook. ❉

Kitchen Organization

THE KITCHEN IS WHERE IT ALL BEGINS. Before the recipe, the ingredients, the equipment, the cooking process, or the completed dish comes your workspace. From tiny kitchenettes to expansive center-island showpieces, the environment in which you cook defines your opportunities and limitations as a cook. How your kitchen is organized plays a major role in your cooking experience.

The Layout of Your Kitchen

The type of kitchen you have is the prime determinant of how you move in the space. Whether you have a huge kitchen with three ovens or a small closet with a mini fridge, the space you have establishes what type and the quantity of kitchenware you need. The layout and appliances also influence the cooking methods you use most frequently.

A kitchen is made of three functional components:

1. **Food storage:** refrigeration and pantry

2. **Cooking:** stove and oven

3. **Preparation and cleanup:** countertop and sink

The components are best integrated in what is known as a **working triangle**, where you move efficiently between the refrigerator, stove, and sink. The principle of triangulation makes any kitchen layout as functional as possible because it centers your workspace and limits superfluous movement.

Expansive kitchens are often less efficient workspaces because the working triangles are so huge that you'll feel as if the triangle doesn't even exist. Like a large closet, a giant kitchen is easy to fill, and since there is abundant space, the same choices do not need to be made as with smaller kitchens—choices that can make you a more competent cook.

If size does not determine how well a kitchen functions, what does? The equipment you have and the way it is organized defines the workspace. The first step in getting organized is understanding what kind of layout you have.

There are five basic kitchen plans.

Single-wall

In a single-wall kitchen, all the appliances, cabinets, and counter space are on one wall. This kitchen design is generally due to space constraints and has no functional benefit to the cooking process. Since there is no working triangle, it's not easy to work in because you have to shuffle back and forth along one line.

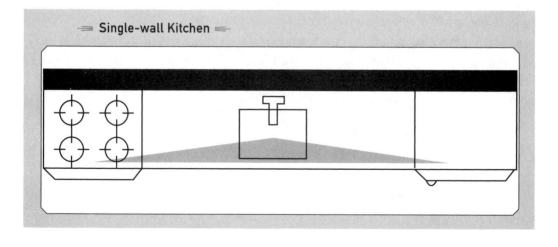

Single-wall Kitchen

L-shaped

In an L-shaped kitchen, two connecting walls form a right angle, and thus a triangle. The main workspace tends to be in the heart of the right angle, with the equipment pushed more toward the ends. The corners are good for deep storage, such as rotating, round "lazy susan" shelves.

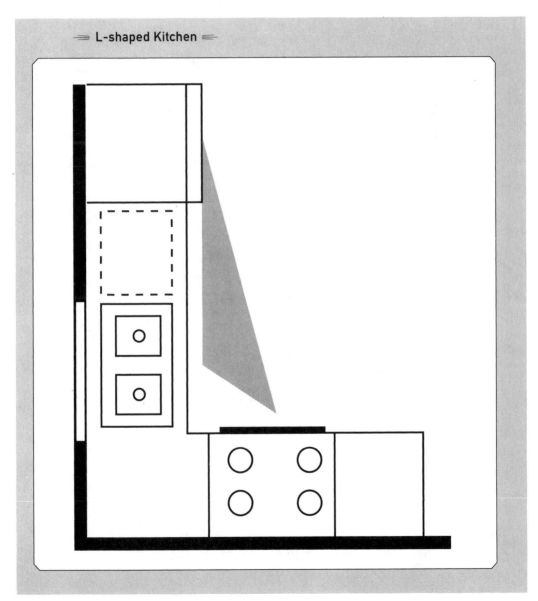

L-shaped Kitchen

Galley

This is a "corridor" kitchen with the cabinets and appliances on opposing, facing walls. It makes the best use of small spaces, and is an exceptional example of triangulation even for large spaces. No matter the size, a galley is basically a hallway, with two points of the triangle on one wall, limiting excessive movement. If too wide, then a galley is just a room without a working triangle.

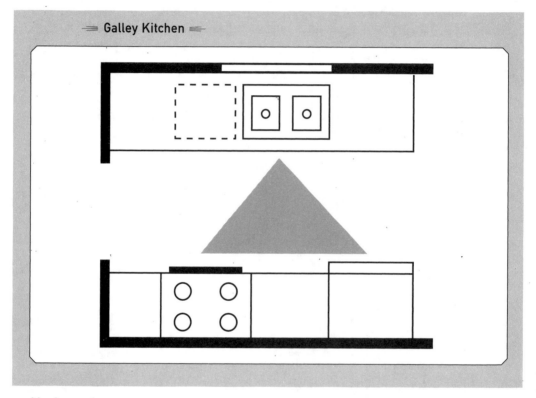

≋ Galley Kitchen ≋

U-shaped

The three-wall, horseshoe layout creates a natural working triangle, which is highly functional for serious cooks. Three adjoining walls create two corners for deep storage and ample counter space.

Island

This layout is generally a U or L with an island in the middle or at the edge. Typically spacious with abundant counter space, the island kitchen might provide multiple working triangles.

U-shaped Kitchen

Island Kitchen

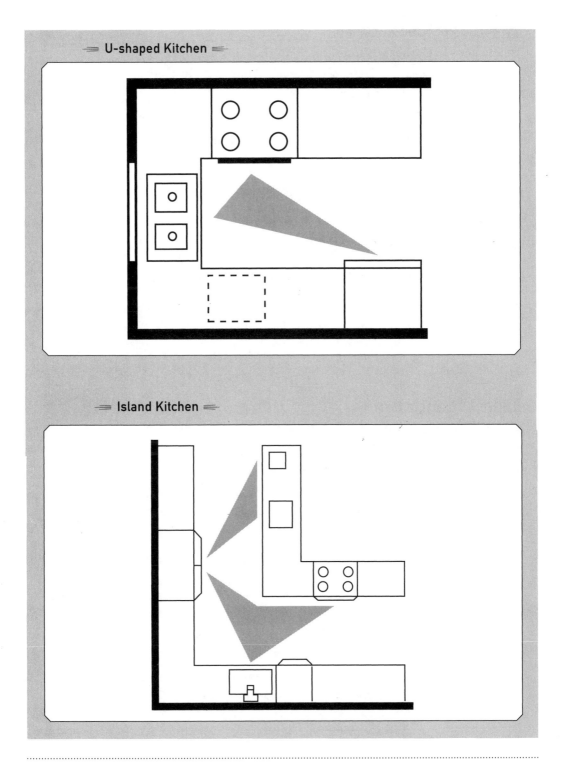

Where to Put What You Need

No matter what layout you have or its size, there is a sensible way to organize your equipment. These general guidelines apply in every kitchen, irrespective of design or activity level:

- Keep spices, oils, and implements within arm's reach of the stovetop.

- Avoid storing oils and condiments near heating elements to prevent them from going rancid quickly.

- Put oven mitts and kitchen towels right next to your heat sources.

- Pots and pans should be stored with the most frequently used pieces on top.

- Store knives in a sheath, block, or drawer tray, but never loose in a drawer.

Cabinet Organization

One of the most important things you can do to be a more competent cook is know your inventory. Be aware of the fresh foods and dry goods you have in stock, and be familiar with and have appropriate access to all your kitchenware. When you know what you have and, more important, can access it easily, you make the right ingredient and equipment choices as you cook in your kitchen.

The Rule of FIFO

We are inclined to use only what is in front of our faces, or what comes to mind when we are planning to cook. However, you'll make better choices if you follow the rule of First In, First Out, or FIFO. Store your perishables with the oldest in front and the newest in back. Along those lines, you should make it a habit of rotating nonperishables from time to time to ensure that you are aware of your full inventory and making the most of it.

The same is true for the freezer and the pantry. Move items in the back to the front so you see what you have. Have you been buying jars of tomato sauce all this time only to discover that you already had two hidden behind some boxes of pasta? Use what you already have, then buy more. You'll avoid clutter, spend money more wisely, and waste less food.

Give Like Items the Same Home

Many people tend to spread kitchen equipment around to make use of all the cabinets available, especially in spacious kitchens. This is not necessarily the best option. It makes much more sense to have all the sauté pans and saucepans on one shelf, for example, than to disperse them between two or more cupboards. If you open Cabinet 1 to find that a certain sauté pan is not there, you will waste time hunting for it in Cabinet 2. Condensing like items also helps with cleanup, since you automatically intuit where to store things when you finish using them.

Identify the Equipment You Use Most Frequently

Placing plastic storage containers high on a shelf out of reach and stacked mixing bowls buried deep below the counter is an inefficient use of space. Your kitchen should not make you work harder—it should be organized to make you work smarter, and ultimately work *for* you.

If you live in a one- or two-person household and end up with leftovers every time you cook, do not keep the storage containers in an impractical spot. If you love to make pasta, why not store the pots and strainers either above the counter at eye level for easy reach, or below the counter at the top of the pile of larger items?

Storing pots and pans can be a challenge because managing the lids that match is often an onerous task. Arrange pot covers and lids in a lid rack on a separate shelf, adjacent to the stacked pots. The separate and designated lid and pot areas prevent tumbling piles every time you reach in to grab a particular piece.

Ask Questions, Then Make Changes

Identify the way you eat and cook, then make the equipment needed available to you to prepare those meals easily. Do you eat lots of salads?

Don't bury your mixing bowls deep within your saucepans. Are you a frequent baker? Place all your muffin tins and cake pans in a place where you can reach them without any frustration. Assess your kitchen real estate, as well as your cooking and eating needs, and then assign storage space for your equipment accordingly. Put the items you use most frequently someplace you can reach easily.

Once you view your kitchen like a workspace, you'll be able to organize it with ease. No one would ever store the telephone in the filing cabinet, or the keyboard on the desk chair. Think of your kitchen inventory as the tools you need to make a meal proficiently and successfully. With a new and improved order, you will become a more competent cook.

tThere are still other considerations to understanding your kitchen layout and knowing your food and equipment inventory. The kitchen's energy sources—even its relationship to the rest of your home—play a role in how you cook.

Gas or Electric

Which is better? There are discernable benefits to both, especially depending on the heat source in question.

Gas stoves provide the greatest control over heat adjustment since the flame is visible and responds instantly to your changes. However, they have many component parts to clean. Newer electric stovetops by comparison are easier to clean thanks to the flat, smooth surface. But the residual heat is slower to dissipate on an electric stove, which makes the heat source in general more challenging to control. That is, the conduction surface of an electric stove gets very hot quickly, but takes much longer to cool down. There are now induction stoves that do not provide any heat at all per se; instead, they produce a magnetic wave above the surface, and require induction cookware with magnetic bases to create the heat. This heat is almost instantaneous and more controllable than regular electric stovetop heat.

convection is just a bunch of hot air

Convection ovens use the physical movement of hot air to blow heat from the source to the food. All ovens have some small amount of convection naturally taking place, but ovens labeled "convection" have amplified air circulation. That means possible shorter cooking times or lower oven temperatures from what the recipe says.

The general consensus on gas ovens versus electric is the opposite. The coils of electric ovens tend to provide more even heat, which aids in browning roasts beautifully and baking breads uniformly. The flame heat of a gas oven cooks food less evenly and less predictably.

Neither gas nor electric heat will make you a better cook. Understanding the heat sources you have and learning how to work *with* them will make you a far more competent one. A recipe made in one kitchen might come out differently in another; the cook's sensibilities, the equipment used, and the heat source are just some of the dozens of factors that play a role.

Cook for the Kitchen You Have

When you buy a piece of beef, you should consider many issues: the number of people you need to feed, your budget, the cut of meat you prefer, and the cooking method you will use. Believe it or not, your kitchen and its appliances also should be a part of your thinking.

Why? If you have a kitchen with no windows right next to your bedroom, broiling a large bone-in rib eye steak is likely not the best idea. Smoke might fill the oven chamber and subsequently the kitchen, flowing right into your sleep space. Perhaps a better choice would be to stir-fry some London broil or braise some short ribs on the stove. That's how you consider the pluses and minuses of *your* kitchen space, and then make wise choices when you cook. ❉

a must-have that hopefully you never have to use

Every kitchen must have a fire extinguisher. There are no exceptions. If you do not have one, go out and buy one immediately. May you never need to use it, but if you do you'll be so thankful you have it.

* Chef's Knife
* Paring Knife
* Bread Knife
* Cutting Board
* Can Opener
* Spatula
* Wooden Spoon

* Ladle
* Tongs
* Peeler
* Kitchen Shears
* Sauté Pans
* Baking Pan
* Sheet Pan

* Saucepan
* Stockpot
* Strainer
* Measuring Cups and Spoons
* Mixing Bowls
* Whisk

The Essential Tools

THERE ARE SO MANY KITCHEN GADGETS available on the market today, it can be hard to know which ones you must have. Surely you do not need the wand that "magically" slices avocado right out of the shell. Do not take a second look at that gizmo shaped like a grid that dices onions *for* you. The preposterousness of the single-task kitchen toy was best satirized in the first "Bridget Jones" movie when Bridget's mother resorts to selling a hard-boiled egg-peeling trinket at the local department store. Do we really need a separate tool for each and every task?

For centuries, competent cooks have produced exceptional results with limited equipment. As Julia Child used to say, your hands are your best tool in the kitchen. Professional cooks do not use garlic presses, asparagus baskets, or tomato knives. A garlic press actually wastes garlic and is a nuisance to clean when all you have to do is smash the clove with the flat side of your chef's knife, peel, and chop. Asparagus baskets are just as silly when you already have a large and deep saucepan to use. When it comes to cutting tomatoes or nearly anything else, the very sharp edge of a well-maintained chef's knife does the job every time.

Space is always at a premium in any kitchen. Nothing could be more wasteful than throwing away time and money along with precious storage real estate. So what does every cook need in order to function? What are the truly essential tools?

"The Essential Top 20" outlines what every kitchen must have at a bare minimum. Whether you dabble between toaster waffles and boxed macaroni and cheese, or sample all the new recipes from your favorite monthly food magazine, the following list is your essential cooking equipment.

⇒ THE ESSENTIAL TOP 20 ⇐

Chef's Knife

If there were room in the world for only one kitchen tool, it would be the knife. Conceptually, knives have been around for at least two million years, dating back to a time when a sharp-edged stone or jagged seashell was a hot commodity. With the onset of the Iron Age only a few thousand years ago, the sharp, strong metallic blade was born.

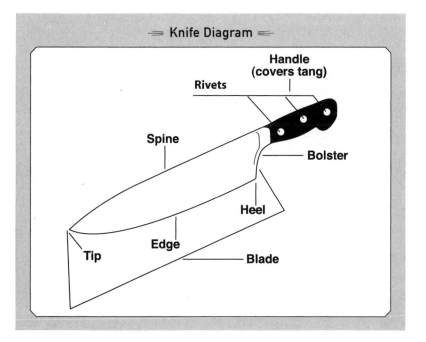

⇒ Knife Diagram ⇐

Knives come in all shapes and sizes, crafted for a variety of uses ranging from chopping to slicing, but the components of a knife are universal:

- **Blade**—the cutting apparatus of a knife, from the tip to the heel

- **Bolster**—the finger guard with which you grip the knife using your thumb and index finger

- **Edge**—the sharp bottom of the blade

- **Handle**—the part of the knife you hold with your last three fingers

- **Heel**—the opposite end of the blade from the tip

- **Rivets**—the pins that hold together the tang and handle

- **Spine**—the top of the blade

- **Tang**—the part of the blade that extends into the handle

- **Tip**—the pointy end of the blade

The chef's, or cook's, knife is the most indispensable culinary tool in both home and professional kitchens. Its primary function, to chop, is accomplished by pinching the bolster with the index finger and thumb while rocking the blade back and forth on the cutting board.

The blade size can range from 5 to 14 inches, but the 8-inch knife is the most common and versatile. Regardless of size, the blade should be deep and somewhat heavy with a straight edge. A deep blade makes it easier to hold the knife properly, and is also more effective in cutting large pieces of food. Full-tang knives (when the blade extends all the way to the end of the handle) provide the best support to the blade.

Shapes vary as well. A traditional western chef's knife has a blade that gradually curves upward with a sharp point at the tip, which allows the knife to rock back and forth across the board. A Japanese chef's knife, called a santoku knife, has a flat edge with a blade that curves downward at the tip (sheepsfoot-style). Many people incorrectly associate santoku knives with hollowed indents along the blade that keep food from sticking to it as the knife cuts. It is the shape of the blade, not a scalloped surface pattern, that defines a santoku knife (*santoku* means "three virtues," as in slicing, dicing, and mincing). The blades of both western and Japanese chef's knives can have hollowed edges to help food fall away easily.

Chef's knives come in a range of materials: low-carbon steel, stainless steel, high-carbon stainless steel, titanium, and even ceramic. Metallic blades can be forged (heated and pounded to form) or stamped (cut to shape and size from cold rolled steel). Forged blades tend to be heavier than stamped blades—a benefit or drawback, depending on your needs. Here are some pros and cons to different materials:

- **Ceramic** blades chip easily and require special sharpening equipment, but are light, exceptionally hard, resistant to stains, stay sharp longer, and impart no flavor to food.

- **High-carbon steel** is the most popular and pervasive chef's knife material in home kitchens. The material does not rust and holds a sharp edge, but it is quite expensive.

- **Low-carbon steel**—the material of knives for centuries—hold a sharp edge, but impart a metallic flavor to food, discolors, and can even stain food.

- **Titanium**, similarly lightweight to ceramic, also imparts no flavor to food, but is not as hard as steel, and thus does not hold as sharp an edge.

Please see Appendix A for more information on knife materials.

It is far better to have one high-quality chef's knife than half a dozen low-quality knives of varying shapes and sizes. This knife will do more than chop—it will carve, slice, bone, and butcher, if need be. Select a knife that feels good in your hand and is made of a material you are comfortable caring for in the long run. Do you like a heavy handle? Check out a traditional chef's knife. Is an even weight distribution between the blade and handle more comfortable to you? Sample some santokus. Like most implements, the knife acts as an extension of your hand, so its size relative to your own is a critical consideration.

There are dozens more knives available, such as filleting knives, butcher knives, cleavers, slicers, oyster knives, and grapefruit knives, to name a few. But quantity and variety are not critical to successful results in the kitchen. The quality and sharpness of the blades, on the other hand, are key.

The key to cutting effectively is using only a sharp knife. A sharp knife does the work for you, making your motions effortless and fluid. A dull knife is ultimately very dangerous: the blade does not provide the cut, forcing you to exert your body to make the blade penetrate. If the blade is not sharp enough to anchor itself in the food, and you have to apply pressure to move through it, then you risk slipping and losing control of the knife. Prevent injury: use a sharp knife.

Never put a knife in the dishwasher, as the heat dulls the blade over time. Wash knives by hand with warm water and soap. Dry them immediately and thoroughly with a cloth or rag, from the spine to the edge, to ensure safety. Avoid scraping the knife against the cutting board repeatedly to pick up the last bits of chopping; turn the knife on its spine and use that flat surface to scrape instead. Store knives in a wooden block, sheath, or drawer tray for safekeeping. If knives are used and maintained properly, they can last a lifetime.

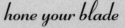

hone your blade

Every home cook should have a tool to straighten and sharpen a knife's edge after each use. Whether it is a steel or stone, a honing tool helps to maintain the investment of a good knife by realigning its edge. Sharpen your knives professionally when the edges are lost.

Paring Knife

The paring knife looks like a miniature chef's knife. The blade is typically about 3 inches long. If it is longer, it is usually called a utility knife. It can be used to slice garlic, remove a tomato core, scrape the skin off a carrot in place of a peeler, or cut eyes from a potato. Wherever the chef's knife is just too big for the job, the paring knife will do. Even though it is a small knife for small tasks, quality is still important. Look for a sturdy blade that will not chip or bend.

Bread Knife

Every cook must have one knife with a long, serrated blade that can cut through foods both crispy and delicate without crushing them. Bread knife blades resemble woodworking tools and are used with the same saw-like motion.

Unlike straight-edged knives (chef's and paring), a bread knife is not easily sharpened. Each individual serration needs to be sharpened. You can tell when you have a dull bread knife, because it tears instead of cuts. However, if you use your bread knife exclusively for its named task, wash and dry it properly, and treat it with care, you will have it for a lifetime and likely won't need to worry about sharpening it. Should it need sharpening, take it to a professional.

Cutting Board

The surface on which you cut and prepare food is as important as any tool. There are several materials available, including wood, plastic, marble, and tempered glass. The best surfaces are those in which the knife's edge anchors itself easily. This provides stability and control, two essential virtues in cutting.

Wood and plastic cutting boards are ideal work surfaces for trimming, cutting, pounding, and rolling. Both materials are soft enough for a sharp knife to grip the surface as it moves across the board. Wood boards are often thick (called butcher blocks) and give the added benefit of additional height. Plastic boards—even the thick ones—tend to be thinner than wooden boards, but are dishwasher-safe. Marble is not appropriate for any use other than baking where it serves as an exceptionally smooth and cold surface for rolling dough. Its hard composition can chip a knife's blade. Tempered glass is never a good option, as it is bumpy, hard, and slippery.

Flexible, light plastic cutting boards are excellent space savers and aid in transferring choppings to vessels. Thick, heavy wooden or plastic boards are the better choice for more substantial tasks like breaking down whole birds, carving heavy roasts, and paring large, dense fruits and vegetables.

You need only one cutting board. To that end, a large, heavy plastic board is the ideal choice since it can go in the dishwasher. Buy the biggest one you can use and store. If you have room for more than one board, buy a few in various colors for sanitation purposes to avoid cross-contamination: red for meat; blue for dairy; green for fruits and vegetables; yellow for fish.

Never put a wooden board in the dishwasher or leave it to soak in the sink; it will warp and splinter over time. Clean it with soap under running hot water. Dry it immediately.

Can Opener

No matter what kind of cook you are, your kitchen is incomplete without a can opener. Whether you live on canned soups and chili, or you often make homemade sauce from San Marzano tomatoes, you must have a can opener.

There are several kinds of can openers on the market, ranging from manual to electric. Space should be your primary concern: if limited, a regular manual can opener does the job. Large, electric can openers are appealingly easy to use, but might not be worth the space they occupy.

All can openers have a circular blade that rotates around the rim of the can. Some are designed to open cans from the side of the can instead of from the lid itself, which prevents the top from having a sharp edge that can cut you.

You can buy a basic "church key" for making holes in the tops of cans as spouts, but this kind of opener is useful exclusively for cans containing only liquid.

Spatula

Without a spatula, you cannot flip flapjacks, turn trout, or lift latkes. A standard spatula, also called a turner, is a flat piece of metal or plastic, possibly slotted, attached to a handle. If you are using a griddle, you always need a spatula. No matter how you cook pieces of fish, you need a spatula to transfer them from cooking vessel to plate.

One spatula is all you need, but there are several kinds worth considering, depending on your kitchen inventory and cooking habits. Ideally the handle should be raised or at an angle, offset from the blade, so that you can keep your hands at a distance from the heat.

The most important thing to remember is that the material of the spatula and pan should match. For example, do not use a metal spatula in a coated pan or you risk scraping and scratching the pan. Metal spatulas are for use with metal pans; heatproof plastic spatulas are a must for use with coated, nonstick surfaces.

Spatulas can be either firm or flexible, whether metal or plastic. Firm spatulas are sturdy enough to lift heavy items like burgers and crab cakes. Flexible spatulas, often curved at the end for additional control and support, aid in turning and lifting delicate items like fish filet.

Wooden Spoon

Doesn't it seem like an image of a wooden spoon is part of every cooking website or company logo out there? That's probably because the wooden spoon is the symbol of cooking. All cooking comes down to movement—that of ingredients, heat, flavors, even the cook herself. The iconic wooden spoon moves, stirs, pushes, and folds food.

Some wooden spoons are traditional hollowed orbs that do not just stir food, but gather it. Others are tapered paddles that hug the pan for increased efficiency in scraping. Short, wide handles are good for stir-frying, while long, thin handles are ideal for stirring in a deep pot. The more serious a cook you are, the greater variety of shapes and sizes you likely need.

Why wood and not metal? Wood does not conduct heat like aluminum or stainless steel (notice how you can stir a hot stew with a long wooden spoon and the handle never gets extremely hot or burns your fingers). Hardwoods like bamboo, cherry, and olive are excellent materials, as they are relatively nonporous compared to softer woods like pine. That means, if cleaned properly (no dishwasher, please), wooden spoons made from hardwoods will not break or splinter.

Wooden spoons of any kind do have one drawback: they are absorbent. They stain and smell of the foods they have touched. Do you like to cook Indian and Italian? Have one for *tikka* and one for tomato sauce. And definitely do not use either spoon for your cake batter. It is best to have a few wooden spoons on hand, especially given how essential and relatively inexpensive they are.

Ladle

There is not much to say about ladles other than that they are the necessary implement to serve soup and stew. Ladles come in stainless steel, plastic, and wood. Stainless steel is the most durable. The best ladles have deep bowls at the base of long handles that curve at the tip so the ladle can hang from the side of the pot. If you are going to own just one ladle, the ideal size is 6-ounce. There are 4- and 8-ounce ladles, too.

get choked up

Most people do not hold a ladle properly. The long handle permits the ladle to hang down in a deep pot. Do not hold the ladle from the top of that long handle. Instead, hold the ladle closest to the cup, at the bottom of the handle. This ensures greater control and fewer spills.

Tongs

Your hands are your best tool—but not when things are hot. Tongs allow you to lift and turn. The shorter the tongs, the greater control you have. But there are instances, like needing to reach across a hot grill, where a long set of tongs helps you grab the food without burning your arm.

Spring-action tongs that lock into place are fairly easy to work with and even easier to store. The spring provides resistance when you pinch, and the lock keeps the tongs closed to fit in a drawer, canister, or dishwasher basket. The downside, of course, is that such tongs can lock in place in the midst of your using them. Tongs that have a sliding ring that locks at the neck to keep them closed for storage, but slides to the bottom to open, avoid the problem of locking mid-use.

Stainless steel tongs are best as they are sturdiest, but plastic or nylon versions are also available.

Peeler

Swivel or fixed? That is the essential peeler blade question. It's all a matter of preference. The swivel blade, whether anchored vertically or horizontally in a plastic or metallic arch, adjusts with the curvature of the item being peeled, but the blade itself is straight. Think of it as power steering. A fixed blade is the original peeler, and requires more effort but yields greater control. The blade itself usually has two slits so you can peel either towards or away from yourself.

If you like to peel towards yourself, anchoring your thumb on the food, then the fixed blade is the only way to go. If peeling away from yourself is more comfortable, a swivel-blade peeler, particularly a vertically oriented one, is best.

> *ginger has its roots*
>
> That's why using a peeler to remove the skin is a tough job. Use a regular spoon from your flatware instead. Hold the ginger in one hand and a teaspoon in the other. Turn the edge of the spoon over the ginger skin and scrape. The skin will come off and there will be little waste.

Kitchen Shears

It is important to have a pair of scissors just for kitchen use—even if you never plan to butterfly a quail. Not only is it more sanitary to use one pair for cutting paper at your desk and another for removing the backbone of a bird, but this ensures a longer life for the blades of both scissors. Use kitchen shears to snip chives, cut the dough of a coffee ring, break bones, or just to open a bag of frozen peas.

Rubberized handles make for easy cleaning and gripping, but many kitchen shears are all stainless steel. Do not put them in the dishwasher; always wipe them dry immediately following a careful manual cleaning. Remember: scissors are essentially two knives held together with a rivet, so the same rules apply to both tools.

Sauté Pans: Regular and Nonstick

Whether you call it a frying pan, skillet, or sauté pan, this piece of equipment almost does it all. When you sauté chicken, sear fish, make pancakes, prepare a pan sauce, or fix a quick stir-fry, a sauté pan is your go-to gear. If it has a heatproof handle, you even can throw it in the oven and roast with it, too.

This all-purpose, shallow pan with flared sides is as perfect for French toast as it is for a veal chop. The low sides relative to the wide base allow for searing and dry-heat cooking. This shape helps moisture to evaporate, preventing it from collecting in the pan. Tight-fitting lids are what really make the pan even more versatile, enabling you to sweat, braise, and steam.

If you have just one sauté pan, buy one that is all-purpose in both material and size. A heavy-bottomed stainless steel pan with an aluminum core conducts heat well, handles high temperatures, and is durable. Sizes generally run from 8 to 14 inches, so a 10- or 12-inch pan is optimal if it is the only pan you buy. Look for a tight-fitting lid and heatproof handle to make the purchase worthwhile.

Nonstick sauté pans are easy to clean and essential for items like scrambled eggs and low-fat cuisine. They work best when used over gentle to medium heat. Use rubber, wood, silicone, and plastic implements to avoid scratching a nonstick surface. The drawback to a nonstick pan is that nothing sticks, so you cannot caramelize and develop *sucs* (those crusty bits) at the bottom of the pan. Use a nonstick pan only for a nonstick task.

Baking Pan

The baking pan is known by more than one name. What you call it is generally guided by what you make in it: a brownie pan, lasagne dish, or casserole, for example. But the cooking technique is always the same: baking in an oven at a moderate temperature for a substantial period of time.

Whether glass, metal, porcelain, enamel cast iron, or earthenware, the baking pan is typically square or rectangular. Standard sizes are 8" × 8", 9" × 9", and 9" × 13", usually 2 inches deep. Ovals and circles are also popular. Some pans are elegant enough to be taken from oven to table for service, and are then usually called dishes. Both sweet and savory things can be made in baking pans, such as cakes or casseroles.

it's all in a name

It's dubbed a pan in the oven but a dish on the table. Did you know that it's called stuffing in a turkey, but dressing when baked solo in a pan? And then, it's dressing in a dish, of course, if the pan makes it to the table!

Sheet Pan

Also known as a baking sheet, cookie sheet, or jellyroll pan, this is the oven version of the sauté pan. You can bake, roast, or broil on this pan. Line it with parchment paper or aluminum foil for a disposable non-stick surface. Sheet pans do come in coated nonstick finishes that make cleanup less of a challenge, but they do not function as well at higher temperatures.

Sheet pans often have a rolled 1-inch rim, ideal for roasting vegetables and preventing juices from dripping on the oven floor. Baking sheets with rimless edges are superb for easy cookie removal. Some sheet pans have one or two open edges for this purpose, with the remaining sides flared for safe and efficient handling.

The standard size of a sheet pan is 18" × 13". But get the biggest pan your oven can hold, which allows you to bake more at once. If you have just one, then opt for a pan with 1-inch rims so you can make the most use of it. If you have room for two baking sheets, then get one with rims and one without. Bakers should have two cookie sheets per oven (if you bake often and have two ovens, then you should have four sheet pans).

Saucepan

This is the all-purpose pot for cooking grains, warming sauces, and heating soups. Classic saucepans have straight, tall sides, but nowadays there are versions with flared and rounded sides. The straight-sided pans are ideal for cooking rice and couscous, while the flared pans are excellent for reducing sauces and making small-portioned braises. The general shape of a saucepan retains moisture since the sides are tall relative to the base.

The ideal all-purpose size for a saucepan is 2-quart. Since this is such a multi-purpose pot, owning both a 1½-quart and a 2½-quart pot is practical, if you have the room. Stainless steel is probably the most versatile metal, since it does not react with any foods, does not rust, and can be put in the dishwasher. However, stainless steel does not conduct heat as well as copper. Aluminum is a fine conductor of heat, like copper, and is far less expensive, but is highly reactive and therefore can discolor easily and taint the flavor of many foods. Enamel-coated cast iron saucepans are easy to clean, but somewhat cumbersome due to their heavy weight.

Many high-end pans are made with a combination of stainless steel and a superior heat-conducting metal like copper or aluminum. These are ideal because they conduct heat, but are nonreactive.

Stockpot

Even if you don't make homemade stock, you must own this pot. A stockpot is a versatile piece of equipment ranging in use from making soup to boiling corn on the cob.

Technically, a stockpot should have very tall sides compared to its surface area. This prevents liquid from evaporating and allows the heat to rise steadily from the bottom up. A heavy bottom is necessary to prevent ingredients from burning and the pan from warping. Aluminum conducts heat wonderfully well but can tarnish easily. Anodized aluminum, or stainless steel with an aluminum core, is the best option.

Stockpots come in a range of sizes, but the 8-quart version is ideal for the home cook. It is large enough to hold big meat bones and vegetables while still reasonably undemanding to move across the kitchen from sink to stove. Look for a stockpot with a snug-fitting lid—metal or glass—and large riveted handles that make it easy to carry.

Strainer

Without a strainer, rinsing and cleaning small food items would be a challenging task. Whether the holes are large or small, the material plastic or metal, the design round (spherical) or cylindrical (tall and straight with a circular opening at the top), a strainer of one kind or another is an essential item. Even if you are a takeout restaurant's best customer, the one day you decide to make a bowl of pasta you will need this piece of equipment.

Buy the largest strainer with a stable base that fits in your sink, and then expand from there with special strainers that might be a boon to the way you cook. For example, if you cook a lot of varieties of rice, you should have a fine-mesh strainer for rinsing that holds the grain without letting it pass through the holes. But if you mostly boil potatoes or pasta, you certainly can live without a fine-mesh strainer.

Strainers come in hard stainless steel, mesh, plastic, copper, enamel, and ceramic. The latter two can chip or break, respectively, and are best used for a casually chic way to serve washed whole fruit. Stainless steel and mesh are the best options in general, since plastic is not as durable, and copper is an unnecessarily high-maintenance material for this item. Stainless steel does not rust or interact with the hot foods for which strainers are so often used.

There are four basic kinds of strainers in the truest sense—tools that are used to rinse foods with water or separate liquids from solids: colander, chinois and china cap, pasta insert, and salad spinner. The colander is the essential strainer for every home cook.

Most colanders are basically bowls that are pierced with a pattern of small holes. The size of the holes varies as does the size of the colander. The liquid drains from both the sides and bottom, leaving the solids inside the bowl. Colanders that have large handles on either side of the bowl are the safest and therefore the best to buy.

But there are smaller strainers—whether stainless steel, mesh, or plastic—that have one long handle and one or more hooks on the opposite side to rest across a pot or sink. These are often used in place of slotted spoons to retrieve small foods in a large pot. The downside to these mesh strainers, if they are small, is that they are not particularly stable in comparison with a colander that has feet or a round circular base. Mesh strainers that go over the sink are sturdier than their scooping counterparts. They are, however, a nuisance to clean if used for pasta, which sticks and breaks when it touches the surface.

Measuring Cups and Spoons

The overwhelming majority of recipes call for volume, not weight, measurements. Every cook must be outfitted with tools to measure both liquids and dry goods. You need three sets of measuring tools: measuring spoons, dry measuring cups, and liquid measuring cups.

Do not reach for a teaspoon or tablespoon from your flatware and think those are precise measures for cooking or baking. Buy a set of measuring spoons, whether plastic or metal, to measure spices, seasonings, leavening agents, and vanilla extract. Sets typically come with ¼-teaspoon, ½-teaspoon, 1-teaspoon, ½-tablespoon, and 1-tablespoon measures.

Dry measuring cups are designed to scoop ingredients and be leveled to the brim. They are often made of metal or plastic, and come in sets of ⅛-, ¼-, ⅓-, ½- and 1-cup vessels. Liquid measures, on the other hand, are almost always made of a clear material, like plastic or glass, so you can measure the liquid as you pour it into the vessel. They are purposefully not measured to the brim to prevent spills, and also have spouts so the liquid can be poured off. Sizes range from 1 cup to 8 cups.

There is one more good reason to buy dry and wet measures: there is a volumetric difference between the two. Yes, that's right. Three cups of sugar is not the same as 3 cups of milk. Below 2 cups, there is no difference, but above 2 cups the dry measure can be in excess of 16 percent larger than the liquid measure.

Mixing Bowls

Mixing bowls are as versatile for preparation as are sauté pans for cooking. They hold trimmings and choppings, batters and doughs, meringues and marinades. Selecting mixing bowls can be a daunting task, especially with so many sizes, sets, and styles in the marketplace. There is much to consider beyond size and style: the material and its durability, heat resistance, reactivity, and storage.

Must you have a copper bowl to beat egg whites to a meringue? No. But copper is the single best material for the task since the protein in egg whites reacts with it to produce the greatest possible volume of a meringue. If you make meringue often, treat yourself to a large, unlined, round-bottom copper bowl. Just be sure not to use it for anything else—certainly not your favorite teriyaki marinade—because it can hold flavors.

For most everyone else, however, glass, metal or plastic bowls will do just fine for any task. Here are some pros and cons to each material:

- **Glass** bowls are excellent all-purpose tools since they are heavy and stable, dishwasher-safe, nonreactive, and heatproof. They can go in the microwave—even in the oven in some cases. And you can see through them. But they can break, too.

- **Stainless steel** bowls are dishwasher-safe, nonreactive, and unbreakable, making them the ideal choice for the home cook.

- **Plastic** bowls are lightweight and dishwasher-safe, and often have rubberized bottoms that help keep the bowls from wobbling as you work.

- **Wooden** bowls, like copper bowls, have limited use. If treated or laminated, they can be used for salads. Unfinished wooden bowls are often used with a mezzaluna to chop foods. But they are porous and should be cleaned by hand with little soap.

Mixing bowl sets are useful for any cook. Since bowls nest, they are easy to store, taking up no more space than the largest bowl. Nesting sets that offer several bowls ranging from a mere tablespoon to 6 quarts are certainly attractive and appealing, but not as utilitarian as, say, a 2-quart, 4-quart and 6-quart trio. Small bowls that hold just tablespoons or cups are best bought in sets themselves, since they are used for *mise en place* (see Chapter 3, page 30), not for mixing.

bigger is better for bowls

Always reach for a bigger bowl than you think you need. It is far easier to whisk a vinaigrette in a large bowl, since it gives you greater range of motion. That means better emulsion and less mess. Consider, then, both the volume of food placed in the bowl, and the action taken to transform it, when selecting a bowl.

Whisk

When added manual power is needed to blend, beat, whip, or emulsify, the whisk is the tool to grab. Made of intersecting wires that curve to form an elongated orb attached to a handle, this tool incorporates air like nothing else. Indispensible to any cook, the whisk evenly integrates dry ingredients, blends eggs, beats batters, whips cream and egg whites, and emulsifies mayonnaise and vinaigrette.

Whisks for home use come in many shapes and sizes, ranging from 5 to 14 inches. A standard whisk, also referred to as a sauce or French whisk, is a narrow, elongated band of thick, intersecting, arched wires used to beat heavy sauces, savory or sweet. By contrast, a balloon whisk, as its name suggests, is a larger wand with a more rotund orb that makes beating cream or egg whites far easier. This bulbous shape, along with lighter and thinner wires, assists in incorporating more air into the food with every stroke. There are all-purpose whisks whose shapes are a combination of the two, an excellent choice for someone looking to buy just one implement.

There are other less traditional versions, such as the flat whisk, coiled whisk, or ball whisk. Flat whisks are a series of wires that do not intersect but arch over one another; their use is generally limited to making *roux*, scraping the *sucs* from the bottom of a pan, and blending eggs. Coiled whisks look like round scrub brushes or cocktail strainers whose chief advantage is fully touching the bottom of the pan. Ball whisks also reach the base of a pot or scrape the curves of a bowl due to the many freestanding wires, each finished with a weighted ball.

Although whisks are now made from plastic, rubber, and silicone, a classic stainless steel whisk is best. It is stronger and more durable, which allows the cook or baker to use the whisk as a true extension of the arm. This is especially useful not just for the act of beating, but also for scraping the bottom of the bowl.

Clean and dry a whisk thoroughly to prevent rust and discoloration. ✳

The Essential Techniques

IF THE RIGHT TOOLS ARE A BOON TO COOKING WELL, then you should know how to use them. It's all in the execution. Cooking, at its essence, is the transformation of food. The ingredients themselves might be what invite us to the kitchen, and their distinct combination is what lures us to the table. But without the proper treatment, we cannot do them justice.

It's so easy to be seduced by the food itself, that the cooking method becomes an afterthought. "Oh, it doesn't matter if I bake the chicken or grill it. It's the rosemary and thyme that makes the dish." Not exactly. The seasoning does matter, but the cooking method matters just as much because it impacts the ingredients' transformation. Do you want a browned, seared exterior to the meat? Then grilling is the right choice. Baking will not produce the same result.

In order to be a truly competent cook, you need to know the basics of all the different ways you can apply heat to your ingredients. If you only know how to bake and sauté, you are limiting yourself and ultimately your food. Think of your favorite piece of fish and imagine it baked or sautéed. Now consider it roasted, poached, braised, fried, and so on. These various applications of heat bring forward different aspects of the food, revealing a variety of textures and flavors.

Choose the cooking method wisely. Know the proper techniques. Find out how to use your essential tools. But before you apply any heat, learn how to get organized and work with a knife. It all starts with how the food is handled before the heat is applied.

Mise en Place

Mise en place (MEEZ ahn plas) is the essential best practice for any competent cook—every other technique depends on it. Meaning "put in place" in French, mise en place is having all your ingredients prepped before you begin cooking. Your labor can be divided into preparation (washing, peeling, weighing, cutting, and measuring) and cooking (applying heat, assembling, and combining foods). Mise en place, then, is everything you do before you start to cook.

Look at any recipe and you'll see instructions for the mise en place. The standard recipe format itself is meant to divide labor into preparation and cooking, two necessarily distinct stages. Think of the ingredient list at the top of a recipe not just as a shopping list, but a to-do list before you start cooking. Consider the quantities and size/shape specifications of the recipe as a plan of what you need to do first.

When a recipe lists ingredients with quantities and sizes ("2 carrots, peeled and diced"), you should have them prepared that way before you follow the second part, the procedure. Do all the measuring, peeling, trimming, and cutting, place each item in individual vessels, then cook.

Speaking of vessels, you should mise en place your tools as well as your ingredients. Most recipes do not list the required equipment as they do the ingredients (though, recipes in this book do). Some equipment is mentioned in the instructions: "heat the oil in a large sauté pan over medium-high heat." Other information can be inferred; when you read, "add the onions, stirring constantly until softened," understand that you'll need a wooden spoon to do the stirring. It's far better to have all your equipment ready before you begin the cooking process than to hunt for it during the action.

To appreciate fully the value of mise en place, think of the simplest dishes. If you want to make a tomato and mushroom omelet, how would it even be possible without mise en place? The tomatoes and mushrooms must be chopped before the eggs hit the pan so that the moment the eggs are ready for their filling, you can be ready to execute. If the tomatoes and mushrooms are not ready at the moment you need them, you will have rubbery or burnt eggs at best. Go one step further back: the eggs must be beaten before you heat the pan and add the fat. If not, you risk overheating the pan and burning the fat while you crack and beat the eggs.

It is critical to prepare the ingredients—wash, peel, cut, measure—and select the equipment before you begin the cooking process. Make sure that you read and understand what the recipe calls for in advance. Follow this foundational principle to competent cooking, and you'll become instantly more efficient and effective.

> ## punctuation matters in recipes
>
> Is there a difference between "1 cup chopped walnuts" and "1 cup walnuts, chopped?" Most definitely. The ingredient "1 cup chopped walnuts" means that you place already chopped walnuts into a dry measuring vessel until you reach the volume of 1 cup. However, "1 cup walnuts, chopped" means that you should measure one cup of whole walnuts and then chop them, which yields perhaps ¾ or ⅔ cup chopped walnuts.

Knife Skills

It is by design that the first four items on the Essential Top 20 tools list are three knives and a cutting board. Cooking begins with the preparation. How you break down your ingredients is the first phase of how you eventually taste your food as a finished dish. The cooking method you plan to use informs the way you must prepare your ingredients.

Holding the Knife

It is surprising how many home cooks have been cooking for decades yet do not actually hold the knife as they should. They might even turn out some exceptionally tasty fare. Imagine a basketball player who can shoot the ball, but cannot dribble or pass . . . nothing truly competent about that. Please refer to the image on page 13 for a refresher on the parts of a knife.

» THE CHEF'S KNIFE

A chef's knife is the most frequently used tool, and there is a specific way to handle it. You must hold it with the thumb and the index finger pinching the blade right next to the bolster, while your fist and remaining three fingers grip the handle. This is the safest and most effective way to use the knife. If you hold the knife with your index finger stretched across the blade's narrow spine then you do not have control over the edge. Improperly handling the knife in this way makes for an unstable and wobbly blade. Should your index finger slip from that slender and slippery surface, your knife might falter and you risk cutting yourself.

Speaking of cutting yourself, never expose your fingers to the blade with your "guiding hand," the hand that is holding the food being cut. You must stabilize the food, but you can do it with your fingers safely tucked away in a "claw grip." Curl your fingers inward so that they are perpendicular to the cutting board, gently anchoring the food. When the knife moves across the board, the surface of the blade can directly touch the backs of your fingers without you ever fearing that its sharp edge will cut your skin.

⟩⟩ **Chef's Knife Grip** ⟨⟨

» PARING AND BREAD KNIVES

Paring and bread knives are a little different, of course. A paring knife often needs to be held with the index finger stretched across the spine of the blade. This is perfectly safe, however, for two reasons: size and application. The blade of a paring knife is roughly the length of an index finger, if not smaller. And the paring knife is used for those special tasks requiring the precision of your finger's guidance matched with the knife's sharpness.

A bread knife cannot be held like a chef's knife. The blade is not deep enough to be held that way and its function is not to move across a board or be pressed through food, but to saw through something with a hard exterior and tender center. Hold a bread knife with your fist entirely on the handle and saw back and forth. Don't press. Cut. You must move gently back and forth through the food to reach the cutting board.

Moving the Knife

The countless preparation methods (slicing, chopping, mincing, dicing, and so on) that you encounter while you cook require different movements of the knife. Following are instructions for some of the most basic methods.

» SLICING

The most basic way to use a chef's knife is to move it front to back though the food, a form of slicing. First, anchor the curved tip of the knife on the cutting board (after all, that's why it's curved); the remainder of the blade and your hand are raised off the board at an angle. Place the food underneath the blade, closest to the tip, and bring the knife down through the food to the board so that the entire straight edge is flush with the board.

To ensure that that cut has been made, move the knife forward, with the entire blade firmly on the board (and the curved tip now decidedly off the board). Cut through the food up to the heel of the blade. The knife is long for this reason. You make the cut in two stages: first by bringing the knife from the top of the food to the bottom, and then from the front of the food to the back. As you slide the knife through to the back of the food, you then return the knife to the start position, with the curved tip anchored on the cutting board.

> ### caveat cutter
>
> Have you ever cut a scallion and then realized it is a row of attached circles? That's because the heel of the blade has not touched the cutting board before you move the knife forward and ultimately upward to make another cut. Pay close attention to the feeling—and listen for the sound—of the board stopping the knife.

With the comfort that comes from experience, you'll find that this action repeats itself quickly as you move the knife across the board. In doing so, the knife never actually leaves the board; some part of the edge is always touching its surface. Keeping the knife on the board at all times enables an organic, steady, swift movement. Unless you are an extremely proficient chopper, lifting the knife off the board with each cut is an awkward, unstable, and tiring waste of time.

Another slicing method is to move the chef's knife back to front, instead of front to back, through the food. The movement is quick and brief, used primarily for slicing small and thin pieces of food. You begin the same way as you do in the aforementioned method, but the heel of the blade never fully touches the board. It is the curved tip of the knife that does the work as you repeatedly move from the back of the food to the front, the tip of the edge never leaving the cutting board.

» CHOPPING

Chopping is an entirely different rocking motion that requires a special way of holding the knife. As in all cutting techniques, the tip of the blade rests on the cutting board. Your guiding hand presses the spine of the blade with the tips of your outstretched fingers (but your thumb). You do not anchor the food with this technique—you are using one hand to hold the knife and the other hand to guide it by spreading your fingers across the spine. Making full use of the curve, you rock the knife up and down over the food (usually herbs), managing the movement with your guiding hand.

Garlic can be treated this way for a very fine mince. In fact, this method (coupled with a few pinches of salt to extract the garlic's moisture) is how you make garlic paste. Never chop onions or shallots like this. They are so important, they have a singular method all their own.

» CHOPPING ONIONS AND SHALLOTS

Onions and shallots are succulent, juicy bulbs whose simultaneously sweet and savory flavor makes them essential foundational ingredients in an endless number of recipes. To keep the juice in the onion and off the cutting board, you must follow a specific procedure:

1 Trim the onion of its tip, and of the fur on its root.

2 Slice the onion in half lengthwise, from top to bottom; peel and discard the skin.

3 Place one half on the cutting board, with the top of the onion facing the knife.

4 Turn the knife on its side so that the sharp edge faces the onion's center from the tip, and the flat blade faces the cutting board.

5 Decide how big you want the chopped onion pieces to be. Keeping the blade parallel with the cutting board, slice several rows (usually at least three) to the root of the onion, but not through it, leaving the root intact. (FIGURE 1)

6 Now turn the sharp edge of the knife to the top of the onion (the outer layer), with the tip of your knife in line with the root. Still leaving the root intact, slice the onion from top to bottom in the same width as the slices you previously made from bottom to top. (FIGURE 2)

7 To make the final cut into diced bits, slice the onion cross-wise. (FIGURE 3)

Mastering this method might take a bit of time, so go easy on yourself. But it is well worth learning. In the end, this is the easiest and most efficient way to cut an onion.

Cuts and Shapes

Slice, julienne, baton (jardinière), macedoine, brunoise, dice, mirepoix, chiffonade, suprême: These are all different shapes into which you can cut a vegetable. Don't

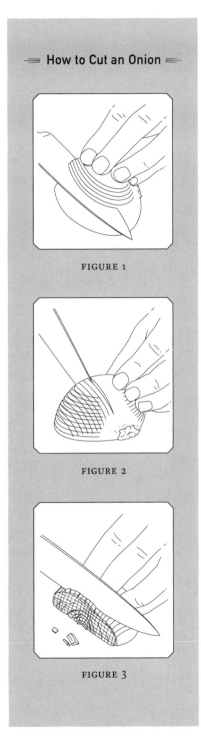

How to Cut an Onion

FIGURE 1

FIGURE 2

FIGURE 3

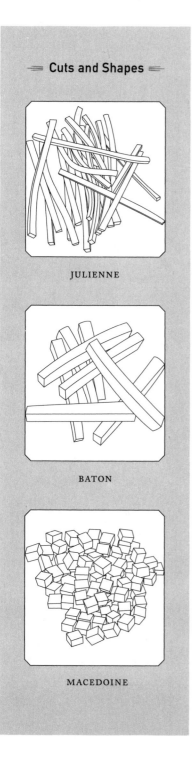

Cuts and Shapes

JULIENNE

BATON

MACEDOINE

be put off by the French terms. These words each stand for a very specific size and shape, and knowing the terms will make you a more competent cook. There is nothing terribly informative about "thin strips"—yet "julienne" means just that, plus the exactitude of a precise measurement.

Slice—a slice is the most basic cut. It is the very first cut made after something has been peeled and pared (trimmed), and can be any shape or size depending on the food being cut and your plans for it. A slice is paring the food: breaking it down so you can begin to shape it. You cannot go from a whole potato to chunks or dices in one or two cuts. You'll always begin with slices, then customize your cuts based on what you need for your end result.

Julienne—both a noun and a verb, this word means to cut food, usually vegetables, into long, thin matchsticks. Technically, the measurement is about 1/16-inch square × 3 inches. To make this shape, cut the vegetable into 3-inch-long sections, then 1/16-inch slices, then trim those slices to have an even edge on all sides, then finally cut those slices into 1/16-inch strips.

Baton—also known as *jardinière*, a baton is a cubed stick, measuring about 1/5-inch square × 2 inches. In order to make proper batons, you must start with slices perfectly trimmed on all sides. The thickness of the slices must match the width of the baton, 1/5 inch, in other words.

Macedoine (mass-eh-DWAN)—this word means to be cut into perfect cubes. Technically the measurement is about 1/5-inch cubed. To make this shape, cut the vegetable into 1/5-inch-thick slices, lengthwise into 1/5-inch-wide batons, then finally crosswise into 1/5-inch cubes.

Brunoise (broo-NWAHZ)—a mini macedoine of sorts, the finest and tiniest of dices (so small their appearance as perfect cubes can hardly be detected). The classical measurement is about ⅟₁₆-inch cubed. To make this shape, cut the vegetable into ⅟₁₆-inch slices, lengthwise into juliennes, then finally crosswise into ⅟₁₆-inch cubes.

Dice—this term is not specific in size or shape. A dice can be very small, or relatively large. The important thing is that the shape and size are consistent and uniform. Almost anything can be diced, from apples and tomatoes to carrots and onions (remember: onions have their own special dicing method; see page 35). It's important to know that to get dices, you first must make slices and strips.

Mirepoix (mir-PWAH)—aromatic vegetables, cut in small, unshaped chunks, used frequently when making stock, soups or sauces, or as a bed on which to braise or roast meat. Mirepoix classically consists of two parts onion, one part carrot, and one part celery. It is often browned in fat before it is used to impart flavor, and is removed before the final product is served.

Chiffonade (SHEEF-oh-nahd)—both a noun and verb, this is a method of cutting herbs like basil, or leafy greens like lettuce that produces ribbons or thin strips. Literally it means "made of rags." Stack clean leaves, roll them into a cigar shape, and slice the roll crosswise into fine strips.

Suprême (soo-PREM)—both a noun and a verb, this method is used to section a citrus fruit. First remove the skin and the pith from the fruit. Then cut away from the membrane by slicing the flesh next to

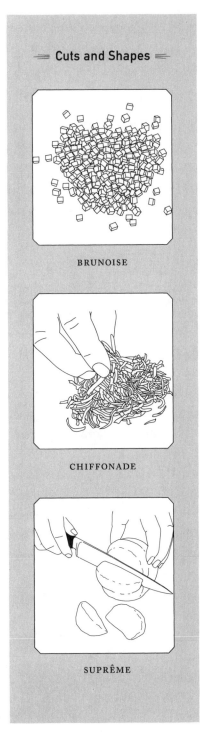

≡ **Cuts and Shapes** ≡

BRUNOISE

CHIFFONADE

SUPRÊME

the membrane on either side. You are left with a suprême. (There is a secondary meaning to the term: a boneless breast of duck or chicken is sometimes called a suprême.)

Sautéing

Sauté literally means "to jump" in French. That is what your food does when it is panfried quickly in a small amount of fat or oil, until brown and thoroughly cooked, in a skillet or sauté pan over direct heat (uncovered). Sautéing involves direct heat from the pan on the surface of the food.

The sauté pan and fat must be hot before the food is added, otherwise the food might absorb oil and become soggy, or stick to the pan. The food must be dry to prevent the fat from spattering when you place the food in the pan. Ideally the food should not be ice cold from the refrigerator, which could cool the pan abruptly. Remove foods from the refrigerator 15 to 30 minutes before sautéing.

Since sautéed food needs to cook quickly and completely (when it leaves the pan it requires no further cooking before it is served), tender cuts of meat in small sizes are good choices.

When you add food to a hot sauté pan, you should hear a sizzle. If not, the pan is not hot enough. The pan is hot when the oil moves quickly and easily across its surface as you tilt it, or when the butter begins to foam. If the oil smokes, it has burned, just like blackened butter. Wipe the pan clean and begin again. Alternatively, you can grease the food instead of the pan, as in brushing a filet of fish before placing it in a hot pan; listen for the same sizzle sound to know the pan is hot enough for cooking. If you lower food into a pan and don't hear the sizzle, remove it immediately if it has not stuck instantly. If the food sticks to the pan, leave the food where it is and let the pan get hot. Don't worry too much about it. Just avoid that misstep for the future.

Never crowd the pan when you sauté, otherwise the food steams instead of sears. Keep the food in a single layer with

stir-frying is sautéing, too

The French have sautéing, but the Chinese have stir-frying. A wok is heated to a high heat and then fat, seasoning, bite-sized meats, and vegetables are quickly added one after the other (those that take the longest to cook are added first). The cook continually stirs the food and then serves it immediately.

ample space between pieces. Work in batches when necessary. Allow the food to respond to the heat—do not shake or move the pan—until the food has first browned. Depending on the size of the item being sautéed, use tongs to lift and turn, or a spoon to move the food.

Grilling

When man discovered fire, he became the first outdoor grill cook. Without a grate but with an ample supply of twigs and branches, he cooked game directly over a flame. Born of this method, grilling is the technique of cooking food over a grate of hot coals, or on a ridged heat source. This dry-heat cooking method leaves food with grill marks from the hot grid. Food cooks quickly when grilled, due to the high, direct heat.

Outdoor grilling can be as rudimentary as holding a gridiron (or grid) filled with food over an open flame in a fire pit, or as high-tech as the turn of a knob on a sophisticated gas grill fueled by a propane tank. Indoor grilling is usually done with a ridged pan on the stovetop or an independent electric heat source like a panini press.

Tender meat cuts like sirloin steak, pork chops, and ground chuck hamburgers are appropriate choices for the direct heat of the grill. Tougher meats like beef brisket and pork shoulder, and larger pieces like whole birds and roasts, cannot be cooked well quickly with such dry, high, direct heat. These items require indirect grilling where they are placed further from the flame and cooked with the cover closed over a much lower heat. Indirect grilling turns the grill into an oven of sorts, with heat circulating the food, not just penetrating from the bottom.

To grill food in any context, the grid must be thoroughly clean and very hot. If either of these two requirements falls short, the cooking process is compromised. Food sticks to dirty and insufficiently hot grids. For the surface proteins of any meat to coagulate and release from the grid, the grid must be clean enough to touch the food directly without any surface crud, and hot enough to make a sear. A dirty grill shows, especially with ridged indoor grill surfaces. Black flecks of burnt crust from previous use "pepper" the food between the grill marks. The problem is, it isn't pepper. It's food residue.

Gas grilling is incredibly easy: no fire to light, no waiting for coals to burn and heat, and no messy ash to clean. The biggest benefit to gas grilling is the adjustable heat source. Just turn on the gas, heat the grill, and turn the switch off when you're done. But the clean-burning gas does not impart that smoky, charred flavor of a charcoal grill. While the white-hot heat of charcoal briquettes cannot be adjusted, it does uniquely flavor the food with an unmistakable outdoor-grill taste.

Considered a healthy cooking method, grilling requires only a small amount of fat. Some foods, such as rib eye steak, are fatty enough without requiring added grease to grill on a hot grate. Leaner foods, like skinless chicken breast, need to be brushed with oil or a marinade to prevent them from sticking to the grill.

Doneness of meat can be tested with an instant-read probing thermometer or the cook's clean fingers. The rarer the meat is, the softer it will be to the touch. The best way to learn what rare versus well-done feels like: use a thermometer and also touch the meat. Over time, you will become competent at sensing when the meat is ready without needing the confirmation of the thermometer.

> ## how hot is high heat?
>
> At least 500°F when you cook on an outdoor grill, whether charcoal or gas. How can you tell if the grill has reached the right temperature? Hold your hand several inches above the grate. If the heat is so hot that you have to remove your hand in under three seconds, you have high heat. Different parts of the grill might be hotter than others, so move the food around accordingly.

Broiling

Broiling differs from grilling in that the food is placed below a heat source. Like grilling, broiling is a form of quick, high-heat cooking that provides a flavorful, charred, and browned surface to meats and fish.

Most ovens (gas or electric) have a broiler section that is used to cook meats, fish, and poultry, or melt or toast other foods like cheese—either right below the ceiling of the oven chamber, or in a separate drawer below. In fact, most oven manufacturers provide a broiling pan with the oven: a shallow, enameled steel rectangular pan without handles, outfitted with a snug-fitting tray with slits.

To broil food, preheat the oven to "broil" or the highest temperature setting available (500°F). If you're broiling in the main oven chamber, place the rack a measured distance (3 to 6 inches) below the direct, dry heat. The broiling pan should be hot before the food is placed on it. Since the heat is so high and direct, you do not need to grease the pan. The food, however, should have a natural fat content or be brushed with fat to cook without sticking.

Broiled food can burn easily, so keep a watchful eye and alert nose. If you smell the food burning, remove it from the oven and perhaps lower the rack one level, or open the broiler drawer a crack to dissipate the direct heat.

lost in translation

In the UK, "grilling" means broiling (cooking under the heat source). To barbecue in Belfast, Ireland is to grill in Grand Rapids, Michigan (think hamburgers and hot dogs). But talk to someone in Greensboro, North Carolina, and they might tell you that barbecue is only made in a smoker (probably pulled pork and ribs).

Roasting

Once upon a time, meat was roasted under an open flame on a turning spit of iron—not terribly different from the rotisserie we know today. Roasting is a form of surround-heat cooking, applying indirect heat to the food. The food is generally uncovered and exposed to dry, moderately high heat in the oven, which produces a well-browned surface and seals in the juices.

Reasonably tender pieces of meat or poultry should be used for roasting. Many fish, root vegetables, and winter squashes are good candidates, too. Food that is going to be roasted for a particularly long time, such as the Thanksgiving turkey, may be tented to prevent it from drying out.

Small cuts of meats and most vegetables can be roasted at a relatively high heat (approximately 400°F) to cook quickly and evenly, and will acquire a browned surface without losing too much moisture. Some recipes call for slow roasting (approximately 325°F), like a turkey or rump roast, to make for a more tender, juicy piece of meat. A combination of the two methods is an ideal approach: first, brown meat quickly in the oven, and then cook it further without drying out the flesh.

After any meat is roasted, it is important to allow it to rest for at least 10 minutes (up to 30 minutes for large whole roasts and birds) so that the internal juices redistribute evenly before carving. If carved immediately from the oven, all the concentrated juices run from the meat, making what could have been very juicy, dry and tough.

Poaching

Poaching, unlike the aforementioned methods, is a form of extraction. Poaching cooks food by gently simmering it, submerged in liquid (water, wine, stock, etc.), just below the boiling point. The amount of liquid and poaching temperature depends on the food being poached. Particularly delicate foods like eggs, fish, and fruit can fall apart easily and require lower poaching temperatures than less fragile foods like chicken breast.

Small pieces of food can be submerged in the already simmering poaching liquid, whereas whole birds are brought to a simmer with the liquid, as in chicken soup. Meat should be cold from the refrigerator in order to allow the natural juices to extract into the cooking liquid, ultimately flavoring the cooking liquid, which essentially self-bastes the food.

> ### "season" means with salt and pepper
>
> Season your savory food with salt, and usually pepper, too. Salt brightens and highlights the natural flavors of foods. Cook with kosher or sea salt and then taste the dish a few times along the way to determine if the flavors are balanced. Season the dish again before you serve it. It takes practice to learn how to season. Like lots of things in life, the best way to learn is by making mistakes.

Blanching

One of the most elementary methods of cooking vegetables is called "blanching" or "parboiling." This is when heavily salted water is brought to a boil and vegetables are plunged into the pot, cooking for a brief period of time. The French refer to this as *á l'anglaise*, meaning "in the English style." The salted water, intended to be reminiscent of the sea, seasons the vegetables and helps to set the color from the moment the vegetables are dropped into the pot. Blanching string beans, for example, makes them tender enough to bend without snapping.

There once was a time when boiling green beans until they were soft and olive-green was in vogue, or at the very least tolerated. Today, that is considered an overcooked preparation that yields an insipid taste and unpleasant texture. But the pendulum can swing too far to the other side sometimes; asparagus should not be so crunchy that it could break with one slight bend of the stalk, or a sugar snap so undercooked that the peas inside are still raw. Green vegetables should be tender to the tooth, not soft. Their cooked color should be a brighter green than the raw state.

So many people, though, continue to make the unfortunate mistake of overcooking their vegetables, turning them brown, mushy, and limp. Nutritionists tout the benefits of green vegetables, in particular, citing them as excellent sources of vitamins and amino acids. When over-cooked, they can lose many of their nutrients and enzymes. Properly cooking these essential foods provides superior flavor and improved nutritional value.

In order to blanch vegetables, you should follow a few simple guidelines:

- For every quart (4 cups) of water, add at least 1 teaspoon kosher or sea salt.

- Do not crowd the pot, so the vegetables can cook evenly and quickly. Make sure you select a vessel that you can fill with ample water to hold your vegetables.

- Let the water come to a vigorous boil (212°F), when the water rolls and bubbles. Once there is active movement in the pot, plunge all the vegetables in at once to ensure even cooking time.

- Once the water returns to a boil, the cooking time begins. (Remove the vegetables from the refrigerator when you put the water on to boil so they are not too cold when put in the pot.)

The blanching process is quick and efficient, so it is critical to stay near the pot while the vegetables are in the water. Most green vegetables cook within 30 seconds to 5 minutes from the time the water returns to a boil. Using tongs, remove one piece of vegetable (e.g., string bean, snow pea, or asparagus) and taste. If the vegetable is still crunchy with a bit of snap, then continue cooking. Another way to test for doneness is to pierce the vegetable (e.g., broccoli) with a paring knife. If the knife penetrates the surface without resistance, the vegetables are ready.

The final step in the blanching process is shocking your vegetables. No, that doesn't mean telling them a secret or confessing your sins. Remove the vegetables when ready either with a slotted spoon or strainer, or drain them in a colander. Then immediately plunge them into an ice water bath or run them under a steady stream of cold water until they are cool. Shocking your vegetables is like an insurance policy for flavor and color. It stops the cooking process and further sets the color.

Braising

This is the quintessential "slow and low" cooking technique, where food is cooked for a long time over a low flame. Known as the mixed method, braising both concentrates and then extracts flavors. Cooks generally braise tougher, "second" cuts of meat. Usually the meat is seared first to concentrate the juices and brown the exterior surface, then submerged partially in liquid to slowly extract those same juices.

Braising is a form of cooking that can be executed either on the stovetop or in the oven. The basic technique is cooking by wet heat—the food is partially immersed in hot liquid in a cooking vessel (as opposed to dry heat cooking, such as roasting). The goal is to integrate the flavors of the solids and liquids in the pot.

The chief principle of this method is the exchange of flavors and juices. The item being cooked gives off juices to the liquid, which in turn imparts flavor to the food item. This is one of the reasons that fattier cuts of meat braise well—the fat renders, giving off flavor to the liquid, which then returns flavor to the meat. Cooking the food slowly over a low heat also helps to tenderize meat by breaking down the connective tissue that otherwise would be too tough to consume if cooked quickly by grilling or sautéing. The difference between braising and poaching: You fully submerge the food

> ## *"medium rare" veggies*
> Blanching vegetables until they are no longer raw but still relatively crisp has many applications. This can be a good place to stop cooking if you are preparing sugar snap peas for crudités and want a taste somewhere between raw and cooked. This is also a good stopping point if you are cooking large batches of vegetables ahead of time and will sauté them later before serving them.

in liquid when poaching, but you do *not* fully submerge the food when you braise.

Frying

Frying is synonymous with fat. When we hear "fried" we usually think of the food as "deep-fried" in a cauldron of piping hot grease. Food can be shallow-fried, too, immersed in enough fat to cover about half the item.

This is probably the one cooking method you think you don't need to know. You might not even eat fried foods in the first place, and if you do, you would rather order them at a restaurant on occasion than dirty your kitchen with grease. The frying thermometer was not listed in the Essential Top 20, and the only recipe in the book that covers frying does not call for deep-frying. All that aside, you cannot claim culinary competence if you do not know the procedure for frying food.

concentration vs. extraction

There are two general ways we cook meat: concentration or extraction. Concentration is the method of cooking in which you lock in, or concentrate, the juices by coagulating the surface protein. Examples of this are grilling, broiling, sautéing, and roasting. Extraction is the method by which juices are drawn out of the product during cooking, such as poaching.

Which Pans to Use

Deep-frying requires a deep vessel so that food can be completely submerged in fat. Shallow-frying is usually done in a regular sauté pan or cast iron skillet where enough oil is placed in the pan to reach half-way up the side of the item(s) being fried. The food must be dry (remember: water and oil don't mix and that is no exception when incredibly hot) and room temperature; cold food dramatically lowers the temperature of the cooking oil, which increases the possibility for the food to absorb the oil. Crowding the pan also can lower the oil temperature since the heat has to be distributed to more individual units, and thus takes longer to rise.

Use Care with Hot Oil

Never plunge food into hot fat, or you surely will burn yourself. Instead, gently lower the food right into the cooking oil, letting at least part of the food touch the hot fat before you release it, even if you are using your hands. It might seem counterintuitive to bring your exposed skin close to something so hot, but this is absolutely the best way to avoid a splash, which is how people generally burn themselves when frying.

Hot fat cooks food quickly, crisping its surface while keeping the inside moist and tender. The texture and flavor of properly fried food is crunchy, rich, and luscious. If the food tastes greasy and has absorbed too much of the cooking oil, then it either was fried for too long or at too low a temperature.

Which Oil to Use

Oil reaches a much higher temperature than water. Depending on the specific type, oil can climb to 500°F. Most fried food recipes call for the fat to be between 350°F and 375°F. The lighter the oil, generally the higher the smoke point (the temperature at which the oil begins to decompose and visible fumes (smoke) are given off). When oil is heated and begins to smoke, the fatty acids in the oil become damaged, even turning into harmful substances. This is why it is important to select the right oil for the proper task.

Olive oil is seldom used for deep-frying foods, as compared to corn or peanut oil, due to its lower smoke point. Grapeseed oil, like olive oil, is one of the healthier fats, but has a higher smoke point than olive oil. Safflower, sunflower, and canola oils all have high smoke points, as does vegetable lard, which is characteristically solid at room temperature. Fats with high smoke points fry food well.

The Process

To fry food, add the fat to a cold pan, leaving at least 2 inches of space between the oil and the top of the pan. When the food is submerged in the oil, the oil rises. The heavier and larger the food, the more fat rises. If you are deep-frying chicken parts, for example, leave several inches between the fat and the top of the pot.

double-fry those fries, please

French fries might be the most pedestrian food, but they actually require careful technique to turn out just right—crispy and golden brown on the outside, soft and tender on the inside without a trace of grease. Fried twice, once at a lower temperature to cook the potato, and then a second time at a higher temperature to provide the crispy golden exterior, French fries are deceptively fussy for such a seemingly simple dish.

Heat the pan and the fat together, and use a deep-fat frying thermometer to read the oil temperature. As the oil gets hot it will shimmer and shine. Once it reaches the desired temperature, gently add the food to the oil. Adjust the heat as needed to maintain as stable a temperature as possible.

Never leave a pot of frying food unattended. It is too dangerous and too risky for the food.

Baking

Baking is an elusive term. On the one hand, we know that it means cooking cakes, pastries, pies, cookies, and breads in the oven. Yet we also consider as baked anything that we toss in the oven at a moderate temperature for a protracted period of time, sweet or savory.

Like roasting, baking is a method of cooking by dry, surround-heat in an enclosed chamber, namely an oven. The distinction, then, is the temperature and length of time the food is cooked. Baking is done at a lower temperature than roasting and for a longer period of time. There is the potential for foods to dry out, so baked dishes are often covered to retain moisture.

Casseroles like lasagne and potatoes au gratin are baked, as are many chicken dishes. Oven-fried foods are essentially baked in the oven instead of fried in a pan (the "fried" part is meant to convey that the food should be crunchy and golden brown). ✳

CHAPTER

4

* Hand Mixer
* Standing Mixer
* Pastry Brush
* Timer
* Spatula
* Pastry Bag and Tip
* Scale
* Pastry Scraper
* Silicone Baking Liner
* Cake Pans: Round and Square
* Muffin and Loaf Pans
* Springform Pan
* Rolling Pin
* Sifter
* Pie Pan
* Tart Pan
* Cookie Cutters
* Ramekins
* Cooling Rack

The Baker's Essential Tools and Techniques

ONCE YOU HAVE THE ESSENTIAL TOP 20 TOOLS (page 13), you can fill in the blanks in other areas of your cooking repertoire. For instance, you might be uninterested in baking in general, but love to make cookies from time to time. Take a look at the Baker's Essential Tools and invest in a quality cookie sheet and silicone baking liner.

THE BAKER'S ESSENTIAL TOOLS

Hand Mixer

Anyone who bakes regularly must have a hand mixer. This tool allows you to stir, mix, whip, blend, and beat ingredients with electric power when you really need the machine to do the work. It occupies a lot less space than a standing mixer, and it does not require you to use a machine-specific bowl. A hand mixer can effortlessly beat eggs, blend cake batter, mix cookie dough, and whip meringue. The best part: cleanup. All you need to do is wash the beaters and wipe the hand-held machine.

A good model has several speeds, ranging from a slow stir to a vigorous beating. It is important that the slowest speed is gentle enough to blend dry ingredients without having powder spatter from the bowl.

Look for a model with a built-in, upward-counting timer. The next time you need to beat cream and sugar for two minutes per a recipe's instructions, you'll know exactly when to stop. Choose a hand mixer that feels comfortable and is not terribly heavy or noisy. Virtually all hand mixers come with a detachable pair of standard beaters as well as a single whisk. Some even come with blender rods (to mix drinks) and dough hooks.

Standing Mixer

If the hand mixer is basic like a moped, then the standing mixer is luxurious like a limousine. Just like the hand mixer, this large kitchen appliance stirs, mixes, whips, blends, and beats. But it also kneads and, with the appropriate attachments, makes fresh pasta, juices fruits and vegetables, and grinds meat. Home bread bakers consider this machine as essential as savory cooks do a chef's knife.

The customary beaters for most standinig mixers are a flat paddle, wire whisk, and dough hook. The flat paddle is used for cake batter and cookie dough, while the wire whisk is used for whipping egg whites to make meringue. The dough hook kneads dough. Bowl size varies.

Standing mixers are heavy by design, generally about 20 pounds or more, in order to stand still while beating dense dough vigorously. If you plan to store your standing mixer on a countertop, measure the distance between the counter and the overhead cabinets to ensure you have enough height for this large appliance.

Pastry Brush

The pastry brush is so utilitarian that savory cooks use it, too, for both dry and wet applications. Whether brushing excess flour from a rolled dough, "washing" a pastry with beaten egg before it goes in the oven, or glazing a cake with simple syrup, the pastry brush is the tool to use.

Just like paint brushes, pastry brushes come in many sizes, but the average size is about 6 inches long, with 2- to 3-inch bristles about 1½ inches wide. The best pastry brushes traditionally have wooden handles and sterilized natural boar hair or nylon bristles. Silicone brushes are popular because they are heat-resistant and do not singe on contact with a hot metal surface, as can natural-hair brushes. They also do not absorb and transfer food flavors. Silicone brushes are acceptable for daubing barbecue sauce on meats on the grill, but not refined enough for delicate pastries, even the ones that have more slender bristles.

Invest in at least two pastry brushes—one large and one small—to accommodate various tasks. Ideally, you should buy two sets—one pair for your baking needs and the other for savory uses.

excellent egg wash

Do what the pros do and add a teaspoon or two of ice water, or heavy cream (one or the other, not both), per beaten egg to make superior egg wash for brushing on doughs before baking. The water gives the crust a golden hue, while the cream helps to add shine.

Timer

The time noted in a recipe is an important benchmark that guides and binds us to the cooking process, even though it might not indicate how long it ultimately takes to make the dish. The most seasoned cooks rely on timers at the very least to help them monitor food. For bakers, however, timers are deeply trusted guides that are a required tool of precise measurement.

Sandglasses, wind-up dials, or digital clocks are common timers. Sandglasses, or hourglasses, are the original version of this essential tool. They are not terribly useful other than indicating when the time has expired; that is, they do not indicate at any given moment how much time has passed or remains, nor do they let you know when the time is up unless you happen to be staring at it as the last grain of sand passes through the glass. What sandglasses lack in precision, they make up for in novelty. But wind-up dials or digital timers are superior implements.

A wind-up dial goes up to one hour, which is not helpful if you are roasting a roast beef for an hour and a quarter. They require no batteries and are noisy, even while counting down the time. While they are more accurate than sandglasses, they lack the benefits of a digital timer.

Yes, digital timers run on batteries, and beep instead of buzz. But they are precise down to the second. And speaking of down, they can count down *and* up. So you can set the timer to 30 minutes and watch it work its way down to zero, as well as start the clock at zero and count the time upwards. This is particularly useful to meticulous cooks who wish to note the time it actually takes them to execute a recipe. The recipe says 20 minutes, but it actually took you 26? If you use a digital timer with a count-up feature, you'll have this information at your fingertips to record it for the future. Plus, you can take the timer with you to other parts of the house—you're not forced to stay within earshot of your oven's timer. For these reasons, it's a good idea to have a separate digital timer beyond what's already on your oven.

Spatula

This can be a confusing word in the kitchen because there are three kinds: one is a lifter and turner, the second is a spoon and scraper, and the third is a cake froster and icer (see Offset Spatula below). The spoon and scraper spatula is an essential item to anyone who works with batters (e.g., cupcake or quick bread).

Spoon and Scraper Spatulas

Stiff or flexible, flat or spooned, a spatula can be made of rubber, plastic, or silicone with either a wooden or plastic handle. Flat spatulas, particularly the flexible variety, are excellent scrapers because they can grab any corner or curve. Spooned spatulas are almost always flexible and scoop things nicely; however, they scrape less efficiently than flat-blade spatulas since they are generally thicker in order to support the spoon shape.

The heatproof silicone flat spatula is ideal should you find yourself scraping a warm custard from a hot saucepan. It comes in a variety of pleasing colors. Handle length and blade size vary. Whichever spatula you select, consider the tasks for which you plan to use it.

Offset Spatula

This, the third kind of spatula, is the baker's best tool for glazing, icing, frosting, and spreading. It is a long, narrow stainless steel blade with a rounded tip anchored in a wooden or plastic handle that resembles a knife with no sharp edge. The standard blade size is a little more than 1 inch wide and at least 9 inches long. There are miniature offset spatulas, just 4 or 5 inches long, and they are used for frosting small items like single-portion pastries and cupcakes.

Why is it called an offset spatula? The blade is angled a bit below the handle. There are flat frosting spatulas, but the offset kind gives you the added bonus of using it to (you guessed it!) lift and turn.

Pastry Bag and Tip

When a spatula or spoon won't do, the baker grabs a pastry bag and tip. You can fill cupcake tins precisely using a pastry bag of cake batter, and then decorate cooled cupcakes using a pastry bag of frosting. The bag holds the food, and the tip (also called a tube) is the cone you push into the small, open end of the bag that gives design and shape as food passes through its mouth.

Pastry bags are traditionally made of canvas, a material that can hold heavy items like thick mashed potatoes to be piped in a twice-baked potato. Canvas, though, is burdensome to clean, so many people today prefer pastry bags made of coated fabric or nylon. Disposable, clear plastic pastry bags are very popular, too. If you select a natural fiber pastry bag, be sure to clean and dry it thoroughly before storing it. Open the pastry bag and stand it on a drying rack like a cone until it is bone-dry.

Tips come in all sizes and designs, ranging from very large to incredibly tiny openings, codified by a special number system. The standard tip is flat, meaning that the opening is a flat circle, yielding a tube of the food passed through it. Star tips—whether open, closed, or French—have many tall, sharp points radiating from the circle, which produce fluted patterns. Plastic tips are available, but they are inferior to their seamless nickel-plated, stainless steel counterparts.

Scale

Due to the superior accuracy of weight measurement, bread bakers and pastry chefs prefer a scale to volumetric devices, such as cups and spoons. Recipes for bread and pastry, unlike savory dishes, often call for grams or ounces, not cups. If you cook with foreign cookbooks, you likely encounter weight measurements, too.

Kitchen scales are either electronic or mechanical. Electronic scales require a battery, of course, but are easy to read thanks to a digital screen. Mechanical scales for home kitchens usually fall in the spring-action category where a bowl is placed on a tray that pushes on a calibrated spring. They hold a lot more weight than the average electric scale, but have dial faces and can be more challenging to read than digital displays.

The best electronic scales let you set a bowl on the scale's tray and then reset the weight to zero so that when you add the food you wish to measure, the weight registered is for the food alone. You can even do this leaving ingredients in the bowl should you want to measure uniquely each ingredient you place in the bowl without having to remove the preceding items.

When you purchase a scale, make sure you are getting one large enough to suit your needs and that it measures in both grams and ounces.

Pastry Scraper

Instead of using your hands to scrape sticky dough from a bowl, use a pastry scraper. Flexible enough to move along every curved line of a bowl but stiff enough to hold the dough, scrapers are like spatulas without handles. Like so many tools, this is yet another example of an implement that serves to enhance the function of the baker's hand.

Select a plastic scraper with a rounded edge for gathering dough from a bowl. A rectangular metal scraper, called a bench scraper, is best used for gathering dough from a flat work surface, like a counter or board (what is called a bread baker's "bench").

Silicone Baking Liner

We used to grease sheet pans or line them with parchment paper. Now the silicone baking liner makes bakers' lives easier in more ways than one.

Silicone can withstand heat up to nearly 500°F. So, when you read a recipe that says to "grease a cookie sheet" or "line a pan with parchment paper," simply think, "use a silicone baking liner." Not only does food slide right off this mess-free mat, but the flexible material makes it a cinch to store. Roll it or leave it flat after a quick sponge wash in the sink or run in the dishwasher. Sizes vary from as small as toaster oven trays to as large as full sheet pan-size for a professional kitchen. An 11" × 16" liner is the best size for most home bakers.

Since this innovation is so new in the general scheme of cooking's long history, there is a brand worth mentioning. What Kleenex is to tissues, Band-Aid is to bandages, and Tupperware is to food storage containers, SILPAT is to silicone baking liners. The distinctive design of the original, a silicone-coated woven fiberglass mat, helps to distribute heat evenly. SILPAT liners last almost forever; they need to be replaced eventually—after a few thousand uses, or so.

the secret life of brownies

How do they get those brownies so perfectly cut in the local gourmet store, with those crisp edges and no crumbs? They freeze them first. Line the brownie pan with aluminum foil hanging 2 inches over two of its sides. Once the brownies have cooled completely, lift them from the pan using the foil and place them in the freezer for about an hour. Peel away the foil, then slice the brownies on a cutting board using a sharp chef's knife. Perfect every time!

Cake Pans: Round and Square

The most important thing to bear in mind when selecting a cake pan is the material. Glass and coated (nonstick) dark metal pans tend to conduct heat very well and bake batters faster with thicker crusts than do earthenware and uncoated light metal pans. Since cake batters are often light, most bakers want a thin crust. However, many bakers are willing to have darker and tougher crusts for the ease of turning out a cake from a nonstick surface. If this is not a fair trade in your mind, then line an uncoated metal cake pan with greased parchment paper instead (see page 187).

Traditional cake pans are 9 inches round, 2 inches deep, and made of aluminum. Today, standard cake pans also come in 8 inches, round or square (2 inches deep), and often are made of a mix of aluminum and steel, coated or uncoated. Square pans are typically used for brownies.

Many cake recipes are for layered cakes, like German chocolate or Birthday Cake with Buttercream Frosting (page 186). These recipes usually make enough batter for two 8- or 9-inch round pans. If you bake a lot of cakes, have two cake pans of the same size and material.

There are other cake pans to consider: tube pans, plain and patterned bundt pans, as well as specialty shapes for almost any occasion.

Muffin and Loaf Pans

Muffin tins and loaf pans, not surprisingly, come in the same materials as cake pans. Since cupcakes are really just tiny cakes, use uncoated light metal muffin tins with paper or foil liners. A superb nonstick option is a silicone muffin tray—flexible for easy, no-liner-needed muffin removal. Quick breads and yeast breads can handle thicker crusts and you want them to release from the loaf pan freely, so a glass or coated nonstick pan is a good choice.

Muffin tins come in a range of sizes, both for the size of the muffin and the number of muffins the pan holds. There are three standard muffin sizes: mini (⅛ cup batter), regular (½ cup batter), and jumbo (1 cup batter). These sizes come in 6-, 12-, and 24-muffin pans. If you are one who prefers the muffin crown to the base, you can even buy a specialized tin that just bakes the muffin tops.

Springform Pan

Cheesecake bakers cannot live without this brilliantly designed cake pan. The separate bottom and spring-action ring make removal possible for moist and heavy cakes with crumb crusts that would otherwise be damaged if turned out from a standard pan onto a cooling rack.

Coated or uncoated, all metal springform pans have clamps on the side that, when opened, widen the ring and release it from the side of the cake. The bottoms have a thin groove along the perimeter to create a tight seal with the ring. Sometimes the bottoms have a waffle pattern to help circulate air, which prevents soggy crusts. Sizes range from individual 4-inch pans, to standard 8- or 9-inch pans, up to 11- or 12-inch pans.

Clean and dry the bottom and ring separately and thoroughly before fastening them back together for storage and future use.

Rolling Pin

Homemade pie, pastry, and cookie doughs chill in the refrigerator in balls, but need to be rolled perfectly smooth and flat before being shaped for baking. The rolling pin is the only tool that can do that.

In an era of new-and-improved everything, the rolling pin remains perfectly unchanged. The original design and material of a French rolling pin—a long and slender cylinder made of hardwood—is still the preferred model among professionals. The iconic American rolling pin, with its two side handles and heavy (usually wooden but occasionally marble) cylinder that rolls freely around ball bearings or a center axle, was once the home baker's standard. More people are now familiar with the French rolling pin and its unquestionable superiority.

While the American rolling pin does not require much muscle to move across dough given its weight and construction, it is cumbersome to control. Though you have to use a little more strength to move the much lighter French rolling pin, you have closer contact with the dough and a better feeling of its transformation as you move the pin across its surface. The French rolling pin enables you to adjust pressure at one end or the other to maintain fluid movement, providing finesse and enhanced maneuverability. This allows you to work faster, which is much better for temperature-sensitive dough.

French rolling pins are about 20 inches long and 2 inches in diameter. They come tapered or untapered, in hardwood or nylon. Both smooth surfaces require a standard dusting of flour. The nylon pin can go in the dishwasher while the wooden one must be manually washed and dried.

Sifter

Long ago, flour was sold loose in barrels at the market. Foreign objects like pebbles or insects needed to be removed, and natural lumps needed to be sifted into fine grains of flour. Thankfully, these are no longer concerns. Today, all-purpose flour is packaged, pest- and lump-free. We now sift flour first to aerate it, lightening it to ensure that the flour does not pack too densely in volume measures, and also to combine it with other ingredients.

Sifters—metal cups with single- or double-layer mesh bottoms—work three ways: a crank handle, squeeze handle, or hold-and-shake construction. A crank handle moves a wheel that pushes the flour through the mesh base, whereas a squeeze handle spins a spider that stirs the ingredients through the mesh. A sifter that is merely a mesh-bottomed vessel with a side handle is the simplest and easiest kind to use; just hold it and gently shake.

Use a sifter for more than just flour. You can dust a cake evenly and beautifully using a sifter filled with cocoa powder or confectioners' sugar.

Pie Pan

Apple pie is the American dessert. Any self-proclaimed baker, then, needs to have a pie pan. Like many other baking pans, the important distinguishing characteristic is the material. Glass, ceramic, or metal (coated or uncoated aluminum) pans are available.

Pie pans have sloped sides for the most part and come in three standard sizes: 8-, 9-, and 10-inch, with a standard depth of 1½ inches. A "deep" pie dish will be about twice as deep. Some pans have straight sides. Most have flat rims, while others have ruffled edges into which you can press and crimp the dough for a decorative look.

Pie pans become pie *dishes* when they make their way to the table. Since pies cannot be removed from their cooking vessels for service (they are sliced right from the pan), earthenware is the more attractive material, but glass distributes heat the most evenly. Nonstick metal darkens dough, which is helpful to a piecrust with a wet filling, but that material also scratches easily.

two pies for the price of one

Piecrust recipes yield two crusts, since so many American pie recipes are double-crusted (top and bottom). If you prefer open-faced pies like pecan or single-crust pies like apple crumb, why not just plan to make two pies at once? Buy two identical pie pans and you will always be prepared.

Tart Pan

If the pie is classically American, then the tart is its European relative. Refined, shallow, and crisp, a tart is a reflection of its pan's size and shape.

Tart pans come in either coated or uncoated metal, but pastry doughs, like piecrust and shortbread, have so much butter in them, they surely will not stick. Sizes range from individual tartlet to extra large, with the standard round pan 9 inches in diameter and just 1 inch deep (there are some rectangular pans, perfect for savory tarts like tomato and goat cheese). Sides can be straight or more typically are fluted. Bottoms are either fixed or loose.

Fixed tart pans are not very useful since a tart is almost always beautifully served free from its cooking vessel. Loose-bottom pans let the fluted sides fall and unearth the tart on its base when the pan is set over a raised item, like a can of soup, smaller than the diameter of the tart base.

blind bake with beans

Some tarts and pies require no cooking, just a finished shell (such as key lime and chocolate cream). "Blind baking" pastry and pie doughs—that is, with nothing in them—produces puffed, misshapen shells if baked unweighted. To maintain the desired hollow shape of an empty pie shell, line it with parchment paper or aluminum foil while raw and fill it with dried beans, or ceramic or metal pie weights before baking.

Cookie Cutters

Kids of all ages love to make shaped cookies. Sugar cookie pumpkins for Halloween, gingerbread men for Christmas, and chocolate hearts for Valentine's Day make holiday celebrations more festive and fun. Cookie cutters come in every imaginable shape and size, and are sold individually or in sets.

The most basic collection is a nesting set of round cutters. Cookie cutters can be tin, plastic, copper, or stainless steel. The important criteria are sharp edges on the bottom for easy, crisp cutting of dough (no stretching or tearing allowed), and rolled edges on top for safe, pain-free pressing.

Scrub cookie cutters by hand to make sure no dough is wedged in any corner or stuck in any seam. Dry metal cutters immediately to prevent rusting.

Ramekins

The ramekin is to the soufflé what the pie dish is to apple pie; you cannot make the recipe without its proper vessel. Both functional and ideally good-looking, a ramekin is made of ceramic. The classic look is clean and crisp, just like the chef's toque (hat): bright white with a ridged outside and smooth inside. Not just for your favorite soufflé, a ramekin can be used to serve puddings, mousses, and custards.

If you buy one ramekin, you might as well buy four, six, or eight. A full set comes in handy. Use them at the table to hold garnishes, or as containers to hold the fillings the next time you make omelets.

Cooling Rack

Every cookie, cake, and pastry needs a safe place to cool. After all, cooling is the final requisite step in the baking process. A cooling rack not only acts as a designated area for your baked goods to rest, it allows them to cool properly.

Hot foods from the oven cool fastest when air can circulate on all sides of the cooking vessel or the food itself. This prevents steam from being trapped between baked goods and pan. Remove cookies from a sheet pan immediately to a cooling rack, but allow a cake to cool first for a few minutes before you turn it from its pan on to a rack.

Rectangular or round, cooling racks are raised from the counter with short feet or taller, collapsible legs that often stack. Standard or coated metal makes for a sturdy and nonstick rack. Choose a cooling rack with a grid, a tighter pattern than parallel lines through which smaller items can slip.

ice a cool cake with frosting

Ice. Cool. Frost. It's no coincidence that all the words are about cold temperature. The cake has to be cooled completely before you ice it with frosting, frost it with icing, or cover it with buttercream (it's your call). If you ice a warm cake with frosting you get . . . drum roll . . . glaze! Of course, you can make glaze (thin icing) from the start and drizzle it on a cool cake.

⟅ THE BAKER'S ESSENTIAL TECHNIQUES ⟆

Baking is all about precision and procedure. Deviating from a recipe's ratios for doughnut dough, or cavalierly combining wet and dry ingredients at once for cake batter, likely will yield a different result from what the recipe writer intended. Measure carefully. Follow the instructions. If the cake box says to beat the batter for three minutes with an electric mixer and you do it for a mere thirty seconds, do not be surprised if the batter is not as light and fluffy as you expected it to be. Process counts. Method matters. If you follow a basic set of principles when you bake, you will achieve success.

Read the recipe carefully.

If you just glance at a recipe and begin cooking, you might miss something important: extra large eggs instead of the standard large, a tablespoon of vanilla extract instead of a teaspoon, or toasting the nuts before adding them to the dish.

Preheat the oven.

Once you have read the recipe but before you begin to measure the ingredients, preheat the oven. Ovens take time to reach temperature. None of your time will be wasted if the oven does its job while you prepare the recipe. And while you're at it, make sure the racks are in the desired position so you can put the pan in the oven quickly without letting all that freshly made hot air escape.

Measure correctly.

There are two aspects of measuring ingredients correctly: using the appropriate vessel and making a level measurement.

Wet and dry measures should not be used interchangeably. Clear glass or plastic measuring cups with spouts are for liquids like milk, oil, lemon juice, and molasses. Dry measures, by contrast, which you cannot see through and have no spouts, are for flour, sugar, butter, and sour cream. *But sour cream is wet!*, you say. True, but it's not a liquid. You cannot make half a cup sour cream level in a 1-cup liquid measure. A half cup of milk poured into a 1-cup measure is level on its own. That is the test of whether a wet item belongs in a wet or dry measure.

Level measurements are the baking standard. Unless the recipe calls for a heaping tablespoon of sugar, it is tacitly understood that you should make the sugar level with the top of the measuring device. Use the tablespoon to scoop the sugar, then take the back of a dinner knife to scrape away the excess sugar. Level measurements are so critical to the baking procedure that there is a specific method used for measuring flour by volume.

"Spoon and sweep" flour.

While brown sugar is supposed to be packed into a dry measuring cup (pressed down to leave no air between granules so that as much sugar as possible is in the cup), flour never should be. The principle is that since volume measurements are less precise than weight measurements, aerating the flour as you put it in the measuring cup provides some context for parity.

Hold the empty measuring cup over the container of flour and gradually place small scoops of flour into the cup using a regular spoon. "Spoon" an excessive amount so that it overflows. Do not use the measuring cup itself to scoop. Never tap the measuring cup so that some of the excess falls away and the flour settles in the cup; this counters the point of aerating it in the first place. Using the back of a dinner knife, "sweep" the excess flour away and make what is left level with the measuring cup.

Cream butter and sugar together until light and fluffy.

Sound familiar? Well, it's a common instruction, good advice, and a necessary procedure in baking. This stage plays a critical role in the quality of the finished product.

Creaming butter and sugar together creates air bubbles in the batter that helps the leavening process, which translates to light and fluffy texture. The air bubbles allow steam to disperse evenly amongst the fat, making cakes and cookies rise (leavening agents like baking soda just make those air bubbles bigger).

Butter should be soft but not warm—slightly colder than room temperature is ideal (about 68°F). Do not liquefy the butter in any way by melting it in the microwave, for example. You want the rough sugar crystals to cut into the soft but solid butterfat. The fat, in turn, surrounds each sugar crystal with air trapped inside.

It does not matter if you "cream" by hand with a whisk or use an electric mixer, though the former will take about twice as long (eight to ten minutes). All that matters is that you achieve the "light and fluffy" part. As long as you reach the destination, it doesn't matter how you get there.

Beat sugar and eggs properly.

Sugar cooks eggs. Yes, that's right. If you pour sugar on eggs and do not stir immediately, the sugar will curdle the eggs eventually. Go ahead . . . try it. You'll see.

When a recipe instructs you, for instance, to beat ¾ cup sugar with 6 eggs (or egg yolks) it is important that you do it immediately. Have the whisk next to the bowl so you are ready to beat the eggs once you add the sugar. Stir vigorously in a circular motion for a few minutes until the eggs lighten in color to a pale yellow hue and fluffy texture.

This technique, known as *blanchir* in formal cooking terms, has the benefit of preventing the sugar from curdling the eggs, and the act of whitening and lightening helps to leaven batters, much like the proper creaming of butter and sugar does.

Combine dry and wet ingredients separately.

There are exceptions to this general rule (most notably, pancakes) and, of course, you should follow the recipe's directions. Most of the time, however, you combine all the dry ingredients, then combine the wet ingredients separately from the dry, and then combine the two mixtures together. ❊

CHAPTER 5

* Food Processor
* Blender
* Spice Grinder
* Microplane
* Mandoline

* Slotted Spoon
* Meat Cleaver
* Box Grater
* Dutch Oven
* Roasting Pan

The Serious Cook's Essential Tools and Techniques

A SERIOUS COOK—someone who avoids taking shortcuts and enjoys digging deeply into the pleasures of the craft—needs serious tools. The Essential Top 20 is all that you need most of the time. But if you like to make your own breadcrumbs and braise meats, you'll need some specific tools to get the job done well. It's just not possible to get the precision of a perfectly ground spice quickly and efficiently without a spice grinder. Velvety smooth puréed soups and sauces are made in a blender or food processor. Even if you do not consider yourself a serious cook or aspire to be one, take a look at the list and consider, at the very least, investing in a Microplane. You'll never buy preground Parmesan again!

⟨ THE SERIOUS COOK'S ESSENTIAL TOOLS ⟩

Food Processor

Big cooking jobs require a lot of preparation. Food processors make it so much easier to grate cheese, shred carrots, slice potatoes, chop nuts, and prepare fresh breadcrumbs. They even make pie dough and mayonnaise! Just as useful in the final stages of cooking, too, food processors purée vegetables and blend soups. They are to serious cooks what hand mixers are to bakers: essential.

Food processors come in several sizes, ranging from mini-choppers to 20-cup machines. The typical size for home cooks is a 10- to 14-cup model. Like a standing mixer, a food processor should be heavy enough not to move on the counter while the motor is running. Speaking of the motor running, food processors are noisy machines. Some are quieter than others, but you should expect it to be loud when the machine is on. Still, it's well worth it since food processors get the job done very quickly.

The clear plastic bowl of a food processor locks into the motorized base. The lid comes with a tall tube feature that allows you to pass food safely through its mouth during operation. Generally outfitted with a chopping blade, dough blade, slicing disc, and shredding disc, food processors come with a lot of parts. There is a lot to clean, but it is dishwasher-safe with the exception of the base that can be wiped clean with a towel. Some models come with several buttons on the base to control the power, but the standard modes are "on," "off," and "pulse."

Blender

There are two kinds of blenders worth considering: standing and immersion. Standing blenders are what most people think of when they say "blender." The motorized base sits on the countertop holding a tall glass, plastic, or metal container with a tight-fitting lid. Pour a soup base into a blender for a velvety smooth finish, or liquefy fruits and vegetables for sauces. Standing blenders crush ice, but cannot chop onions due to the vertical nature of the blade and the vessel. They blend wet things very well, but are not designed to grind dry things.

Immersion blenders are compact, lightweight motorized wands that can purée soup right in the pot. Their chief advantage over traditional countertop blenders is that they do the job in the container of your choosing. No need to transfer a hot soup to a blender's pitcher in batches. Just immerse the wand in the vessel, press the button on the handle, and *voila*: the rotating blade purées the soup. The motorized handle separates from the bottom blade attachment for easy cleaning and storage. Some models even come with a cup attachment for small tasks like chopping nuts and garlic, or crushing ice.

Standing blenders are more powerful than noncommercial immersion blenders, and therefore do a better job, in general. But they take up a lot more space and are more cumbersome to clean. If you love making smoothies, buy a blender. If soup is a favorite, consider the simplicity of working with an immersion blender.

Spice Grinder

Freshly ground spices are more fragrant and powerful than the pre-ground bottled kind. But what do you do when you want to toast whole cumin seeds and then grind them to a fine powder like the untoasted version found in little bottles in the supermarket?

Think mini coffee grinder. That's what a spice grinder is. Sure, a salt or pepper mill is a spice grinder of sorts. But it can never make a superfine powder that an electric grinder can. Today manufacturers market these little machines specifically as spice grinders. If you cannot find one, use a mini coffee grinder that you solely designate for spices. You do not want your next batch of morning brew to taste like stew.

Microplane

Cooks who uses this tool swear they cannot live without it. Also known as a rasp, the Microplane was originally used to shape and smooth a variety of building materials, ranging from wood to rubber. Fitted with hundreds of tiny stainless steel razors, this hand-held tool revolutionized cooking when a frustrated home cook borrowed her husband's woodworking tool to zest an orange. Bless her.

Microplanes come flat, box, or rotary. Whatever the shape, Microplanes can zest citrus fruit, grate hard cheese and carrots to the finest

a food processor for the Flintstones

Thousands of years ago, people used the mortar and pestle, a small bowl with a stubby pounding implement (perhaps a hunk of tree and well suited stone?). Today we have food processors, blenders, spice mills, and grinders that do the job effortlessly in seconds. However, do not overlook the tactile delight of working with a mortar and pestle. You can feel your food transform and slowly develop flavors as you physically mash, grind, and pound the ingredients together. That's exactly why so many cooks still rely on this ancient tool.

grade, or turn whole nutmeg into powder. They are easy to clean and occupy little space considering how much value they add. Go out and get one.

Mandoline

Even the most adept cooks can use a little help sometimes to achieve precision and save time. A mandoline (man-doh-LEEN) is a manual apparatus that does the fancy cutting for you. Julienne, waffle cuts, and paper-thin slices are easy; just slide vegetables across a blade mounted on a rectangular surface. This is an especially appealing tool if you are an adventurous cook with a sophisticated aesthetic who is still developing those knife skills. With a mandoline, the cook moves the food over the blade instead of moving a knife blade over the food.

There are two kinds of mandolines: French and Japanese. The French mandoline is the clunkier, heavier version. Typically made of stainless steel, though some models are plastic, an elongated tray holds two blades across from one another. Small handles on the underside of the tray adjust the position and texture of the blades to make distinct cuts (only one blade is used at a time). The tray itself stands securely at an angle on collapsible legs.

The Japanese mandoline is a streamlined version of the French, lightweight with a less complex construction and therefore a considerably lower price tag. Made of plastic with three removable blades (straight edge, fine tooth, and wide tooth) that can be adjusted with the simple turn of a knob, the Japanese mandoline is easy to clean and store. Since it has no legs, it can be more difficult to stabilize while you work, although some models come attached to a plastic container that steadies the device and simultaneously gathers the trimmings. Try both kinds and select the mandoline that's more comfortable for you and fits in your storage space.

the namesake

Yes, a cook's mandoline was named after the stringed musical instrument. And like a musician playing particular notes on a mandolin, the cook can use a mandoline for particular cuts. Other food-related gear named after musical instruments include the drum sieve (called a "tamis" in French), "cloche" (bell-shaped dome for upscale food service named after the French word for bell), and champagne flute. One more fun food homograph: "flageolets" are both beans and recorder-like woodwind instruments.

Slotted Spoon

Is a spoon with holes an essential tool for a serious cook like you? Yes. Every major ethnicity boasts a dumpling as a staple dish. No matter the cuisines you like to cook, you will come across a dumpling.

With a slotted spoon you can lift the dumpling from the pot of boiling water, or hot oil, at the same time you strain it. Without a slotted spoon—a strainer of sorts—you would have to pour the pot of water or oil over a colander to retrieve the dumplings. This can be done with boiling water, but absolutely out of the question with hot oil. Even if safety were not a concern, most dumplings are too delicate to be handled this way. Lifting them gently from their cooking pots prevents them from being crushed or torn.

Slotted spoons can be wooden, plastic, or metallic. Their shapes and sizes vary, as do their perforations (slits versus holes). A shallow, slotted oval spoon is ideal for lifting wontons, whereas a perforated ladle is better for matzo balls due to its corresponding contours.

Skimmers are large, flat, slotted spoons with extra long handles specifically used to remove fried foods from hot oil. If you deep-fry foods, a skimmer is a must-have. Whether it is made of twisted or coiled wire, mesh or perforated stainless steel, select a skimmer for the task at hand (i.e., twisted wire is the Chinese standard while coiled is best for doughnuts).

around the world in 80 dumplings

Maybe there aren't 80 varieties exactly, but the list is undeniably extensive: Italian raviolis and meatballs, German knodels, Indian koftas, French quenelles, Chinese wontons, Jewish kneidls (matzo balls) and kreplach (meat-filled noodle dumplings), Japanese shumai and gyoza, Korean mandu, Middle Eastern falafel, Brazlian coxinha, Russian pelmeni and vareniki, Polish pierogi . . . can you name a few more?

Meat Cleaver

A meat cleaver is used in Chinese cooking the way a chef's knife is employed in the western kitchen: for slicing, dicing, chopping, and mincing. Though not an all-purpose knife for the typical American cook, the meat cleaver is an essential piece of equipment for the serious cook who wants to do some butchering.

The heavy blade cuts through bones with one decisive chop. Butterfly a chicken and remove the backbone, section ribs effortlessly, or pound a chicken breast into a *scallopini* or *paillard* using the flat body of the blade. You can ask your butcher to do this for you, but you certainly can do it yourself with this tool.

Select the heaviest cleaver you can find with a handle you can grip securely. The majority of the weight should come from the stainless steel blade, which might feel a bit unbalanced compared to the even weight of a chef's knife. Some blades have a hole at the top corner furthest from the handle for hanging. Blade size ranges from 6 to 8 inches.

Box Grater

A box grater is useful for small jobs when taking out the food processor isn't worth the effort. Shred cheese and carrots for salads, or grate them for pasta sauces with this basic and timeless tool. Move the food across a sharp blade as you do when using a mandoline.

There are many graters with just one blade, and yet there are many blade styles available. That's why a box grater is such a well-conceived tool. With four tall sides, the box grater has four distinct perforated blades that shred, finely shred, grate, and, in some cases, slice (some box graters even have five or six sides).

Look for a model with a removable base that collects the shavings. Confirm that the handle at the top is comfortable to grip. Stainless steel is the best material for the blades, but the handle can be rubber.

Box graters are convenient for cutting but, due to their protruding sharp punctures, are predictably difficult to clean. A good scrub brush and some "elbow grease" do the trick. Just don't put the box grater in the dishwasher without a good manual scrubbing first, or you might find caked-on carrots that are even more challenging to remove.

> ### roll with it
>
> The Chinese "roll" cut exposes the maximum surface area of a vegetable to heat, making the food cook more quickly (a requirement of stir-frying). It is a beautiful bias cut for large items like Japanese eggplant, carrot, radish, and zucchini. Using a cleaver or chef's knife, make one diagonal slice at the beginning of the vegetable, then roll it a quarter of the way and cut again. Repeat until the vegetable is cut and you have large diamond-shaped pieces.

Dutch Oven

The Dutch oven is the original slow cooker. A deep and wide round or oval cooking vessel with a tight-fitting lid, this wonderfully practical pot is perfect for braising in the oven and can be used even for deep-frying on the stovetop.

The iconic Dutch oven is made of enameled cast iron, and is actually called a French oven per its most popular manufacturer, Le Creuset. These pots have matching lids of the same material with a knob that is heatproof up to 450°F, far higher than the typical braising temperature. Since this Dutch oven encases the food entirely in cast iron with a shiny, nonstick enamel finish, food stays very hot and cooks very evenly when used in the oven. If used on the stovetop, the bottom of the vessel can scorch foods at the base since the pot holds heat so well. The handles are made of the same material as the pot, so never touch them without an oven mitt or towel.

There are several brands of Dutch ovens, some of which are not necessarily enameled cast iron. Stainless steel, cast aluminum, and copper pots are also available, though they might be called stew pots, braisers, or casseroles. Sizes range from a modest 2 quarts up to 12 or more quarts. Usually such a vessel is used for big cuts of meat made at holidays or for family gatherings, so buy the biggest one you can for your space and budget (5 to 7 quarts is a useful yet manageable size).

burn a pan? boil it

If you burn a thick crust onto the bottom of a pan, do not race to the sink to clean it. That's the worst thing you can do. All that scrubbing further sets everything below the top layer of crud. Instead, fill the pot two-thirds of the way with water, bring to a boil over high heat, then simmer over low heat for an hour on the stovetop. This loosens all the caked-on crud from the top to bottom. Then take the pot to the sink to scrub it clean. The crud will come right off.

Roasting Pan

You might only use this pan for turkey (you can use a rolled sheet pan for chickens, rib roasts, and pork loins), but if you are a serious cook you probably are on duty Thanksgiving Day.

A typical roasting pan is rectangular and shallow with straight sides and rounded corners, has angled or vertical handles, and is large enough to hold the turkey, but shallow enough to let it brown. Dimensions range anywhere from 14 to 20 inches long, 10 to 14 inches wide, 2 to 4 inches deep. It must be sturdy enough to hold a heavy hunk of meat, but light enough to maneuver. Classic materials include stainless steel, lined copper, anodized aluminum, and stainless steel with aluminum cores.

Most roasting pans come without racks, and depending on what you are cooking, the recipe, and its methods, you might not even need one. Some roasting pans, however, do come with racks: a shallow rack that resembles a footed cooling rack but shaped to fit perfectly in the pan; a V-shaped rack (2 sloped sides); or a basket rack (1 flat bottom and 2 sloped sides).

Pick up a roasting pan to gauge how heavy it is before you buy it. Imagine it with the bird, ham, or roast beef you plan to cook in it. Remember that the pan will be much heavier and hundreds of degrees hot. You need to be able to carry it from oven to stovetop or counter. As for handling the pan, upright handles perpendicular to the length of the pan are the easiest to manage since they give your mitted hands room to grip.

THE SERIOUS COOK'S ESSENTIAL TECHNIQUES

Cooking is a lifelong pursuit. Knowing how to season properly with salt, sensing when to adjust the heat, or recognizing how to turn tribulation into triumph is something you grow into over time. You never finish learning how to work with food or improving your ability with a chef's knife. Beyond basic knife skills and cooking methods, serious cuisine involves the special touches and fine accents of a dish. If you aspire to this level of competence, there are several techniques you need to know so you never need to buy bottled salad dressing, and can make your own sauces.

Create an emulsion.

If you've ever mixed oil and vinegar together, you know it's true: they don't mix. You can shake a bottle as hard as possible, but the oil and vinegar never stay blended. That's because they lack a liaison—a stabilizing binder that helps to suspend the two liquids. Mustard is a classic liaison for making vinaigrette. Egg yolk is the liaison for making mayonnaise.

To properly emulsify oil and vinegar for vinaigrette, add some mustard to the vinegar. Then, very slowly, pour the oil in a thin, steady stream as you continuously whisk the vinegar and mustard in the bowl. The mixture will go from translucent to opaque as the oil and vinegar come together, bound by the mustard. As you continue to pour and whisk, the mixture becomes thicker.

Following this "slow and steady" procedure is essential to emulsion, a relevant technique in competent cooking. If you just dump the oil, vinegar, and mustard in a bowl and stir, you won't get a stable emulsion (one that never breaks once it has been made).

Deglaze a pan.

When you sauté or roast meats and vegetables, lots of crusty browned bits called sucs (SOOKS) are glazed on the bottom of the pan. These are the foundation of exceptionally good pan sauces. After you remove the meat and vegetables from the pan, you can deglaze it to retrieve the sucs. All you need is a wooden spoon, liquid, and heat.

To deglaze, return the empty pan to a medium-high heat and add wine, stock, juice, vinegar, or water (depending on the ingredients in the dish you're preparing). Scrape vigorously as you remove the sucs from the pan and disperse them in the liquid, which will cloud and darken. All the flavors of the food that was prepared in the pan now permeate the liquid you added, which is the perfect foundation for a quick and refined sauce.

Reduce to concentrate and thicken.

Once you have deglazed a pan, you can begin to develop the flavors you have married with the sucs and the liquid. Reduction is the process of intensifying flavor and thickening texture through evaporation. In other words, when you reduce a sauce, you concentrate and heighten the flavors by allowing the water to cook off from the pan, decreasing the volume with which you started, in turn thickening what is left.

Note that you can reduce a pan sauce only so far. There is a tipping point at which you lose too much of what is in the pan, and not just in volume—it's when the sauce becomes too thick, too little remains, or the flavors are too concentrated. Experience, unfortunately, is the best way to tell that you've reached that point. If you reduce a pan sauce too much, you can cook away some of the fundamental flavors you're aiming to develop.

Thicken sauces with fat and starch.

If you have reduced a pan sauce as much as you can without losing too much volume or flavor, but it just isn't viscous enough, add something to bind and thicken.

There are several ways to do this. Sometimes just swirling some cold butter in the pan does the trick when a pan sauce is almost as thick as you want it. If the sauce is simply too thin, add a slurry—a combination of a raw starch (arrowroot, potato starch, or corn starch) and cold liquid (water, white wine, or stock)—to the liquid, slowly, over heat while stirring constantly until the sauce thickens. Alternatively, you can whisk in a mixture of equal parts flour and room temperature butter, called *beurre manié* or kneaded butter. When the butter melts, it suspends the flour particles in the sauce, thickening without lumps. Reducing heavy cream by half its volume and whisking it into a warm reduced stock thickens as well.

Sometimes you need to build a sauce with the thickening agent as the foundation, and the liquid as the building block. *Béchamel*, or white sauce, is a sauce made entirely of milk and seasoning, thickened with a roux. A roux is also equal parts fat and flour, except that instead of being added to a pan of hot liquid, the butter and flour are combined first in an empty pan, cooked for a minute or two, and then hot liquid is added. ✳

The Health-Conscious Cook's Essential Tools and Techniques

THE AT-HOME MODERN COOK is conscious of health and nutrition. Delicious food does not have to be decadently prepared; indulgence in flavor trumps fat and calories. Inherently healthy techniques like steaming become foolproof with the proper tools. Even if healthy cooking is not a priority for you, all the recipes are worth sampling for brightly flavored fare.

THE HEALTH-CONSCIOUS COOK'S ESSENTIAL TOOLS

Steamer

Steamed food is synonymous with health food primarily because you don't need to use any fat. Water and heat work together in a covered vessel to produce a vapor that quickly cooks the food. Nutritionists tout the benefits of steaming, including the retention of nutrients and enzymes.

There are four basic steaming tools: a steamer basket, a steamer insert, an electric steamer, or a bamboo steamer. Following is more information about each type.

Steamer Baskets

Steamer baskets are wonderful contraptions: stainless steel discs with perforated overlapping petals that close like flower buds for storage and expand to fit the pot perfectly. When fully open, they are almost flat and can be washed in the dishwasher. Steamer baskets usually have three legs and a center handle, all four of which are removable for cleaning. Easy to use and maintain, steamer baskets make steaming food as easy as can be.

Steamer Inserts

Steamer inserts are special accessory items from the manufacturer just like the saucepans in which they are bulged to fit, but with perforated bottoms. Sometimes an insert and pan are sold as a set (pasta inserts can be used as steamer baskets). The water goes in the bottom pot and the food to be steamed rests in the perforated pan. Sizes range from a few to several quarts.

Electric Steamers

Electric steamers are bulky appliances with electric water tanks for bases and clear stacking or side-by-side compartments for the food. They have digital display buttons and touch-pad controls for convenience, but can weigh up to 10 pounds.

Bamboo Steamers

Bamboo steamers, by contrast, are shallow, round, stackable vessels made of natural bamboo with lattice-weave lids that trap steam without creating condensation that would otherwise fall back on the food and make it soggy. Food sticks to bamboo, however, so the steamer must be lined with a large leaf (banana, cabbage, lettuce) or plate.

Electric Juicer

Juicing raw fruits and vegetables retains even more nutrients than does steaming. An orange sliced in half is easy to juice by hand, but how about an apple, raspberry, carrot, or cucumber? An electric juicer lets you juice anything you like, from pineapple to peas.

Electric juicers work by extracting juice and pulp from the food, leaving behind the fibrous matter. A motorized centrifuge typically pushes juice through the front spout of the mixer and the waste into a separate receptacle in the back.

Look for a model with a wide feeding tube to accommodate sizable chunks, as well as a splash-guarded spout to prevent splattered juice on your counters and walls. Electric juicers are quite noisy, but they juice most foods very quickly so the sound is bearable.

Electric Grill

Thanks to compact electric grills, indoor countertop grilling is possible, enjoyable, and healthy. The nonstick surface allows you to grill food without added fat for leaner, lighter fare.

Electric grills are either open or closed, with one or two nonstick cooking surfaces. Open models resemble an outdoor grill with a rack that rests above a heating element, or a grid that is the heating element itself with embedded electric coils. Food needs to be turned to cook on both sides. Closed electric grills, like waffle irons and panini presses, have heated electric coils on the base and the top to provide direct heat contact, cooking both sides of food at once.

Ridges and their widths vary. Some grids are detachable and dishwasher safe. Others are slightly angled forward to let unwanted fat drip from the cooking surface. Most electric grills come with a light that indicates when the machine is hot—beneficial for letting you know when the grill is ready for use, and whether it has cooled down for cleaning.

The greater the wattage, the stronger the machine, which means the better the grill marks you'll get in less time. After you determine what size you and your kitchen can handle, select the machine with the most power. Grills range in power from 700 to more than 2000 watts.

Salad Spinner

To enjoy lettuce, it must be clean, crisp, and dry. Damp lettuce might not be so terrible on its own. Add salad dressing to a wet leaf, though, and watch it fall away or become watered down at best (remember the old adage that water and oil don't mix). A salad spinner beats filling the sink with cold water and giving some Bibb a bath any day. Outfitted with two bowls—an internal plastic basket in which to rinse and hold the lettuce, and a larger bowl to hold the excess water—the salad spinner takes your rinsed greens and spins them dry.

As the internal basket spins faster and faster, the centrifugal force pushes the lettuce from the middle of the basket to the sides, pulling all the unwanted water with it. The most popular salad spinners today work with a pump that activates the spinning motion with a few manual pushes. The spinning can be stopped at once with a button that doubles as the lock to keep the pump down for storage. Other models work with a pull-cord mechanism, which is gentler on the greens but takes a few more tugs than pushes of the pump. A crank salad spinner requires you to turn a crank to spin the basket.

Select the size that best suits your daily needs and work in batches when necessary. Prewashed baby lettuces are lovely and exceptionally convenient, but with a salad spinner you can clean and dry fresh heads of lettuce for a lot less money.

take herbs for a spin

The salad spinner is useful for more than just lettuce. Fresh, leafy herbs like parsley, cilantro, basil, and dill can be quite dirty. Trim herb bunches of their roots and long stems, and rinse them in the salad spinner basket until clean. Spin them dry and store them tightly rolled in a slightly damp paper towel in the refrigerator. They will remain crisp and vibrant for days.

Oil Mister

Every health-conscious cook carefully monitors fat content. A nonaerosol mister (healthier for you and the environment) helps you add oil lightly and evenly by spraying with a fine mist. This gives you a lot of control over how much fat you use.

An oil mister also gives you control over *what kind* of fat you use. Unlike the ubiquitous aerosol cans sold in supermarkets, an oil mister enables you to select the quality and type of oil that suits you. Would you like a touch of toasted sesame oil flavor on that sesame-crusted salmon? You cannot find a spray bottle of toasted sesame oil unless you fill it yourself.

≋ THE HEALTH-CONSCIOUS COOK'S ESSENTIAL TECHNIQUES ≋

Healthy cooking encompasses so many aspects of food preparation: the ingredients, the ratios, the cooking methods, and the portions. It's critical to employ colorful fruits and vegetables, lean proteins, and low-fat or fat-free techniques. With the exception of deep-frying, a health-conscious cook should use every basic Essential Cooking Technique (page 29). In addition, steaming, juicing, and cooking in parchment paper are excellent methods to master.

Steam vegetables until crisp-tender.

"Crisp-tender" means that the broccoli should be easily penetrable with a knife, but firm enough to hold its shape with a toothsome bite. Neither crunchy nor mushy, a perfectly steamed vegetable retains many of its nutrients and natural taste while taking on a pleasing, cooked texture.

Steaming works by water and heat acting together—along with the natural moisture of the vegetable, poultry, or fish—to create a vapor that cooks food gently. No added fat is needed for steam heat, and there is obviously no possibility for dried-out results. Procedures vary depending on the apparatus you use, but the principle is always the same.

If you are using a steamer basket, place the basket in a saucepan large enough to hold the food to be steamed. Fill the pot with water just below the surface of the basket (about an inch or two). Bring the water to boil and place the food in the basket (broccoli florets, sugar snap peas, carrot slices, etc.). Cover the pot with a tight-fitting lid. Most vegetables cook in a matter of a few minutes. Test for doneness by piercing one of the vegetables with a paring knife. If the vegetable resists the knife, cover with the lid and continue steaming. When the vegetables are ready, season them with whatever you and your doctor allow.

Use your juicer for more than just drinks.

If you are a health-conscious cook, it's likely you are already an expert on fruit juice concoctions and exotic vegetable elixirs. Have you tried using these juices to marinate, or make sauces and soups?

It probably seems obvious to marinate sea bass in a mixture of freshly squeezed orange juice and olive oil for a healthy, flavorful dish. It might not be as apparent that you can make a creamy, colorful sauce from vegetable juice. As an accompaniment to your favorite steamed fish, make a deceptively creamy yet light sauce. Juice two sweet potatoes and one carrot, let the starch fall to the bottom of the vessel, pour off the juice, and heat the nectar over low heat until it thickens a bit. Add a touch of low-fat coconut milk with a small dollop of curry paste, and spoon the sauce over the fish.

Experiment with fruit and vegetables juices you like to drink. Poach fish or chicken in a dilution of your favorite mix with water or stock for a subtle flavor boost. Reduce fruit juice from 2 cups to just ¼ cup for a thick and syrupy drizzle on roast meats or fish. They contain a high concentration of natural sugar, so a little bit goes a long way. Starchy vegetables like sweet potatoes, peas, corn, and several winter squashes thicken when their juice is heated slowly.

Cook en papillote.

There is a very special way to steam food without using any steaming equipment. Cooking with lightly greased parchment paper, or *en papillote* (ehn-pahp-ee-YOHT) as the French say, is a fun and creative way to cook a healthy meal. The method simply involves placing vegetables and fish in a large piece of tightly sealed, greased parchment paper and baking in the oven until it puffs.

Take a large piece of parchment paper, about 12 inches long, and fold it in half lengthwise. As if you were making a heart-shaped Valentine in grade school, draw a large semicircle that tapers in at the bottom toward the fold. Cut through the paper so you have a heart when unfolded. Put the paper on a sheet pan, and place julienned vegetables and fresh herbs in the center of one half of the heart close to the fold, leaving plenty of room around the edges (at least one inch). Top with a piece of fish seasoned with a slice of lemon and a splash of white wine.

Fold the top of the paper over the food and seal by making a double fold along the edge, each new fold overlapping the one before it. The key to success is in making sure the package remains sealed, otherwise it will not trap steam nor puff. Brush the pleated edge with egg white to "glue" it together if need be. Brush the top of the parchment parcel lightly with olive oil to attract the heat and place in a 425°F oven for approximately 10 minutes until the parchment is golden and—hopefully—puffed. The food will be cooked even if the package never puffs, for whatever reason.

Don't be disappointed if you see a beautifully puffed parcel in the oven only to watch it deflate as you move it to the counter. The high oven heat is what activates the steam and holds the puff. The cold kitchen air cannot sustain it over time. ✳

CHAPTER

7

✳ Cleaning Brush
✳ Meat Thermometer
✳ Skewers
✳ Meat Fork
✳ Grilling Plank

The Grill Master's Essential Tools and Techniques

MANIPULATING HEAT ON A LARGE GRILL is not dissimilar to controlling the flame of a stovetop burner. Nevertheless, there are special tools and techniques for the outdoor cook. Certain techniques amplify the flavor and appearance of grilled food, such as proper marinating and marking meat. Grilling is more fun when you have the tools you need to do it well and know how to use them properly.

⟹ THE GRILL MASTER'S ESSENTIAL TOOLS ⟸

Cleaning Brush

You cannot hide a dirty grill. It shows all over the food: charred black bits crusted on the chicken, or tears in the meat because the food stuck to the dirty grill when it should have released itself from the clean, hot grid. Any cooking surface needs to be cleaned thoroughly after each use, and the grill is no exception.

Look for a long-handle brush with brass bristles and a metal scraper at its tip. The handle can be wood, heatproof plastic, or metal. The metal scraper does the tough job of removing large bits of food from the grid after cooking; the brass bristles are strong enough to brush away the smaller pieces. Clean a grill twice, before and after each use.

Meat Thermometer

Temperature is both a health and individual concern: no one wants pink chicken, but lots of people rightly like lamb that way. There are lots of tricks to testing the doneness of meat (poke the meat, then pinch your fingers or tap your face to compare doneness to hand or facial areas . . . believe it or not, that technique is not nearly as senseless as slicing open the food and judging juice and flesh color midway through cooking). Only a thermometer inserted into the center of the meat flesh, far from the bone, can provide a reliable literal reading of internal temperature.

All food thermometers (as opposed to appliance thermometers for ovens and refrigerators) have probes and come either with dial or digital faces. Instant-read thermometers are ideal tools for testing the temperature of meat at the end of the cooking process. Mechanical dial thermometers have a hand that moves clockwise along a numbered (0–220°F) face and stops at the meat's temperature. Electronic digital devices take the reading and display the number once it has been reached, in a matter of seconds.

There are other kinds of meat thermometers that let you monitor the temperature of the meat as it cooks. These are best used for large roasts and oven cooking in general, if you require a constant reading.

Thermometers must be correctly calibrated, otherwise the reading is inaccurate and therefore useless. If you suspect your thermometer might not be working, boil water and stick the probe in the pot. If you get within a degree of 212°F or 100°C, your thermometer is working properly.

> *mercury rising*
>
> The internal temperature of meat typically increases anywhere from 5 to 10 degrees while the meat rests, depending on the cut and its size. That means from the time you take the steak off the grill and take it to the table it has continued cooking, perhaps going from medium rare to medium.

Skewers

Metal skewers are essential grilling tools because they do not burn or break as do the bamboo variety. Skewered meat, with its small and uniform pieces, cooks quickly and evenly. Depending on the size of the skewer, the food comes off the grill in service-ready portions. Who doesn't love a tasty kebab?

The majority of metal skewers are stainless steel, though some have nonstick finishes or are made of cast iron. Skewers can be straight or circular, flat or round, single- or double-pronged. The softer the item you are grilling, the wider and flatter the spear should be if the skewer is single-pronged. The handles are often decorative, but a simple loop design is just as comfortable.

Meat Fork

Don't lift a steak by stabbing it with a long metal fork. You'll pierce the flesh and lose some of the succulent juice that makes steak so luscious. Use your tongs instead. Reserve the meat fork for the final and critical stage of carving.

Most meat forks are at least one foot long with two exceptionally sharp stainless steel tines that can be flat or curved, straight or bowed. There are three-tine forks, but they tend to be shorter and thus best left for indoor tasks. You can also find special bayonet-style forks that have particularly long prongs.

Anchor meat with a cooking fork and carve with your best nonserrated blade once the meat has had ample time to rest, after all the interior juices have had a chance to redistribute throughout the meat.

Why not just use a dinner fork? Because it is simply too small and would make carving an unwieldy enterprise. The substantial size of the cooking fork with its gigantic tines provides you the room and comfort you need to carve with an appropriately large knife. The cooking fork, then, matches the size of the knife's blade. The dinner fork belongs with a table knife.

a fork's first duty

Forks were originally used in the ancient world strictly as cooking and serving implements, making their way to the table in the Middle East more than a thousand years later. It was not until the sixteenth century that using the fork as an eating utensil became widespread in Europe amongst the nobility. What did everyone else do? What they had always done—used their hands to eat.

Grilling Plank

Grilled salmon sounds so delicious—that is, until you try to make it. Even though salmon is one of the fattier—and tastier—fish on the menu, grilling it can result in burnt, torn, or ripped flesh. Rectangular planks made of fragrant woods like cedar, alder, apple, cherry, and maple make grilling fish a much more inviting prospect.

Grilling planks provide the fish (or meat) a large, flat surface that produces smoke, which ultimately flavors the food. They are single-use items (no cleanup!), and usually come in sets of four for just a few dollars each.

Wood, as you know, catches fire. So, a grilling plank must be properly soaked for two hours or more prior to use. A side of salmon, for example, might take 20 to 30 minutes on the grill to cook. If the plank is sufficiently soaked, it won't catch fire before the fish is cooked.

Place the fish on the soaked grilling plank, put the plank on the grill, and cook.

THE GRILL MASTER'S ESSENTIAL TECHNIQUES

Marinate properly.

Marinating serves two purposes:

1 **Flavor:** First and foremost, it adds flavor and seasoning to meat prior to being cooked.

2 **Tenderize:** Since marinades are applied anywhere from half an hour up to more than a day before cooking, they also tenderize meat by breaking down the protein's connective tissue. This process makes meat more moist, juicy, and pleasant to the tooth.

A proper marinade should have a balance of flavors and tenderizers. Citrus juices, vinegars, oils, and even alcohol tenderize protein. Herbs and spices also are important. A good rule of thumb is to pair seasonings and flavors that you like. If you enjoy garlic and ginger together, they will certainly make a desirable marinade. Are jalapeños and lime more your speed? You have the beginnings of a tasty tenderizer.

Marinate food in a nonreactive, nonmetallic container (plastic, glass, ceramic, or sealed food storage bag) in the refrigerator. It's potentially hazardous to marinate foods outside the refrigerator, since bacteria can grow in a room-temperature environment. Marinades should be evenly distributed to cover as much of the food as possible. To this end, turn the food at a few intervals in the marinating process. For example, if you prepare a beef marinade midday to be cooked the following day, turn the meat before you go to bed, and once more in the morning.

Marinating time is determined by the ingredients in the marinade and, more important, by the type of protein for which the marinade is being used:

- **Fish and seafood** generally should be marinated anywhere from 20 minutes to one hour.

- **Chicken** should be marinated for at least half an hour, but typically no more than six hours.

- **Pork** should be marinated between two and four hours, or overnight for big roasts.

- **Beef,** by contrast, may be marinated overnight no matter the cut.

The connective tissue in the protein can break down too much if meat is marinated for too long. The meat will taste mealy and lose its natural texture. In some cases, marinating protein for too long actually begins to cook the product. Ingredients play a major role. If a marinade is too acidic and the protein has been sitting in it for too long, especially where fish is concerned, the product will begin to cook in those juices (as in ceviche).

Marinade should not be used as a sauce for the finished dish. However, if it has been brought to a boil and cooked for at least five minutes, any bacteria that might have been transmitted from raw meat, poultry, or fish would be destroyed.

Mark your meat.

Those perfectly square criss-cross marks branded on grilled meat make any steak look more appetizing. It's like finishing the look of a handsome suit with a pocket square—that special, extra touch that signals a competent cook at work.

Marking your meat (known as *quadrillage*) refers to a series of perfectly vertical and horizontal lines, or squares. Place the axis of the steak at a 90-degree angle from the lines of the grid. After a minute or two—just enough time for the surface proteins to coagulate so you can lift the meat without it sticking to the grid—lift the meat and turn it 90 degrees.

Only one side of the steak needs to be marked. The diner only sees the presentation side of any plated food. So, when you turn the steak over for the second phase of cooking, it does not matter where it lands (not for aesthetic reasons, that is). ⚏

CHAPTER 8

* Knives
* Tools to Chop, Separate, and Cut
* Pots and Pans and Appliances
* Utterly Irrelevant Equipment Miscellany

Nonessential Equipment Miscellany

THE FOLLOWING ARE PERFECTLY USEFUL, respectable tools, just nonessential in general. A few of them might interest you, or perhaps virtually all of them suit your personal cooking needs. Before purchasing anything from the list below, ask yourself if you can get the job done perfectly with the tools you already have. If the answer is no, add any of these items to your equipment inventory as long as you will use them.

Knives

Boning Knife

This knife has a stiff, narrow blade and sharp point, used to remove bones from meat, poultry, and fish. If you like butterflying your own leg of lamb, use a boning knife. Alternatively, use your large chef's knife to get the job done.

Carving Knife

This knife's blade is even longer than a chef's knife (anywhere from 8 inches to 15 inches) and much thinner, which is useful in slicing large roasts, hams, and other meats. You can cut very precise, thin slices with this implement, but a chef's knife will also do the trick.

Fish Knife

This knife has a long, flexible blade, used to remove the skin from fish and cut the flesh. The flexibility allows you to keep the knife parallel with the cutting board as you slide the fish across the blade to remove the skin. For most at-home cooks, a chef's knife will work fine.

Utility Knife

This knife is a little bigger than a paring knife and a bit smaller than a chef's knife. It's perfectly utilitarian, but not any more advantageous than either of those essential tools.

Tools to Chop, Separate, and Cut

Apple Corer

This tool is used to remove the apple core while keeping the rest of the apple intact, with one swift push of the sharp, hollow, cylindrical blade through the apple. This is only useful if you plan to keep the apple whole; otherwise, you can quarter the apple with a chef's knife, and slice away the seeds and core from each piece.

Baster

A clear plastic syringe with a rubber or silicone bulb top, this tool resembles a gigantic medicine dropper, and is used to baste roasts with pan drippings created during the cooking process. Alternatively, simply use a long-handled spoon.

Biscuit Cutters

These specialty cookie cutters tend to have arched handles across the top of the ring, for pressing and twisting the cutter to ensure a clean cut, as opposed to a tear, in the biscuit dough. Instead of a biscuit cutter, you could use several other tools: a plain round cookie cutter, the open top of a juice glass, or even a knife.

Candy Thermometer

This implement—whether digital, dial, or liquid—measures the temperature, and subsequently the stage, of a sugar solution. It also can be used to measure hot oil when deep-frying.

Chaneller

A channeling tool scrapes out a defined ribbon of skin and flesh as you run the sharp point down the length of, say, a cucumber. This repeating pattern is particularly decorative when the vegetable is cut crosswise, making flower-like slices. Such frivolity is lovely but certainly not essential—you could use a peeler to make some simple, decorative cuts.

Cheese Plane

This tool slices through hard and semihard cheeses, as well as chocolate. It works the same way a peeler does, except that you keep what you slice.

China Cap

Also a conical sieve, but with small holes. Stocks typically are passed through a china cap first, then through a chinois, if necessary, to catch the finer-grade waste. Alternatively, you can line a standard strainer with a double layer of cheesecloth to strain the stock.

Chinois

A conical fine mesh sieve used to strain stocks, sauces, and custards. It's easy to push liquid through this specialty strainer because of its shape. It's not essential for a home cook who doesn't make stocks and sauces frequently, especially since you can line a standard strainer with a double layer of cheesecloth for a similar effect.

Egg Slicer

This contraption holds a peeled hard-boiled egg in place in a slotted dish and then cuts through the flesh with a plate of blades or wires. It produces clean, evenly cut egg slices—but so would your chef's knife.

Fluted Pastry Wheel

Also known as a "jagger," this tool is useful to pasta makers and bakers alike. It rolls across dough like a pizza wheel, but makes a decorative jagged edge, perfect for pretty lattice crusts or ravioli edges.

Food Mill

This tool purées fruits and vegetables while straining out skins, seeds, and fibers. It is more versatile than a ricer, even if a bit unwieldy to use. Food is placed in a bowl with a slotted bottom. A slanted disc attached to a handle pushes the food through the mill as you crank. Instead, just use your chef's knife and a cutting board.

Funnel

A plastic or metal cone with a cylindrical opening at the bottom, this tool helps pour liquids from wide-mouthed vessels into containers with small openings. If you don't have a funnel, simply pour carefully and realize that you might spill a little.

Gravy Separator

This specialty measuring cup with a low spout helps separate fat from pan juices. When you pour the drippings into this cup, the fat rises to the top and the juice sinks to the bottom. Since the spout is so low, it pours off mostly juice. You could use a spoon instead, of course.

Meat Mallet

A metal or wood "hammer" with a head that has one smooth side for pounding and flattening meat, and one pointed side for tenderizing meat. This is a useful tool for cooks who frequently prepare veal dishes that require thin cutlets, called scallopini. Instead of using a meat mallet, you could lay a chef's knife sideways on top of the meat and carefully pound the knife with your hand.

Melon Baller

This short stick with one metallic scoop at each end (one larger than the other) makes perfectly round balls of melon flesh. Another aesthetically pleasing touch that certainly is not essential for serving bite-size pieces of melon.

Mezzaluna

As in the Italian words for "half moon," a tool made of a curved steel blade with a horizontal handle used to chop food by rocking back and forth in a depressed cutting board or wooden bowl. Using a chef's knife on a cutting board will do the same job, however.

Mini-chopper

Literally a miniature version of a standard food processor, this tool chops small quantities of food with a single blade. It's perfect for chopping half a cup of nuts when you don't feel like lugging out the big one. They call it a mini-chopper for a reason: it only chops. There's no dough blade, or slicing and grating discs. Once again, your chef's knife and a cutting board can get the job done.

Olive Pitter

Also known as a cherry stoner because it does the same thing for cherries it does for olives. For people who cook frequently with fresh olives (or cherries) in large quantities, this tool sure beats carving out the pit with a paring knife. It deftly pushes out the pit while leaving the olive or cherry intact.

Pasta Fork

Typically made of metal or plastic, this implement is really a slotted ladle with teeth used to grab long noodles like spaghetti or linguine. It's not an essential tool since tongs do the same job with greater control.

Pastry Blender or Cutter

This tool has a wooden, metal, or rubber handle with several arched metallic blades attached that form a "D" shape. It's used to cut solid fat into a flour-based mixture when making any variety of pastry dough. It's a useful tool that keeps your fingers clean, but does the same job your fingers would!

Pizza Peel

This giant wooden (or metal) paddle easily slips underneath a pizza to remove it from the pizza stone or brick oven floor. Instead of bothering with this large tool, simply use gravity, and let the pizza slide off the pan or stone and onto a cutting board.

Pizza Stone

This flat piece of stone or ceramic is used to bake pizzas in a regular oven by evenly distributing heat to the crust and absorbing excess moisture. It's intended to provide the same effect of a brick oven (a crisp crust). If you make your own pizza dough and take pride in the craft, then this tool might top your list. If not, a sheet pan works just as well.

Pizza Wheel

This sharp-edged wheel riveted to a handle rolls and cuts as it moves across a pizza to divide a "pie" into slices. Your knife can do the same thing, and is less likely to tear the dough.

Reamer

Usually made of plastic, wood, or metal, this tool makes it easy to juice citrus fruit. It has a fluted, pear-shaped top with a small handle. Push half a lemon over the tip, twisting and turning as you go. It really helps release all the juice. You could use a dinner fork, as well.

Ricer

If you make mashed potatoes often, this is a wonderful tool. It looks like a giant garlic press. This gadget pushes the flesh through a slotted disc with a steady squeeze of the handle. As you apply pressure, the potatoes emerge looking like rice, hence the name. People find all sorts of clever ways to mash potatoes without one of these tools.

Turkey Lifters

These tiny pitchforks are used, predictably, once a year when the Thanksgiving bird needs to go from the roasting pan to the serving platter. Stab the bird from both sides on the bottom and lift. Or use your hands with rubber oven mitts, or two wooden spoons through the cavity, or two spatulas (all of which have uses other than simply lifting a turkey).

Pots and Pans and Appliances

Double Boiler

This is a pot within a pot. One saucepan sits directly on top of another saucepan. The bottom pot is filled with water and the top pot holds something that needs heat, but might scald or burn from a direct heat source, such as chocolate to be melted. It's a handy concept, but a mixing bowl on top of a saucepan works even better if you need to whisk, since every inch is curved.

Fish Poacher

The elongated, rectangular shape of this pot with rounded corners is a boon to anyone who wants to poach a whole side of salmon. There is a perforated rack with handles within the pot that enables you to lower and lift the fish into simmering water. But how often do you poach a whole side of salmon?

Griddle

This flat metal plate is used on the stove to cook pancakes, eggs, and any other food that could be cooked in a sauté pan. The singular benefit of a griddle is that it usually fits over two burners, instead of one, and thus accommodates twice as much food.

Pasta Machine

This is available as an attachment to an existing appliance (standing mixer), as a hand-cranked apparatus, or as an electric machine. Since most of us survive on dried pasta from the box, a pasta machine doesn't generally warrant "essential" status.

Rice Cooker

This is an electric pot designed to cook just rice. For the large family that eats rice two times a day, a rice cooker is a useful piece of equipment. Otherwise, why not use a saucepan?

Slow Cooker

Also called by the brand name CrockPot, this electric device is hugely popular for making one-pot meals since it cooks while you sleep or work. Throw some meat, stock, vegetables, and seasoning in the slow cooker, plug it in and turn it on, and go about your day (or night). Depending on the recipe, the food cooks anywhere from 4 to 8 hours. However, you could get the same effect by cooking in a dutch oven over very low heat on your stovetop, or in an oven set to a very low temperature.

Waffle Iron

An electric device with two hinged metal plates that have the honeycomb pattern characteristic of waffles. When the pancake-like leavening batter is poured on the bottom plate and the top plate is closed, the waffles form and cook.

Wok

A round-bottomed vessel traditionally made of carbon steel, used in Chinese cooking, especially stir-frying. It's basically a deep sauté pan with high sides, without the flat bottom. If stir-frying is a fixture in your cooking repertoire, then a wok is a useful pan to own. Otherwise, for the occasional stir-fry, you can get by with a sauté pan.

Utterly Irrelevant Equipment Miscellany

Steer clear of these single-use gadgets, doodads, and thingamajigs. They are dust collectors that take up too much valuable space in an already crowded cupboard or jam-packed drawer.

If you previously own and love any of these items, please take no offense. It isn't that some of them don't do something useful. It's just that they do not do anything better than *you* can do yourself with a superior tool (almost always a knife or your hands).

You are the competent cook. Remember that the next time one of these shiny, new trinkets calls out your name at the local "toy" store.

Asparagus Pot

This tall, narrow pot allows asparagus to cook vertically, boiling the stems while the tips steam. However, if properly trimmed of the tough stem, asparagus will steam or blanch evenly while horizontal in a decidedly essential sauté pan or stockpot.

Avocado Slicer

These wands with two working ends both pit and slice the avocado. The bottom of the handle pits the avocado; the top resembles the head of a tennis racket with several sharp wires that produce uniform slices. You can also prepare an avocado using the paring and chef's knives you already have. Cut the avocado in two, and stab the pit with the paring knife and twist (it comes right out). Then peel the skin off the avocado, or spoon out the flesh in one swift motion with a spoon. Slice the avocado as thick or as thin as you like with your chef's knife.

Cake Tester

A probing tool to be inserted in a cake to test for doneness, it's simply a round plastic paddle or metal ring that holds a long thin wire. Yes, testing a cake before you permanently remove it from the oven is a good thing. But any toothpick can handle the challenge.

Corn Zipper

We all love corn cut fresh off the cob. Just stand an ear of corn in a large mixing bowl and run the chef's knife down the side of the cob to remove the kernels. Or, use this tool that looks like a horizontal vegetable peeler equipped with a pair of sharp teeth to do the same job pretty much the same way.

Garlic Peeler

This flexible rubber cylinder holds a garlic clove, and removes the peel when you roll it back and forth with the palm of your hand. You could also smash the garlic with the flat side of your chef's knife, or trim the root and peel back the skin with a paring knife when you need to keep the cloves whole.

Garlic Press

This tool has come a long way: now you can press or slice garlic if the garlic press has two compartments. When you press the garlic through the perforated disc, it emerges mashed. Well, part of it emerges mashed. The rest stays stuck inside the press, unless you pry it out with your fingers. (So much for avoiding smelly hands with this tool!) If you run your chef's knife over a garlic clove again and again, adding a light pinch of salt once or twice, you will eventually have paste, or mashed garlic. As for making paper-thin slices, use your paring knife, take your time, and practice, as any competent cook would do.

Herb Shears

These specialty scissors distinguish themselves from standard kitchen shears with their unique handle that has two circular openings (one large, one small) designed to pass through stems to remove leaves, as with rosemary, thyme, and oregano. Both your knife and fingers can do the job better: use your knife to cut and chop the herbs, and your fingers to pinch the stem and pull back and remove the leaves.

Mango Pitter

This tool looks a lot like the kind of apple corer that both cores and slices the apple into wedges. It's a plastic ring with two handles on opposite sides, with a sharp, oval blade in the middle. Stand the mango up and press the pitter down to excise the pit. You need to align the mango with the tool so the thin and narrow pit is parallel with the blade—something you have to do anyway when you slice the mango with a chef's knife.

Mozzarella Slicer

This oversized egg slicer, as it were, holds the mozzarella in a slotted base and cuts the cheese in uniform slices with a hinged metal plate set with several wires. Hard-boiled eggs can be very tricky to slice since the yolk might not be centered in, and slides easily from, the white. But mozzarella—even the fresh buffalo kind—can be sliced with a chef's knife as easily as any other food.

Onion Dicer

This plastic base with a hinged, sharp metallic grid dices an onion in one shot. You can do that just as well with your chef's knife, and you can control the size of the pieces, too. You are, after all, a competent cook!

Pineapple Slicer

Once the pineapple is trimmed of its exterior, you can core and slice the fruit with one twist of this gadget's handle. Unfortunately, this tool wastes a lot of perfectly edible pineapple flesh. And what if you want chunks or wedges or a fine dice? You'll need to use your chef's knife for that. Of course, you're eminently qualified.

Rolling Herb Mincer

This is like four pizza wheels attached to one handle. The idea is to roll the tool back and forth to mince the herbs. It's a pretty clunky shape, sure to jam any drawer. Your chef's knife was meant to mince herbs, so use that instead.

Salad Scissors

Another specialty pair of scissors, this tool's curved blades chop through salads in a bowl. Lettuce has to be trimmed, its leaves separated from the core, in order to be washed. So, the cutting board and knife are already on the counter. If you are using a prewashed mix like mesclun or baby romaine, then you have nothing to cut.

Tomato Knife

This tool is designed with a serrated blade strictly to cut tomatoes. It would be a better use of space and money to maintain your chef's knife so it is always sharp, in which case it would never fail to slice a tomato.

Tomato Slicer

Just when you think you've seen it all! This tool works in the same way as the nonessential egg slicer and utterly irrelevant mozzarella slicer. Only tomatoes up to a certain size fit in this bulky contraption. A chef's knife never discriminates. If cared for and maintained, it will cut anything. ✳

How to Shop for Food and Store It Properly

EVERY ASPECT OF THE COOKING PROCESS MATTERS. Earlier chapters covered how your kitchen and equipment play important roles in the food you put on the table. The techniques and recipes you apply are equally relevant, of course. The food you use—and when you buy it and how you store it—is just as impactful.

The Essential Pantry

Certain tools and techniques are required to cook competently, so it naturally follows that you need a certain baseline of ingredients and supplies, too. There are foods so pervasive in recipes from across the globe that they always should be on hand in your pantry and fridge. And certain supplies also should be stocked in your kitchen.

Of course, your own tastes, preferences, and health concerns inform your sense of "essential" ingredients. Perhaps you come from a Mediterranean background and a cupboard without olives just won't do. If your family is Chinese, you better have garlic and ginger on hand at all times. Should an allergy preclude you from cooking with almonds, you won't buy any nuts. Gauge essential supplies by your cooking routine or aspirations.

The following lists are a good start to competent cooking, including making the recipes in this book and improvising on your own.

The Cupboard

- all-purpose flour
- baking powder
- baking soda
- balsamic vinegar
- basmati rice
- breadcrumbs
- brown sugar
- canned beans (chickpeas, black beans, or cannellini)
- canola or grapeseed oil
- chicken stock
- cinnamon
- coarse sea salt in a mill
- dried fruits (raisins, currants, cranberries, apricots, or prunes)
- dried oregano
- dried pasta
- dried thyme
- fine kosher salt
- garlic powder
- granulated sugar
- honey
- olive oil
- paprika
- precooked couscous
- red wine vinegar
- rice wine vinegar
- tamari or soy sauce
- toasted sesame oil
- Tabasco sauce
- tomato paste
- vanilla extract
- whole black peppercorns in a mill
- Worcestershire sauce

The Refrigerator

- Dijon mustard

- fresh ginger

- fresh herbs (parsley, basil, thyme, rosemary, or mint)

- head of garlic

- lemon

- mayonnaise

- nuts (slivered almonds, pecans, and walnuts) stored in the freezer

- pitted kalamata olives

- unsalted butter

Supplies

- aluminum foil

- bamboo skewers

- cotton twine

- dish towels

- oven mitts

- parchment paper

- plastic storage bags

- plastic wrap

- rubber gloves

- wax paper

The Shopping Schedule: Daily, Weekly, Monthly, Yearly

Knowing what to buy and when to buy it is easy, as long as you follow a simple schedule. Some foods are best bought on a day-to-day basis, as needed, while others can be purchased just once or twice a year. As a general guideline, see the frequency with which you buy each item as an indication of its shelf life. The following chart will give you an idea of how often you'll need to buy certain items. Keep in mind that you don't have to buy the items in the categories "daily," "monthly," every single day or every single month; it means that the items will only stay fresh for a full week or a few months, respectively.

DAILY	WEEKLY	MONTHLY	YEARLY
items will stay fresh for one to six days	**items will stay fresh for one to three weeks**	**items will stay fresh for one to several months**	**items will stay fresh for one to two years**
Fresh leafy herbs: parsley, chives, cilantro, mint, basil, tarragon, and dill	Fresh woody herbs: rosemary, thyme, sage, and oregano	Butter	Dried herbs: Salt, pepper, and spices
		Canned goods: pasta sauce, beans, and soups	
Lettuce	Milk		Oil
		Flour	
Freshly baked breads and pastries	Eggs	Nuts	Vinegar
	Fruits and vegetables		Soy sauce
Seafood: fish and shellfish		Fresh olives	
	Packaged breads		Worcestershire sauce
		Cereals	
	Beef, pork, and poultry		Dried beans and legumes
		Crackers and cookies	
	Cheese		Rice
		Coffee and tea	
	Deli meats		Pasta and couscous
		Sodas	
	Ice cream and sorbet		Condiments: mustard, ketchup, mayonnaise, maple syrup, relish, chutney, and capers
	Juices		
			Honey
			Sugar

The Storage Guide: Fridge, Freezer, Cupboard, or Counter

You can buy the best ingredients in the world, but if you don't store them properly, it's all a lost cause. There are four places dry and fresh goods can be stored: the refrigerator, freezer, cupboard (pantry), or counter. The grocery store provides one of the best cues. How was the food stored when you purchased it? You didn't find the whole butternut squash in the refrigerator, so there's no need to store it that way at home. Once fresh fruits and vegetables are cut and flesh is exposed, however, they must be stored in the fridge.

Refrigerated food should be kept at or below 38–40°F; frozen food should be maintained at or below 0°F. If you are not sure if your appliances are at the proper temperature, use designated thermometers to test them. Avoid storing any food in a warm place, such as near a hot oven, frequently running dishwasher, or sun-filled window. "A cool dry place" is the phrase to keep in mind for the cupboard and counter. "Cool," in this case, means nowhere north of about 70°F. And when it comes to oils, that cool, dry place should be dark, too, to inhibit the oil from turning rancid. Here are some other tips:

- Before you place your leftover macaroni and cheese in the refrigerator, make sure it has cooled down (to at least 90°F) to make sure it doesn't negatively impact the temperature, and therefore everything else, in the refrigerator. Don't crowd the fridge or freezer, so that air can circulate freely and effectively.

- Shelve your raw foods below your cooked foods. You never want the juice from a package of chicken breasts to drip onto last night's sesame noodles that you hope to enjoy for lunch tomorrow. You can easily avoid such careless cross-contamination.

- Label foods so you know what's in the container and how long it has been there. Leftovers stored in the refrigerator need to be eaten within a week. Always wrap foods for the freezer tightly in plastic wrap first, then in aluminum foil for added protection. Such foods should never be left there for more than six months, no matter what.

the sniff test

How long should you keep spices? Should you throw the milk out if it's two days past the "sell by" date on the carton? Do eggs ever expire? Spices are generally good for one year. You should only throw the milk out if it has gone bad (remember, it's a "sell by" date, not a "consume by" date). Yes, eggs do expire . . . eventually. For most foods, you can tell if they have gone bad by smelling them. Dried herbs and spices likely won't smell bad—they just won't smell like much of anything at all. Milk smells rotten when it has gone bad. If it isn't malodorous and also tastes good, then it has not yet spoiled. Eggs have a shelf life of a few weeks. If you have a carton from a few months back, just get rid of it.

The following chart provides a general guide for what types of foods should be stored where. You'll see certain items in two categories if they can be placed in either location depending on when you plan to use the item. Nuts go in the freezer because they can go rancid quickly; since they defrost quickly, freezing them ensures that you can use them as needed. Peaches and all the other stone fruits (nectarines, plums, apricots) are best left on the counter. The cupboard is completely dark, whereas the counter is exposed to ceiling and indirect outdoor light (if you have windows in your kitchen). Never place any groceries to be stored on the counter in direct sunlight. When in doubt, of course, store food in the fridge.

FRIDGE	FREEZER	CUPBOARD	COUNTER
Milk	Ice cream and sorbet	Canned goods: pasta sauce, beans, and soups	Freshly baked bread
Eggs	Butter	Salt, pepper, and spices	Bananas
Butter	Beef, pork, and poultry	Dried herbs	Apples
Broccoli	Nuts	Honey	Peaches
Cucumbers		Oil	Pears
String Beans		Vinegar	Citrus fruit
Carrots		Soy sauce	Melons
Grapes		Worcestershire sauce	Avocados
Fresh olives		Rice, pasta, and couscous	Tomatoes
Fresh leafy and woody herbs		Cereals	Onions
Lettuce		Crackers and cookies	Potatoes
Seafood: fish and shellfish		Tea	Mangoes
Beef, pork, and poultry		Sodas	Berries (if consumed right away)
Cheese		Condiments: maple syrup, unopened relish, chutney, and capers	
Deli meats		Flour	
Packaged breads		Sugar	
Juices			
Coffee			
Condiments: mustard, ketchup, mayonnaise, opened relish, chutney, and capers			

Get to Know Your Grocer

The best way to make the local grocery store feel more like *your* grocery store is to speak up! Get to know the management and staff by letting them know what you want and like. Grocers want to serve their customers and earn a profit. If they know what you buy regularly, they can stock it and both of you will benefit.

Talk to the manager about items you want to buy. Have you always wanted to make short ribs but they don't have them at the butcher counter? Is there a fish you want to try but never see available? Would you like more seasonal organic produce but don't yet see it in your local grocery store? Let the manager know about it. If you need something for a party or big dinner you are planning, but have never seen it where you shop, call the manager and ask if he can help. Just because it's not something your grocer regularly stocks doesn't mean it can't be ordered for you.

When you develop a relationship with your grocer, butcher, and fish-monger, you'll get more than just the produce, meat, and fish you'll buy. Once the staff knows you, they'll be more likely to alert you to specials and particularly good meat and fish that come their way. And if you let them know your cooking preferences, they'll keep you in mind when they place orders. After all, they aim to maintain the same relationship with their vendors who sell them the food as you do with them. If you take an active role, the benefits can trickle down to you. ✳

Part 2

Essential
Recipes

WHAT MAKES A RECIPE ESSENTIAL? As a competent cook, you should know how to make classics, like roast chicken and apple pie. Such timeless dishes never go out of style, and continue to satisfy us, generation after generation. Ease of preparation is another important characteristic that makes a recipe essential. When something is simple to make but impresses both your palate and the dinner guests, then you know you have a keeper. A good recipe also details exactly what you need—and what you should expect—for the dish.

Making a recipe your own, however, is one of the more gratifying aspects of the cooking process. After all, a recipe is merely a record of what one cook created—a set of instructions and suggestions of how to repeat the process. Any number of small changes you make here and there turns someone else's recipe into *your* recipe.

Take lasagne, for example. Virtually any lasagne recipe has been made countless times and will be reinvented again and again. The creation of a unique recipe, then, comes from the selection of ingredients (Parmesan instead of pecorino), the particular ratios used (30 ounces of crushed tomatoes to 8 ounces of tomato sauce rather than another alternative), and the nuances of the cooking method (adding noodles dry instead of soaking or boiling them).

Don't diminish your role by treating a recipe as gospel. Instead, look at a recipe as a concept—an idea—for a combination of flavors and a method of preparing ingredients. With this attitude, you might find yourself more willing to experiment. After all, you know what you like to eat, and you have spent a lifetime doing it. You know what flavor pairings you favor, and what ingredients you dislike. This makes you more than qualified to trust your instincts when working with a recipe.

There is one exception to all this creativity and experimentation. Baking is much more scientific than savory cooking. Strictly follow baking instructions, especially where the chemistry of the recipe is concerned. For example, don't tamper with the baking soda, salt, egg, and flour ratios of a cake batter, but feel free to add a pinch of ginger, or some toasted nuts to add a new dimension. In other words, it is generally safe to adjust the flavor of a baked good, but not the basics of the batter.

So, what are the essential recipes worth mastering and reinventing? These are dishes so evergreen and timeless, that all competent cooks must have them in their repertoire. All cooks can and *should* put their own twist on these favorites; variations are conveniently noted here for inspiration. Applying the proper techniques, and employing the right equipment, will guarantee successful results and, in turn, satisfying classics. Trust your instincts and your palate. Try the Essential Recipes on the pages that follow and make them your own. ✻

CHAPTER 10

Breakfast

* The Ultimate Omelet
* Decadent Granola
* Buttermilk Pancakes
* Challah French Toast
* Blueberry Sour Cream Muffins

The Ultimate Omelet

The ultimate omelet is French, rolled as opposed to flat, generally has a completely smooth, unbrowned surface, and is slightly runny in the middle. Taste and preference prevail, of course, but this is the classic preparation. The key to making a superb omelet is scrambling the eggs first, then setting the omelet. Never overstuff it, or you'll have a hard time rolling it. If egg white omelets are more your speed, try making the following recipe with 3 large egg whites and just one yolk. You'll never go back to just egg whites again!

For the omelet:

3 large eggs (ideally, room temperature)

2 teaspoons unsalted butter

salt and pepper to taste

For the filling, choose one of the following per omelet:

¼ cup grated cheese

3 tablespoons caramelized onions

¼ cup chopped tomatoes

2 button mushrooms, sliced

1   Break eggs into a bowl and mix well with a fork. Heat a nonstick 8-inch skillet over medium heat with 2 teaspoons butter. When the butter foams, add the eggs and let them be, just until they start to set along the edge. Stir continuously with a wooden spoon until they are at a runny scramble stage. Spread them evenly in the pan. When the omelet is lightly set, stop stirring and remove the omelet from the heat. (The point at which you stop stirring is the key to having a smooth omelet.)

2   Place the filling in the middle of the omelet. Using a wooden spoon, fold the edge of the omelet over onto itself, tilt the pan from the handle, and lightly tap the pan so that the omelet moves down to the edge of the pan. Form the omelet with a wooden spoon.

3   Roll the omelet onto a warm plate seam-side down. Adjust the form if necessary by shaping with a clean towel. Serve immediately. ✳

ESSENTIAL EQUIPMENT

measuring spoon

dry measuring cup

small mixing bowl

fork

nonstick 8-inch sauté pan

flat wooden spoon

ESSENTIAL TECHNIQUES

mise en place

sauté

DON'T GET WHISKED AWAY

Do not use a whisk to beat eggs for omelets or scrambling. Your goal is simply to combine thoroughly the white and the yolk, not to incorporate air. Mix with a fork, but do not overbeat the eggs. Your omelet will be remarkably lighter and fluffier this way.

MAKES 1 OMELET.

Decadent Granola

When granola is sweet and nutty, it is irresistible morning, noon, and night. Use it for breakfast with yogurt, as an afternoon snack, or as a sundae topping for vanilla ice cream. A little bit of this decadent granola goes a very long way. It is rich and luxurious in ingredients, flavors, and textures. There's no reason why you can't have your granola and eat it, too!

For the syrup:

½ cup (1 stick) unsalted butter

½ cup canola oil

½ cup light brown sugar

½ cup honey

For the dry ingredients:

1 cup oats

3 cups All Bran Flakes

2 cups corn flakes

½ cup wheat germ

½ cup shelled sunflower seeds

½ cup sesame seeds

½ cup desiccated coconut (unsweetened and shredded)

½ cup pecans

½ cup walnuts

½ cups cashews

½ cup sliced almonds

ESSENTIAL EQUIPMENT

dry and wet measuring cups

small saucepan

mixing bowl

wooden spoon

sheet pan

spatula

fork

ESSENTIAL TECHNIQUES

mise en place

baking

MAKES 10 CUPS.

1   Preheat the oven to 350°F.

2   In a small saucepan, combine the syrup ingredients and bring to a boil over low heat. Meanwhile, combine all the dry ingredients in a large mixing bowl. Pour the syrup over the dry ingredients and mix well to coat. Pour the mixture onto a large, rimmed sheet pan and spread evenly.

3   Bake until all the syrup has been absorbed and the dry ingredients have recrisped, tossing every 5 minutes, for about one hour. Remove from the oven and set aside to cool. Loosen the granola with a fork continually until the mixture has cooled completely (otherwise it will set into one giant slab). ✳

Store in an airtight container for up to two weeks.

Buttermilk Pancakes

Whether you call them flapjacks, pancakes, griddlecakes, or hotcakes, these fluffy breakfast skillet creations are part of our American culinary heritage. There is undoubtedly an art to making the perfect pancake—one that is fluffy, yet tender and spongy enough to soak up all that sweet maple syrup. Buttermilk has a distinct and slightly sour flavor. If you prefer, use whole milk for an equally tasty pancake.

2 cups all-purpose flour

¼ cup sugar

2 teaspoons baking powder

¾ teaspoon salt

2 cups buttermilk

¼ cup butter, melted

2 extra large eggs

1 teaspoon vanilla extract

1   Preheat a nonstick sauté pan or griddle.

2   In a large bowl, whisk together the flour, sugar, baking powder, and salt. Make a small well in the center of the bowl. Add the buttermilk, melted butter, eggs, and vanilla. Gently whisk the wet and dry ingredients together, just until thoroughly combined, but not lump-free.

3   Using a dry measuring cup, pour ⅓-cup batter onto the hot pan (with or without sizzling fat, such as butter or oil) for each pancake. Cook until the top of the pancake bubbles, about 1 to 2 minutes. Turn the pancake with a spatula and cook just until the underside is golden brown, aboout 1 minute. ⧋

ESSENTIAL EQUIPMENT

dry and wet measuring cups

measuring spoons

mixing bowl

whisk

nonstick 10-inch sauté pan, cast iron skillet, or griddle

spatula

ESSENTIAL TECHNIQUES

mise en place

sautéing (searing)

MAKES ABOUT 16 4-INCH PANCAKES.

batter basics

Making pancakes is highly procedural. Here's some helpful advice:

Do not overbeat the batter. Believe it or not, lumps in pancake batter are not only acceptable; they are desirable because it indicates that the ingredients have been gently combined. The lumps settle as the batter sits and as the pancakes cook. When the batter is beaten too vigorously, the results might yield a flatter, thinner, and certainly tougher pancake.

Make sure the pan is hot. There are many ways to test a dry pan to see if it is ready for batter. The easiest method is to drop a few bits of water on the dry pan. If those drops bounce and sizzle, then the pan is ready. If the water sits still and holds its shape, the pan is too cool. In the event that the water evaporates the second it hits the pan, then the pan is most likely too hot.

Don't count on the first pancake. Often the first few pancakes don't come out as well as the rest. This usually has to do with the heat of the pan. We turn on the heat and expect it to be ready in just moments, but the truth is it can take several minutes for a pan to come to temperature.

Use fat on cast iron, but not with a nonstick surface. Once the pan is hot enough, small amounts of fat can be added before spooning the batter onto the pan. If you are using a nonstick skillet, you'll find that adding fat makes for a patterned skin, whereas cooking pancakes in a dry nonstick pan results in an even hue. Fat is needed on a cast iron pan, which makes for a crisp exterior to the pancake.

Use a measuring cup to pour the batter. To achieve the standard 5-inch size and an even circular shape, use ⅓ cup dry measure (silver dollars require a mere tablespoon of batter). Fill the measuring cup with batter and pour it onto the pan, just a few inches from the pan's surface. Once you begin pouring the batter, keep your hand steady and do not move. This helps to make a fluffy pancake.

Turn a pancake just once. If you turn a pancake over and over, it can toughen. When the top of the pancake bubbles, it is ready to be turned with a spatula. Once turned, it takes only about half as long for the second side to cook.

Keep pancakes warm while you finish cooking. Preheat an oven to 200°F before you begin cooking. As the pancakes come off the sauté pan or griddle, place them on a sheet pan in a single layer and hold them in the oven. They can be slightly overlapped if they won't fit in a single layer.

Challah French Toast

Challah is a tender, golden egg bread, the perfect base for an egg-soaked panfried breakfast dish. You may substitute any bread you like with this recipe. Just be sure to follow the technique of thoroughly soaking the bread in the egg mixture before toasting it in the pan so that every bite is moist. The subtle hint of vanilla, cinnamon, and freshly grated orange zest makes this a truly scrumptious dish.

1 loaf braided challah, cut in ½-inch slices

6 eggs

⅓ cup half and half

2 teaspoons vanilla extract

1 teaspoon cinnamon

zest of an orange (optional)

4 tablespoons butter

1   In a large mixing bowl, combine the eggs, half and half, vanilla, cinnamon, and orange zest.

2   Soak the bread slices, one by one, in the egg mixture, stabbing them several times with a fork to help the bread moisten. Turn each slice in the egg mixture to coat well and transfer to a sheet pan or casserole.

3   Once all the bread has been coated in the egg mixture, place a tablespoon of butter in a large sauté pan and heat over medium heat. Once the butter begins to foam, add a few slices of bread to the pan and cook for 2 to 3 minutes, or until the bottom of the bread is golden brown. Turn and continue cooking for another 2 minutes. Repeat this process until all the slices are cooked.

4   Serve immediately with maple syrup and fresh fruit. ✳

ESSENTIAL EQUIPMENT

wet measuring cups

measuring spoons

cutting board

bread knife

large mixing bowl

whisk

fork

rimmed sheet pan or casserole

sauté pan

spatula

grater or Microplane (optional)

ESSENTIAL TECHNIQUES

mise en place

sautéing

KEEP IT TOASTY

It is nearly impossible to keep the first slice of French toast as warm as the last while you're cooking. Before you begin preparing the recipe, preheat the oven to 250°F. As the French toast comes out of the sauté pan, place it on a sheet pan, either flat or slightly overlapping and hold it in the warm oven until the last piece is done. Then serve everyone at once.

MAKES 4–6 SERVINGS.

Blueberry Sour Cream Muffins

This recipe comes together so quickly that you can prepare these muffins fresh for breakfast the same morning. Use the base of this recipe to bake any kind of muffin you like: substitute the blueberries with raspberries, chocolate chips, etc.

For the crumb topping:

½ cup light brown sugar

⅓ cup all-purpose flour

¼ cup unsalted butter (half a stick), cubed

1 teaspoon ground cinnamon

For the muffins:

3 eggs

2 cups sugar

1 cup vegetable oil

1 cup sour cream (8-ounce container)

1 tablespoon vanilla extract

2½ cups all-purpose flour

½ teaspoon baking soda

½ teaspoon baking powder

½ teaspoon salt

1½ cups fresh blueberries

ESSENTIAL EQUIPMENT

muffin tin

dry and wet measuring cups

measuring spoons

large, medium, and small mixing bowls

hand mixer

whisk

rubber spatula

ESSENTIAL TECHNIQUES

mise en place

beating eggs and sugar (blanchir)

baking

MAKES 18 MUFFINS.

1   Preheat the oven to 350°F. Line a muffin tin with paper muffin liners and set aside.

2   Make the crumb topping first. In a small bowl, mix the sugar, flour, butter, and cinnamon with your fingers, pressing the butter so it combines with the other ingredients. Set aside.

3   In a large mixing bowl, beat the eggs and sugar using a hand mixer (beat them together until thick, creamy and lighter in color). Beat in the oil, sour cream, and vanilla.

4   In a medium mixing bowl, combine the flour, baking soda, baking powder, and salt. Add it to the egg mixture, and mix well. Gently fold in the blueberries using a rubber spatula.

5   Fill the paper-lined muffin tin three-quarters with batter. Sprinkle each muffin with some crumb topping. Bake for 25 to 30 minutes, or until a toothpick inserted into the center of a muffin comes out clean. Remove the pan to a rack to cool. ✳

Nibbles and Starters

Classic Tuna Tartare

Ruby-red tuna flesh cut into jewel-like little cubes is one of the simplest and more luxurious hors d'oeuvres. Served on toast points or thinly sliced baguette, this dish is the ideal start to almost any meal. Ask your fishmonger for a center cut of tuna. You don't want any grey or black flesh. Cut the tuna as fine as you can—the smaller the better—for a refined appearance and texture.

> 1 pound sushi-grade tuna, finely diced
>
> 1 shallot, minced
>
> 2 tablespoons extra virgin olive oil
>
> 2 tablespoons minced chives
>
> juice of half a lemon
>
> splash of Tabasco sauce
>
> salt and pepper to taste

1 Combine the tuna, shallot, and oil, then gently fold in the chive, lemon juice, and Tabasco. Season to taste with salt and pepper. Cover and refrigerate until ready to serve.

2 Serve on toast points, crackers, or baguette. ✳

Tuna tartare must be served within 24 hours of preparation.

ESSENTIAL EQUIPMENT

measuring spoons

cutting board

chef's knife

mixing bowl

rubber spatula

ESSENTIAL TECHNIQUES

mise en place

knife skills

TUNA TARTARE TWO WAYS

Tuna tartare can be enjoyed as above, or with an Asian twist. Replace the olive oil with toasted sesame oil, and swap out the shallots for scallions. Use lime juice instead of lemon. Skip the Tabasco and add toasted black and white sesame seeds instead. Now you have a brand new recipe!

LUCKY LEFTOVERS

Didn't finish all the tuna tartare? Beat an egg, fold in the tuna tartare along with a handful of breadcrumbs, and form into a patty. You have just prepared an elegant tuna burger. Sauté it in a little olive oil in a nonstick pan. Enjoy it over greens or on a toasted brioche bun with sliced avocado.

MAKES 8–12 SERVINGS.

Cheese Fondue

Preparing classic cheese fondue at home requires only one thing: high quality, freshly grated Gruyère cheese. A special fondue pot is elegant but not necessary for service. Rubbing a garlic clove along the inside of the pot perfumes the cheese mixture. Dry white wine adds depth of flavor and helps to break down the cheese as it melts. Cornstarch provides an even and thick texture that perfectly coats and holds onto the bread. Crusty freshly baked bread is the best accompaniment to cheese fondue, but tart apples and boiled potatoes are appropriate alternatives.

8 ounces grated Gruyère

8 ounces grated Emmentaler

2 tablespoons cornstarch

1 clove garlic, smashed

1½ cups dry white wine

1 tablespoon fresh lemon juice

freshly ground pepper, to taste

freshly ground nutmeg, to taste

2 loaves bread with thick crust cut into 1-inch cubes

1 Combine the grated cheeses with cornstarch in a large mixing bowl. Toss well to coat and set aside.

2 Rub the inside of a fondue pot or small Dutch oven with the smashed garlic. Pour wine into the pot and heat over medium heat until warm. Add the lemon juice. Then add the cheese by the handful, stirring constantly with a wooden spoon. Once each handful is melted, add more cheese until all the cheese has melted and the mixture has the consistency of a creamy sauce. Add pepper and nutmeg to taste.

3 Bring to a boil, then remove the pot from the heat and transfer to a table burner. Adjust the flame so the fondue continues bubbling lightly. Alternatively, bring the pot to the table and set on a trivet.

4 Serve with cubed bread on fondue forks or long skewers. Dunk and stir well to cover bread with cheese mixture. ✳

ESSENTIAL EQUIPMENT

cutting board

chef's knife

bread knife

box grater or food processor

dry and wet measuring cups

measuring spoons

stockpot, Dutch oven, or fondue pot

wooden spoon

ESSENTIAL TECHNIQUES

mise en place

SWISS BORN WITH A FRENCH NAME

Fondue literally means "melted" in French. It was Swiss mountain herders who created this dish of necessity, getting by on what they had available. Scraps of cheese and wine were melted in a clay pot called the "caquelon," and bread was dipped in the liquid cheese. Fondue eventually made its way down the hills of Switzerland to domestic servants who improved the dish by using finer cheeses and wines accessible to them where they worked. The well-traveled aristocracy helped to spread this dish across Europe.

MAKES 8 SERVINGS.

Mushroom Ragout Crostini with Truffle Oil

Savory, sautéed mushrooms and salty melted cheese finished with a hint of truffle oil is a mouth-watering combination. Any selection of mushrooms will work. The key is to let all the moisture released by the mushrooms evaporate before adding the cheeses so the final product is thick and creamy, not runny and wet.

ESSENTIAL EQUIPMENT

cutting board

bread knife

chef's knife

dry measuring cups

measuring spoons

sheet pan

large sauté pan

wooden spoon

ESSENTIAL TECHNIQUES

mise en place

knife skills

sautéing

MAKES APPROXIMATELY
2 CUPS.

For the crostini:

1 French baguette, sliced on bias in ¼-inch slices

For the mushroom ragout:

2 tablespoons vegetable oil

1 shallot, finely diced

3 cups mushrooms, such as shitake, crimini, oyster, and chanterelles

¼ cup grated Parmesan cheese

¼ cup soft goat cheese

1 teaspoon kosher salt

1 teaspoon freshly ground black pepper

2 tablespoons chopped parsley

2 tablespoons truffle oil

1   For the crostini, preheat the oven to 400°F. Place the thinly sliced baguette on a sheet pan and bake until crisp, about 8 to 10 minutes. Cool on a wire rack and set aside (or store in an airtight container for up to one week).

2   For the mushroom ragout, heat the vegetable oil over medium-high heat in a large sauté pan. Add the shallots and sauté until tender. Then add the mushrooms and sauté until tender and the excess moisture has evaporated, about 10 minutes. Add both cheeses, stirring until melted.

3   Remove the pan from the heat, season with salt and pepper, then add the parsley and truffle oil. Top each crostini with the warm mushroom mixture and serve at once. ❖

The mushroom ragout can be made several days in advance—without the truffle oil. Reheat the mixture in the microwave, then stir in the truffle oil right before you serve it.

Asian Beef Salad in Cucumber Cups

This is the perfect hors d'oeuvre for a summer dinner party. The citrus and herbs in the beef salad marry the subtle spice of the Thai bird chili pepper with the coolness of the cucumber. A melody of flavors and contrasting textures make this attractive and colorful dish an essential recipe for any competent cook.

> 1 pound London broil
>
> 1 tablespoon soy sauce
>
> zest and juice of 1 lime
>
> 1 tablespoon oyster sauce
>
> ¼ teaspoon sugar
>
> ½ cup cilantro, chopped
>
> ½ cup mint, chopped
>
> ½ Thai bird chili pepper, finely diced
>
> 1 tomato, seeded and diced
>
> 1 teaspoon toasted sesame seeds
>
> 2 hothouse cucumbers

1 Preheat the broiler with the pan in the oven. Season the steak with kosher salt and freshly ground pepper. Place the steak on the hot broiling pan and cook until rare to medium rare, about 8 to 10 minutes (do not overcook). Remove the pan from the oven and transfer the steak to a plate to rest for 10 minutes before slicing.

2 In a large mixing bowl, combine the soy sauce, lime zest and juice, oyster sauce, sugar, fresh herbs, pepper, tomato, and sesame seeds. Set aside.

3 Slice the steak against the grain in thin slices. Then cut those slices into short, thin strips. Toss the sliced steak with the citrus-herb mixture in the large mixing bowl. Set aside.

4 Cut cucumbers into 2-inch pieces and place flesh-side down on a sheet pan. Using a small spoon (or melon baller), remove the center of each cucumber piece to make a cup, leaving some flesh at the bottom to hold the salad. Divide the steak salad among the cucumber cups and serve. ❄

Make the filling up to one day in advance, but add the fresh herbs only up to one hour before serving. Cover and refrigerate.

ESSENTIAL EQUIPMENT

dry measuring cup

measuring spoons

cutting board

chef's knife

grater or Microplane

broiling pan

large mixing bowl

rubber spatula

regular teaspoon

ESSENTIAL TECHNIQUES

mise en place

knife skills

broiling

SEEDING A TOMATO

Seeding a tomato is very easy: Simply quarter the tomato from top (where the vine is) to bottom, then use a small spoon to scrape out the seeds from between the ribs.

MAKES APPROXIMATELY 12 SERVINGS.

Italian Vegetable Tartlets

These tartlets are tasty whether warm or at room temperature. Caramelized onions, sautéed squash with tomatoes, and briny olives practically melt into the buttery, flaky puffed pastry. Store-bought pesto adds a basil brightness while binding the vegetables to the pastry with its component Parmesan cheese. A competent cook probably prefers to make her own pesto, but using the jar for this recipe is a worthy time-saver.

2 tablespoons olive oil, plus extra for drizzling over the tarts

1 large onion, finely chopped

1 zucchini, small dice

1 yellow squash, small dice

6 plum tomatoes, seeded and small dice

½ cup pesto

36 pitted nicoise olives, about 1 cup

fresh thyme leaves for sprinkling on tartlets, to taste

1 sheet puff pastry

kosher salt and freshly ground pepper to taste

ESSENTIAL EQUIPMENT

measuring spoons

dry measuring cup

cutting board

chef's knife

large sauté pan

wooden spoon

sheet pan

parchment paper

ESSENTIAL TECHNIQUES

mise en place

knife skills

sautéing

baking

MAKES 12 SERVINGS.

1 Preheat the oven to 400°F.

2 Heat a large sauté pan over medium high heat, and add oil. Add onions and a generous pinch of kosher salt, and sweat until tender, stirring constantly. Continue to cook over medium high heat for 10 minutes, scraping up the brown bits that form at the bottom of the pan, or until the onions begin to caramelize. Add the squashes and tomatoes, and continue to cook until tender, about 5 minutes. Set aside.

3 Cut the puff pastry sheet into six strips, and cut each strip into six squares. The squares will be approximately 1½ to 2 square inches. Place the pastry squares on a sheet pan lined with parchment paper.

4 Taste the vegetable mixture and season with kosher salt and freshly ground pepper to taste. Spread a small dollop of the pesto in the center of each pastry square, then top with a tablespoon of the vegetable mixture, leaving a small border. Place one olive in the center of each tartlet.

5 Sprinkle tartlets with fresh thyme leaves and a light drizzling of olive oil. Bake for 15 to 20 minutes or until the pastry has puffed and is golden brown. ❉

Soups and Salads

Classic Chicken Soup

What is broadly known as "chicken soup" can be stock, broth, or consommé garnished with meat, vegetables, noodles, rice, or dumplings. In its most basic form, chicken soup is water, meat, and bones simmered for maximum flavor. When the arctic chill of winter gets the best of you, the best thing you can do is eat a bowl of chicken soup. Packed with nutrients and loaded with flavor, chicken soup can ease the common cold and soothe the soul.

1, 4-pound chicken

water to cover

2 onions, washed and cut in quarters with skins on

2 tablespoons salt

2 whole carrots, peeled

2 whole celery stalks, cut in half

1 turnip, peeled and quartered

½ bunch fresh parsley

1 bunch fresh dill

1   Rinse and clean the chicken thoroughly, inside and out, with cold running water. Discard, or reserve for later use, the heart and liver. Combine the chicken and the onions in a large stockpot and cover with water by 2 inches. Bring to a simmer and cook over medium-low heat, uncovered, for 1½ hours.

2   Add the remaining ingredients except for the dill. Cover and cook over low heat for one more hour. Remove the chicken and vegetables with tongs or a slotted spoon and strain the soup into another stockpot or storage container. Add fresh dill and let the broth stand for 30 minutes. Meanwhile, reserve the chicken meat and chop vegetables to serve with the soup. Discard the dill and chill the soup, covered, overnight. The fat will come to the top of the soup and will be easy to skim with a spoon. ✳

Reserve the fat in the refrigerator for cooking as a flavorful alternative to butter or oil. Use the chicken meat for salad. Save vegetables for garnish in the soup, or discard.

ESSENTIAL EQUIPMENT

measuring spoon

cutting board

chef's knife

peeler

stockpot

tongs or slotted spoon

strainer (with cheesecloth)

ESSENTIAL TECHNIQUES

mise en place

poaching

JUMP IN FEET FIRST

The secret to exceptional soup: chicken feet. Please do not be discouraged by this seemingly strange and old-fashioned ingredient. It really does make the very best chicken soup. Feet are high in gelatin, which makes for a viscous stock. If you can add half a dozen chicken feet to your soup, it will dramatically strengthen the flavor and color of your broth. Ask your butcher to order some for you. They are very inexpensive, if not free, and easy to get.

MAKES 8 SERVINGS.

time-tested technique

Making the very best chicken soup is a work in progress for a cook. Every time you make chicken soup, it should get a little better. Mastering the technique is within reach if you follow a few rules:

Begin with a large stockpot. The flavor comes from the meat and vegetables you put in the soup. You want to pack in as much as possible and cover with water. It is important to cook chicken soup over a low heat for a long time to get the most from the meat and bones. This guarantees the best possible flavor and richer color.

Rinse the chicken carefully. If you're using a whole bird, ensure that no blood or additional residue ends up in your soup. If you prefer using chicken quarters or eighths, that's perfectly fine. Some people like to use a bunch of wings and bottoms (legs and thighs), since dark meat is a bit fattier and decidedly more flavorful.

Use the skin. Whether you use a whole bird or chicken parts, you must keep the skin on the meat. Without the skin, the soup will not have much depth of flavor or color. Fat always can be skimmed once the soup has been made.

Check the cavity. You may add the neck from an organic bird only, but do not use the heart or liver from any bird for soup, often found sealed in the cavity of a prepackaged chicken.

Balance the vegetables. The essential aromatic vegetables of onions, carrots and celery—officially referred to as mirepoix in the chef world—round out the flavor of the soup. Mirepoix is virtually always 50 percent onion, 25 percent carrot, and 25 percent celery. The problem with many chicken soups and stocks is that they often have too much carrot or celery in relation to the onion. Too much carrot makes a soup sweet, even though it might enhance the color. Celery is a flavor that should not be identifiable on its own in meat broth. Make sure you use at least the same amount of onion as you do of carrot and celery combined.

Season the soup at the end. Once the soup has been made, season it with salt and pepper. Any seasoning you add at the beginning weakens by the end of the cooking process. Reseason before you serve the soup.

Roasted Corn and Cod Chowder

This recipe is a quick soup that has the depth and flavor of an all-day-on-the-stove stew. A chowder is traditionally a chunky seafood soup with potatoes and cream. The version here includes a fusion of flavors and nontraditional ingredients, including ginger, sweet potatoes, and cilantro. Use the recipe below and its procedure as a baseline to make a fish soup with your favorite foods.

¼ cup olive oil

2 onions, chopped

2 cloves garlic, minced

1 tablespoon grated, peeled fresh ginger

1 tablespoon ground cumin

2 celery stalks, finely diced

4 tomatoes, seeded and diced

1 jalapeno, seeded and minced

6 cups fish, chicken, or vegetable stock

2 potatoes, peeled and diced

1 sweet potato, peeled and diced

3 ears corn, kernels roasted then removed

1 cup frozen sweet peas

1 cup heavy cream

2 pounds skinless cod, cut into small chunks (or other firm white fish, such as red snapper or halibut)

juice of one lime

salt and pepper to taste

3 tablespoons chopped cilantro

ESSENTIAL EQUIPMENT

dry and wet measuring cups

measuring spoons

cutting board

chef's knife

peeler

grater or Microplane

stockpot

wooden spoon

ladle

ESSENTIAL TECHNIQUES

mise en place

knife skills

poaching

MAKES 8 SERVINGS.

Roasted Corn and Cod Chowder

1   Heat a stockpot over medium-high heat for 2 minutes, and add the olive oil. Add the onions and sauté, stirring until tender and translucent (about 10 minutes). Add the garlic, ginger, and cumin, and sauté for 2 minutes. Then add the celery, tomatoes, and jalapeno, and sauté for 2 minutes longer.

2   Add the stock, potatoes, and sweet potatoes, and bring to a boil over high heat. Reduce heat to medium and simmer, uncovered, until the potatoes are cooked half-way (still somewhat resistant when pierced with a knife), about 10 to 12 minutes.

3   Add the roasted corn kernels, sweet peas, cream, and fish. Simmer, uncovered, until just cooked, about 5 minutes. Add the lime juice, then season to taste with salt and pepper, then sprinkle with cilantro. Serve immediately. ✳

To roast corn all year-round, place cobs directly on the stovetop over an open flame. Cook for about 30 seconds a side or until charred, turning with tongs. If you have an electric range, put them under the broiler for a few minutes, turning as needed.

FROM SOUTHWESTERN TO SOUTHEAST ASIAN

If a recipe is a canvas, paint it any way you want. Take the Roasted Corn and Cod Chowder and move it from Santa Fe to Saigon. Replace the ginger with galangal, the cumin with green curry paste, the jalapeno with a Thai bird's eye chili pepper, and the cilantro with mint and basil. Swap the cream with some coconut milk, and use carrots instead of potatoes. You can even trade the cod for shrimp. Take whatever you want from the recipe and make it work for you.

Classic Vinaigrettes: Red Wine and Balsamic

The salad dressing is just as important to the flavor of a salad as are the other ingredients. The right salad dressing can make basic greens and tomatoes taste seasoned and refreshing. It should be used somewhat sparingly—just enough to lightly coat each component of the salad, never weighing it down, nor turning it "wet." Dressing is not a sauce, but more like moist seasonings for your greens.

For the red wine vinaigrette:

½ cup red wine vinegar

1½ cups vegetable oil

1 large garlic clove crushed

1 teaspoon Dijon mustard

kosher salt and freshly ground black pepper to taste

Crush the garlic clove with a chef's knife and remove the skin. Pour the vinegar into a large bowl and add the garlic clove. Let it sit for at least 20 minutes to infuse the vinegar. Remove the garlic. Add the mustard and seasoning to the vinegar, and blend with a whisk. Then add the oil very slowly to the vinegar mixture, a bit at a time, as you whisk vigorously, to emulsify. Serve immediately, then store tightly sealed in the refrigerator.

For the balsamic vinaigrette:

½ cup olive oil

¼ cup balsamic vinegar

2 teaspoons Dijon mustard

1 teaspoon finely chopped fresh thyme leaves

1 teaspoon finely chopped fresh rosemary leaves

kosher salt and freshly ground black pepper to taste

Combine the vinegar, mustard, and herbs. Slowly add the oil and whisk vigorously until the mixture emulsifies. Add kosher salt and freshly ground black pepper to taste. A pinch of brown sugar or teaspoon of honey may be added if the vinegar is too sharp. ✻

ESSENTIAL EQUIPMENT

cutting board

chef's knife

wet measuring cup

measuring spoons

large mixing bowl

whisk

ESSENTIAL TECHNIQUES

mise en place

emulsion

YOUR INGREDIENTS COUNT, SO COUNT YOUR INGREDIENTS

No salad made with wilted, tired lettuce is good. The same holds true for the vinaigrette—it can only be as good as what goes into it. High quality vinegar and oil absolutely make a difference. If a vinaigrette tastes bitter or harsh, there are only two reasons: either the ingredients are of a poor quality, or there is too much vinegar in proportion to the oil. The ratio is usually one part vinegar to three parts oil.

2 CUPS OF RED WINE VINAIGRETTE AND ¾ CUP OF BALSAMIC VINAIGRETTE.

Market Salad for Four Seasons

Buying produce fresh from the market is the surest way to enjoy what's in season. Fresh berries and summer squashes are bountiful in warm-weather months, while citrus fruits and root vegetables peak in winter. A market salad that changes with the seasons is guaranteed to be delicious all year-round.

Winter:

¼ cup freshly squeezed orange juice (from 1 orange)

½ cup extra virgin olive oil, plus 2 tablespoons

1 small butternut squash, peeled, seeded and cut into large dice

4 large beets

1 head of frisée

4 ounces soft goat cheese

kosher salt and freshly ground pepper to taste

1 Preheat the oven to 400°F.

2 In a mixing bowl, whisk the orange juice and ½ cup olive oil. Season with kosher salt and freshly ground black pepper. Set aside.

3 Put the butternut squash on a sheet pan and toss with 2 tablespoons olive oil and a generous pinch of kosher salt. Roast in the oven for 20 minutes, or until golden and tender.

4 Meanwhile, prepare the beets. Scrubs the beets under cold running water. Trim and discard the stems. Do not peel the beets. Fill a small saucepan two-thirds with water and set over high heat. Once the water begins to boil, add the beets and a large pinch of kosher salt. Cook until the beets are fork tender, about 45 minutes. Strain the beets, and cool until easy to handle. Wearing gloves, rub the skins off the beets under cold running water.

5 Slice each beet into five slices and divide among four plates along with the roasted butternut squash. Using a spoon, drizzle a bit of orange-olive oil dressing over the beets and butternut squash. ✳

ESSENTIAL EQUIPMENT

dry and wet measuring cups

measuring spoons

cutting board

chef's knife

mixing bowls

whisk

peeler

sheet pan

parchment paper

saucepan

strainer or colander

regular spoon

ESSENTIAL TECHNIQUES

mise en place

knife skills

roasting

blanching

emulsion

EACH SALAD MAKES 4 SERVINGS.

Market Salad for Four Seasons

6 Trim and discard the root of the frisee, and add the leaves to the remaining orange-olive oil dressing. Divide the leaves among the four plates on top of the beets and butternut squash. Sprinkle each plate with one ounce of crumbled goat cheese.

Spring:

4 slices pancetta

1 cup shelled sweet peas, blanched

5 ounces mesclun salad mix

½ cup mixed fresh herbs, such as dill, parsley, chervil, cilantro, and mint

⅓ cup classic vinaigrette, page 126

1 Preheat the oven to 400°F.

2 Line a sheet pan with parchment paper, then add the pancetta slices. Cook in the oven until crisp, about 10 minutes.

3 In a large mixing bowl, toss the mesclun and blanched peas with the vinaigrette. Divide among four plates and top each salad with a crumbled pancetta crisp.

Summer:

2 tablespoons white wine vinegar

1 tablespoon fresh lemon juice

1 tablespoon Dijon mustard

⅓ cup extra virgin olive oil

kosher salt and freshly ground pepper to taste

5 ounces baby romaine

1 pint red and yellow grape tomatoes

½ pound haricots verts, trimmed and blanched

1 zucchini, cut in half lengthwise and very thinly sliced in half moons

Market Salad for Four Seasons

1 In a large mixing bowl, combine the vinegar, lemon juice, and mustard with a whisk. Slowly add the olive oil, whisking continuously, until the mixture emulsifies. Season with kosher salt and freshly ground black pepper to taste.

2 Add the baby romaine, grape tomatoes, haricots verts, and sliced zucchini. Toss well to coat and serve.

Fall:

¼ cup balsamic vinaigrette, page 126

5 ounces arugula

6 fresh Mission figs, sliced in half, or 1 pear, quartered and each quarter sliced into thirds

⅓ cup toasted whole hazelnuts

⅓ cup crumbled Gorgonzola

1 In a large mixing bowl, toss the arugula with the balsamic vinaigrette. Divide the dressed greens evenly among four plates.

2 Place three fig halves or pear slices on each plate, then sprinkle each plate with toasted hazelnuts and Gorgonzola.

3 Serve immediately. ✳

Quick Caesar Salad

The classic Caesar salad is made with a coddled egg, an egg in its shell briefly immersed in simmering water to thicken and slightly cook the yolk. Most people don't have time for that, and worry about the potential presence of bacteria in the egg. This quick version makes a creamy dressing using store-bought mayonnaise. You can buy the croutons, too, but the following recipe is so easy, it's worth giving it a try. Throw in some grape tomatoes and crumbled bacon for a new twist on the old classic, BLT!

For the croutons:

½ French baguette, ¼-inch slices

¼ cup olive oil

For the Caesar salad:

3 romaine hearts, leaves separated, washed, and dried

¼ cup mayonnaise

juice of one lemon

2 tablespoons olive oil

6 anchovy filets, finely chopped

1 garlic clove, minced

2 tablespoons grated Parmesan cheese

1 tablespoon Worcestershire sauce

extra Parmesan for garnish

1   To make the croutons, preheat the oven to 400°F. Cut each baguette slice into quarters and place on a sheet pan. Brush with olive oil and bake for 10 to 12 minutes or until golden brown and crisp. Cool on a wire rack and set aside (or store in an airtight container at room temperature for up to one week).

2   To make the salad, stack the romaine leaves, trim away the top and bottom, and cut the rest into bite sized pieces. In a large bowl, combine the mayonnaise, lemon juice, olive oil, anchovies, garlic, Parmesan, and Worcestershire. Add lettuce pieces and toss well to coat. Add croutons and garnish with Parmesan shavings. ✦

ESSENTIAL EQUIPMENT

cutting board

bread knife

dry and wet measuring cups

measuring spoons

sheet pan

pastry brush

chef's knife

mixing bowls

whisk

peeler

ESSENTIAL TECHNIQUES

mise en place

knife skills

baking

PEEL YOUR PARMESAN

It's easy to make those stylish Parmesan curls you sometimes see in restaurants. Peel a chunk of Parmesan cheese the same way you would a carrot, and you'll have the perfect finish for salads and pasta. Use the same technique with a bar of chocolate to garnish desserts.

MAKES 4 SERVINGS.

Main Dishes

Great Grilled Cheese

Buttered, toasty bread. Oozing, milky cheese. The grilled cheese sandwich is simple yet perfect in every way (except for its name: grilled cheese is not actually grilled, it's panfried or sautéed). Somehow, though, it is possible to mess up this timeless and modest dish. Any competent cook should know the secrets to making great grilled cheese every time.

> 2 slices bread
>
> 1 tablespoon butter, softened
>
> 1 or 2 slices cheddar, Swiss, Munster, or other cheese

1   Heat a pan (regular or nonstick) over medium-low heat and allow it to get hot before you cook.

2   Meanwhile, butter each slice of bread on one side with ½ tablespoon of butter.* Once the pan is hot, place a slice of bread in the pan buttered side down. Lower the heat, and top the bread with one or two slices of cheese, then top with the second slice of bread, butter side up.

3   Immediately place a lid on top of the skillet to help melt the cheese while the first slice of bread turns golden brown. After about 2 minutes, flip the sandwich to toast the second slice of bread. If the cheese still needs to melt a bit more, cover the pan with a lid again. If the cheese is melted to your satisfaction, at this point you may finish the cooking process sans lid. ❉

This might seem counterintuitive, but it is the best way to achieve a uniform taste and color. It actually helps to reduce the amount of butter needed to get the job done. If you spread soft butter on the outside (the side that touches the pan) of each slice of bread, you apply only as much as is needed.

ESSENTIAL EQUIPMENT

cutting board

knife

small sauté pan or cast iron skillet with lid

spatula

ESSENTIAL TECHNIQUES

mise en place

sautéing

ATTENTION, TOMATO LOVERS!

If you enjoy a slice of tomato with your grilled cheese, use two slices of cheese and place very thin slices of tomato (without too many wet seeds) between the cheese slices. This keeps the tomato from moistening the bread, and allows the cheese to melt better by being closer to the toasting bread and thus the heat source.

MAKES 1 SANDWICH.

Macaroni and Cheese

The key to making this classic is selecting quality cheese. Experiment with everything from goat cheese to Gorgonzola. Once you make macaroni and cheese from scratch, the boxed version will never do again.

1 pound uncooked elbow pasta or macaroni

½ cup (1 stick) butter

½ cup all-purpose flour

1 teaspoon kosher salt

½ teaspoon freshly ground black pepper

2 teaspoons Dijon mustard

2 teaspoons Worcestershire sauce

4 cups whole milk

¼ teaspoon nutmeg

2 cups shredded Gruyère cheese

2 cups shredded sharp Cheddar cheese

1 cup fresh breadcrumbs or extra shredded cheese for topping

ESSENTIAL EQUIPMENT

dry and wet measuring cups

measuring spoons

box grater

large saucepan or stockpot

small saucepan

colander or strainer

wooden spoon

whisk

casserole or baking pan

ESSENTIAL TECHNIQUES

mise en place

thickening sauces (with a roux)

baking

MAKES 8 SERVINGS.

1 Preheat the oven to 350°F.

2 Cook noodles as directed on the package. Rinse with cold water once drained to prevent them from sticking together.

3 Warm the milk in a small saucepan and set aside.

4 Melt the butter in a large saucepan over low heat. Stir in the flour, salt, black pepper, mustard, and Worcestershire. Cook over low heat, stirring constantly, until the mixture is smooth and bubbling. Remove from the heat and slowly whisk in the warmed milk.

5 Return to the heat and bring to a gentle boil, stirring constantly to create a smooth, lump-free sauce. Reduce the heat to a simmer and stir the mixture until thickened to the point of coating the back of a spoon. Add the nutmeg. Remove from heat. Stir in cheeses until melted and well incorporated.

6 Gently stir drained macaroni into the cheese sauce. Pour into a casserole dish. Top with breadcrumbs or extra cheese. Bake for 25 to 30 minutes uncovered, or until bubbly and lightly browned. ✳

Hams and Hots (Hamburgers and Hot Dogs)

Experimenting with flavors and techniques for even the most basic dishes makes you a more competent cook. There are literally hundreds of ways to season hamburger meat and dozens of ways to garnish the hamburger bun. Hot dogs are perhaps a little less versatile, but there is certainly more to a hot dog than mustard and sauerkraut.

For the hamburgers:

2 pounds 85 percent lean ground chuck or sirloin

1 tablespoon Worcestershire sauce

2 teaspoons salt

1 teaspoon ground black pepper

2 cloves garlic, minced

2 tablespoons barbecue sauce (optional)

6 hamburger buns

For the hot dogs:

6 all-beef frankfurters

6 hot dog buns

ESSENTIAL EQUIPMENT

measuring spoons

cutting board

chef's knife

mixing bowl

paring knife

saucepan

cast iron skillet, griddle, electric grill, or outdoor grill

spatula

tongs

ESSENTIAL TECHNIQUES

mise en place

grilling, broiling, or sautéing

poaching

MAKES 6 SERVINGS.

1 To make the hamburgers, combine the ground beef, Worcestershire, salt, pepper, minced garlic, and barbecue sauce with your hands. Divide the mixture into sixths, and form six round patties, each slightly larger than the size of the bun (the burgers shrink during cooking).

2 Heat a cast iron skillet, griddle, electric grill, or outdoor grill. If you are using a skillet or griddle, heat the pan over high heat to start, but then lower to a medium-low heat so that the burgers do not burn as they cook. Turn the burgers when juices appear on the surface—only once. Do not press the burgers down repeatedly, or turn them over and over. This removes moisture and toughens the meat.

3 Serve the burgers on buns with your favorite toppings.

4 To make the hot dogs, fill a large saucepan two-thirds full of water and bring to a boil. Run a knife around each frankfurter, making a spiral cut top to bottom around the body. Place them in the boiling water and reduce to a simmer. Once the spirals open up, after about 10 minutes, remove the hot dogs from the water and place them on a hot grill, cooking them until they are lightly charred.

5 Serve the hot dogs on buns with your favorite toppings. ✳

hamburger helper

A grilled, juicy beef burger on a bun with all the fixings is so appetizing. Even the most unadulterated burger—a plain unseasoned beef patty—cooked over an open flame can be so darn good. What makes a burger even better?

Meat selection is essential. Ground beef that is more than 90% lean is too lean for a juicy burger, especially if you like your burger medium to well done; it just won't be that flavorful or moist. 80 to 85 percent lean is ideal for a grilled hamburger. If you are going to make a burger, remember that a little bit of fat is your friend.

Season the meat. Salt and pepper are basic seasonings for any meat, and a hamburger is no exception. Adding ketchup, barbecue sauce, or Worcestershire to the meat adds moisture and flavor. A pat of butter in the center of the burger permeates the cooked patty, which translates to the tastiest moisture there could be. Crumbled blue cheese lends a sophisticated flavor and unexpected ooze to a hamburger patty. Liquid smoke (for those nonpurists who would consider using it) is a fun and easy way to add a hickory wood chip accent. Any flavor you customarily enjoy on top of the burger can go inside—onions, tomatoes, crumbled bacon, and cheese. There is really no limit to how creative and decadent you can be.

Garnish the burger and the bun. Topping a burger is even more fun than filling it. Ketchup, lettuce, tomato, onions, and pickles are classic options. Cheese, of course, is a perfect match. Some people like mayonnaise, while others like mustard. Fried eggs, chili, and bacon are good protein picks. A sandwich bun is traditional, but there are lots of ways to hold a burger. A toasted English muffin is delicious, as is toasted rye bread (one of the key ingredients in a patty melt). Lettuce leaves are an appropriate choice for those carb-counters.

Broiled Flank Steak

Flank steak is a long and flat cut from the cow's belly, with a moderate amount of fat. Since it comes from working muscle, the meat is naturally tougher than other cuts and benefits from a lengthy marinade. The marinade permeates the steak due to the meat's porous texture, making it tender and flavorful when cooked. Flank steak's texture and taste is best when rare or medium rare.

¼ cup vegetable oil

¼ cup Worcestershire sauce

¼ cup soy sauce

2 tablespoons brown sugar, or ¼ cup maple syrup

1 tablespoon dry/ground mustard

4 cloves garlic, mashed into paste

1 teaspoon kosher salt

½ teaspoon ground black pepper

2 pounds flank steak

1 Combine all the ingredients in a shallow casserole and add the steak, turning to coat several times. Marinate the steak in the pan, or in a sealed plastic bag, for at least one hour up to overnight, turning periodically to coat both sides evenly.

2 Preheat the broiler to high. Place an oven rack just below the broiler. Put the broiling pan in the oven for five minutes to become hot. Place the meat on the broiler pan and return to the oven for anywhere from 8 to 12 minutes (ranging from very rare to well done).

3 Remove the meat from the oven and pan, and place it on a cutting board. Allow the meat to rest for 5 minutes before slicing. ✳

ESSENTIAL EQUIPMENT

wet measuring cup

measuring spoons

cutting board

chef's knife

casserole

whisk

broiling or sheet pan

ESSENTIAL TECHNIQUES

mise en place

broiling

GO AGAINST THE GRAIN

Yes, you should be creative and break from convention from time to time. But never when it comes to slicing beef. Going against the grain, in this case, is to follow strictly a culinary commandment. Always slice beef against the grain of the meat. If you fail to cut perpendicular to the lines in the beef, it will be tough and chewy.

MAKES 4 SERVINGS.

Roast Chicken and Potatoes

How can something so simple be so good? It's the "simple" that makes this recipe a favorite comfort food. This perfect pair brings out the best in each other. When chicken is well seasoned, trussed, and roasted in the oven, it releases its fat, browning and crisping its skin for an authentically savory flavor. The excess chicken fat then flavors the potatoes, almost frying them in the oven for a truly mouthwatering side dish.

1, 4-pound chicken

kosher salt

freshly ground black pepper

3 thyme sprigs

3 garlic cloves

4 large Idaho potatoes

1 teaspoon dried rosemary

1 teaspoon garlic powder

¼ cup olive oil

1 teaspoon kosher salt

ESSENTIAL EQUIPMENT:

wet measuring cup

measuring spoons

cutting board

chef's knife

large mixing bowl

wooden spoon

metal spatula

sheet pan or shallow roasting pan

tongs

kitchen twine

ESSENTIAL TECHNIQUES

mise en place

roasting

MAKES 4 SERVINGS.

1 Preheat the oven to 450°F.

2 Rinse the chicken, if necessary, and pat it dry inside and out. Remove any excess fat and trim the wings. Sprinkle the chicken cavity with ½ teaspoon salt and ½ teaspoon pepper, then add the fresh thyme leaves and garlic cloves inside. Sprinkle the outside of the chicken with ½ tablespoon salt and pepper. Truss the chicken and place it in a large, shallow roasting pan. Drizzle the chicken with 2 tablespoons olive oil.

3 Peel the potatoes and cut them lengthwise into sixths. In a large bowl, toss the potatoes with rosemary, garlic powder, olive oil, and 1 teaspoon kosher salt. Arrange the potatoes around the chicken in a single layer.

4 Place the pan in the oven, with the legs facing the back, at 450°F degrees for 30 minutes. Do not open the oven door. After 30 minutes, remove the pan from the oven and shut the door. Lower the heat to 350°F. Turn over each potato wedge using tongs, or a metal spatula if necessary, and return the pan to the oven to roast the chicken for another 45 minutes, or until the internal temperature of the chicken thigh reaches 170°F.

5 Allow the chicken to rest at least 10 to 15 minutes before carving. Serve the chicken with the potatoes. ✳

Lasagne al forno

Lasagne "from the oven" is easy to make, and best when prepared in advance. It feeds a crowd, and travels well when you need to bring a dish to a family gathering or potluck dinner. The key to any good lasagne is the quality of the ingredients. Sauce made from scratch, fresh ricotta and buffalo mozzarella, and garden-picked herbs make all the difference.

For the meat sauce:

3 tablespoons olive oil

2 medium onions, finely diced

3 garlic cloves, minced

2 pounds sweet Italian sausage, casings removed (or 1½ pounds sweet Italian sausage and ½ pound hot Italian sausage for a little "kick")

2, 15-ounce cans crushed tomatoes

1 8-ounce can tomato sauce

1 6-ounce can tomato paste

1 tablespoon chopped fresh oregano

½ bunch fresh basil, chiffonade

1 teaspoon kosher salt

½ teaspoon freshly ground black pepper

For the cheese filling:

22 ounces fresh ricotta cheese (or 16 ounces ricotta, plus 6 ounces mascarpone)

1½ cups Parmesan, divided (1 cup and ½ cup)

1 large egg, lightly beaten

3 tablespoons chopped flat-leaf parsley

½ teaspoon kosher salt

¼ teaspoon freshly ground pepper

10 no-boil, oven-ready lasagne noodles

1 pound fresh buffalo mozzarella, thinly sliced

ESSENTIAL EQUIPMENT

dry measuring cup

measuring spoons

cutting board

chef's knife

large saucepan or stockpot

fork

can opener

large mixing bowls

rubber spatula

casserole or baking pan

ESSENTIAL TECHNIQUES

mise en place

knife skills

sautéing

baking

A PINCH OF RED PEPPER WILL DO

If you only have access to pre-packaged sausage, you might find that you can buy the sausage in 1- or 2-pound portions. If you don't feel like buying more sausage than you'll use (since the recipe calls for 1½ pounds sweet Italian sausage and ½ pound hot Italian sausage), just buy 2 pounds of sweet Italian sausage and add ½ teaspoon of crushed red pepper flakes to the sauce for the same effect.

MAKES 8 SERVINGS.

Lasagne al forno

1 Preheat the oven to 400°F and position the oven rack in the middle.

2 To make the meat sauce, heat the olive oil in a large saucepan. Add the onion and cook over medium-low heat until translucent (about 5 minutes). Add the garlic and stir for one more minute. Then add the sausage and cook over medium-low heat, breaking it up with a wooden spoon, for 10 to 15 minutes, or until fully cooked and no longer pink. Add the crushed tomatoes, tomato sauce, tomato paste, oregano, basil, kosher salt, and freshly ground black pepper. Simmer uncovered over medium-low heat for 20 minutes.

3 While the sauce is simmering, make the cheese filling. In a large bowl, combine the ricotta, 1 cup of Parmesan, the beaten egg, chopped parsley, kosher salt, and freshly ground black pepper. Set aside.

4 Ladle one third of the meat sauce into a 9" × 12" × 2" casserole or baking pan. Spread the sauce over the bottom of the dish. Then add approximately half the pasta (in one layer, cover the sauce with the noodles), half the sliced mozzarella, half the cheese mixture, and one third of the sauce. Add another single layer of noodles, mozzarella, ricotta, and the remaining sauce. Sprinkle with the remaining ½ cup of Parmesan.

5 Bake uncovered for 35 minutes, or until the sauce is bubbling. ✳

This dish can be assembled up to one day in advance before baking. Even better, bake the lasagne a day or two before you want to serve it to allow the casserole to settle.

Sautéed Sea Scallops in Brown Butter

This wonderfully simple recipe, with just two components apart from the salt and pepper, is all about applying technique to bring out the best in the ingredients. Sea scallops are plump, pinkish white, and tender, pleasingly smooth in texture and taste. Toasting butter in a pan until the milk solids turn golden brown adds a nutty depth that pairs perfectly with the distinctly sweet flavor of sea scallops. Serve this dish with a simple green salad, or with String Beans Almandine (page 159).

> 1 pound sea scallops, approximately 20
>
> kosher salt
>
> freshly ground black pepper
>
> 6 tablespoons (¾ stick) unsalted butter

1 Pat the scallops dry on the cutting board using a paper towel. Sprinkle the tops and bottoms generously with kosher salt and freshly ground black pepper.

2 Place 2 tablespoons of the butter in a cold sauté pan and melt over high heat. Once the butter has melted and begins to foam, add the sea scallops. Cook for 1 to 2 minutes per side to achieve a golden brown surface without overcooking the scallops.

3 Remove the scallops to a serving dish, and tent with foil to keep warm. Set aside.

4 Add the remaining 4 tablespoons of butter to the pan and reduce the heat to medium low. As the butterfat melts, the milk solids will sink to the bottom of the pan and turn golden brown. Remove the pan from the heat, and spoon the brown butter sauce over the sea scallops. Serve immediately. ❖

ESSENTIAL EQUIPMENT

cutting board

sauté pan

spatula

ESSENTIAL TECHNIQUES

mise en place

sautéing

BUTTER THAT GOES FROM BROWN TO BLACK

Brown butter is often called "beurre noisette," named after the hazelnut color and nutty flavor achieved in browning the butter. Black butter ("beurre noir") is not really black; if it were, it literally would be burnt, toxic, and unfit for consumption. It's just one stage past brown butter, darker brown and even more nutty. Add a splash of lemon juice, rinsed capers, and some chopped parsley to black butter for savory sauce for fish and vegetables.

MAKES 4 SERVINGS.

Poached Salmon with Pickled Cucumber Salad

As healthy as it is colorful, this is a classic cold main course, perfect for a summer lunch or a light dinner. Prepare both the salad and the fish the day before you plan to serve it, giving the cucumbers time to pickle and the fish time to chill.

For the fish:

1 quart cold water

1 bottle dry white wine

1 lemon, thinly sliced

1 bay leaf

12 black peppercorns

8, 6–8-ounce salmon filets, skin-on

For the cucumber salad:

1 cup white wine vinegar

1 cup water

½ cup sugar

2 teaspoons kosher salt

1 teaspoon black peppercorns

½ teaspoon yellow mustard seeds

1 bay leaf

4 hothouse cucumbers, cut in ⅛-inch slices

2 tablespoons chopped dill

½ cup finely diced red onion

salt and black pepper to taste

ESSENTIAL EQUIPMENT

dry and wet measuring cups

measuring spoons

cutting board

chef's knife

deep sauté pan, shallow stock pot, or Dutch oven

spatula

saucepan

strainer

ESSENTIAL TECHNIQUES

mise en place

knife skills

poaching

EXTERIOR DESIGN

When it comes to salads, it's up to you whether you want to peel a cucumber or leave the skin. You do have the option to make a design, highlighting the contrast between the opaque, dark green skin and the translucent, light green flesh. Use a vegetable peeler to remove alternating strips of skin. If you like the cucumber to have fluted edges that resemble a flower, use a channeling tool to dig thin strips of skin and flesh.

MAKES 8 SERVINGS.

Poached Salmon with Pickled Cucumber Salad

1   To make the fish, add water, wine, lemon, and spices to a deep pan and place over low heat. Bring to a simmer just below the boiling point. Rinse and dry the filets, then place them skin-side down into the poaching liquid. Cover and simmer until done, approximately 10 minutes. To check, poke gently with a sharp skewer. If it passes through readily, the filet is done.

2   Remove the pan from heat and allow the contents to cool for several minutes before removing the filets. Lift the cooled filets from the pan with a spatula. Carefully transfer the filets onto a cutting board and peel off skin. Store the filets in the refrigerator (discard the poaching liquid).

3   To prepare the cucumber salad, combine the vinegar, water, sugar, kosher salt, peppercorns, mustard seeds, and bay leaf in a large saucepan and bring to a boil. Remove from the heat immediately and strain the pickling liquid into a storage container, discarding the peppercorns, mustard seeds, and bay leaf. Stir for a few minutes to help release the heat. Let the mixture rest until it is no longer hot, or chill immediately over an ice bath.

4   Add the cucumbers, pepper, dill, and chopped red onion to the cooled pickling liquid. Cover and chill overnight in the refrigerator. The next day, season with kosher salt and freshly ground black pepper to taste.

5   Serve the chilled salmon filets with the pickled cucumber salad. ✳

BBQ-Glazed Turkey Meatloaf

Meatloaf and potatoes might be from another era, but they can be prepared with today's diet in mind. Use lean ground turkey instead of the more fatty beef option, and sauté onions and apples to make the loaf lighter and more substantial. Lots of fresh herbs and a light glaze of a quick homemade barbecue sauce make this dish a hit with the grownups as well as the kids. Serve with a green salad and Baked Lemon Potatoes (page 201).

1 small onion, diced

½ Fuji apple, peeled and finely diced

2 tablespoons olive oil

1 pound ground turkey

1 egg, lightly beaten

½ cup breadcrumbs

1 teaspoon chopped fresh thyme

½ teaspoon kosher salt

¼ teaspoon freshly ground black pepper

¼ cup smoky barbecue sauce (page 146)

ESSENTIAL EQUIPMENT

wet and dry measuring cups

measuring spoons

cutting board

chef's knife

peeler

sauté pan

wooden spoon

large mixing bowl

sheet pan or loaf pan

pastry brush

ESSENTIAL TECHNIQUES

mise en place

knife skills

sautéing

baking

MAKES 4 SERVINGS.

1   Place a rack in the middle, and preheat the oven to 375°F.

2   Heat a small sauté pan over medium heat and add the olive oil. Add the diced onion and apple, cooking for about 5 minutes, until the onion and apple have softened. Remove from the heat and set aside.

3   In a large mixing bowl, combine the ground turkey, egg, breadcrumbs, thyme, kosher salt, and freshly ground pepper. Fold in the sautéed onions and apples.

4   Lightly grease a sheet pan or loaf pan with olive oil. Form the meat mixture into a loaf and place in the pan. Brush the top with barbecue sauce. Bake uncovered for 30 minutes, or until the turkey is cooked and the loaf is firm.

5   Remove from the oven and let the loaf rest for 5 minutes before slicing into ½-inch thick pieces. ✹

Beer-Braised Beef Short Ribs

Short ribs are meaty and tender pieces of beef from the rib section of the cow. You can get them cut either with or without the bone, but leaving the bone in is better because it adds a depth of flavor and viscosity to the cooking liquid.

1 tablespoon vegetable oil

¼ pound bacon, chopped

4 large, meaty beef short ribs (about 4 pounds), cut in 4-inch pieces

kosher salt and freshly ground black pepper

2 garlic cloves, minced

2 tablespoons chopped ginger

2 cups pearl onions, skins removed

1 carrot, peeled and finely diced

1 celery stalk, finely diced

2 to 3 cups beef stock

1 can stout (such as Guinness)

1, 28-ounce can diced tomatoes

1 tablespoon balsamic vinegar

ESSENTIAL EQUIPMENT

dry and wet measuring cups

measuring spoons

cutting board

chef's knife

peeler

can opener

Dutch oven or stockpot

tongs

ESSENTIAL TECHNIQUES

mise en place

knife skills

braising

MAKES 4 SERVINGS.

1   Preheat the oven to 300°F. Pat the ribs dry and season all sides generously with kosher salt and freshly ground black pepper. Set aside.

2   Heat a Dutch oven or stockpot over medium-high heat and add the oil. Add the bacon and cook until crisp and the fat renders. Remove the bacon from the pan to a dish lined with a paper towel and set aside. Cook the ribs in the bacon fat in batches until they are nicely browned on all sides, about 20 minutes.

3   Remove the ribs to a plate and set aside. Drain off all but two tablespoons of fat, and add the garlic, ginger, onions, carrot, celery, and additional kosher salt and freshly ground black pepper to the pot. Cook, stirring occasionally, until the vegetables begin to soften, about 10 minutes.

4   Return the ribs and bacon to the pot. Add the stock, beer, and diced tomatoes (the liquid should come up the sides of the ribs, but not over the ribs; add more beef stock or water, if necessary). Bring the braising liquid to a simmer, then transfer the pot to the oven and cook for 2 hours, turning the meat once.

5   Once the meat is tender and comes away easily from the bone, transfer the ribs to a plate and set aside. Bring the braising liquid to a simmer and skim off the fat. Reduce the liquid to thicken the sauce a bit, then add the balsamic vinegar. Season to taste.

6   Return the ribs to the pot to reheat them, then serve. ✳

Roasted Rack of Lamb with Herbed Breadcrumbs

Rack of lamb is the ideal elegant dinner for two. Lamb is tender and juicy, well paired with crisp herbed breadcrumbs and a hint of Dijon mustard. Serve rack of lamb with seasonal sides like Roasted Root Vegetables (page 1+0) in autumn and winter, or Steamed Asparagus with Red Pepper Coulis (page 202) in spring and summer.

1 rack of lamb, frenched

1 tablespoon vegetable oil

sea salt

freshly ground black pepper

1 tablespoon Dijon mustard

½ cup fresh breadcrumbs

1 tablespoon chopped parsley

1 tablespoon chopped chervil

1 teaspoon chopped thyme

1 teaspoon chopped rosemary

1 garlic clove, finely minced

1 tablespoon olive oil

1   Preheat the oven to 375°F.

2   Rub the rack with the vegetable oil and sprinkle it generously with fine sea salt and freshly ground pepper. Heat a large sauté pan over medium-high heat until hot, and add the rack, meat-side down. Sear for 3 minutes, then turn the rack upright (holding on to it with your tongs if necessary) to sear the bottom of the meat as well. Remove the pan from the heat and remove the rack to a cutting board.

3   Coat the top of the meat with the mustard. Combine the breadcrumbs, herbs, garlic, and olive oil in a small bowl. Spread this mixture over the top of the mustard-coated meat. Put the rack on a sheet pan in the oven and roast for 15 to 18 minutes.

4   Remove the rack from the oven, and let it rest for 10 minutes before carving it into four double chops. The lamb will be medium rare and warm for service. ✳

ESSENTIAL EQUIPMENT

dry measuring cup

measuring spoons

cutting board

chef's knife

large sauté pan

mixing bowl

rubber spatula or wooden spoon

sheet pan

tongs

ESSENTIAL TECHNIQUES

mise en place

sautéing

roasting

PITCH A TENT

Whole birds and roasts need to rest before being served so the juices can redistribute in the flesh. They are large enough to hold on to the heat that they acquired in the oven for some time. If you worry about the roast losing heat, or need to shield the chicken from the draft of a cracked window, tent it with foil. Take a large piece of foil creased down the middle and make a roof open on all sides. This helps to retain heat, but also releases steam so the food does not become soggy or overcooked.

MAKES 2 SERVINGS.

Panfried Chicken Fingers with Three Dipping Sauces

Homemade fried chicken fingers are almost always much healthier and tastier than those available in restaurants.

For the smoky barbecue sauce:

1 cup ketchup

2 tablespoons brown sugar

1 tablespoon molasses

1 tablespoon liquid smoke

1 tablespoon soy sauce

1 tablespoon Worcestershire

1 teaspoon powdered ginger

1 teaspoon garlic powder

1 teaspoon chili powder

½ teaspoon cumin

For the chili orange sauce:

½ cup orange marmalade

2 tablespoons orange juice

¼ teaspoon red pepper flakes

For the honey mustard:

⅔ cup mayonnaise

¼ cup honey

2 tablespoons Dijon mustard

kosher salt and freshly ground black pepper to taste

For the chicken fingers:

4, 6-ounce split chicken breasts

½ cup flour

1 teaspoon kosher salt

½ teaspoon freshly ground black pepper

2 eggs, lightly beaten

⅓ cup buttermilk (optional)

1 cup homemade breadcrumbs or panko

vegetable oil for frying

ESSENTIAL EQUIPMENT

dry and wet measuring cups

measuring spoons

small saucepans

wooden spoons

mixing bowls

cutting board

chef's knife

fork

cast iron skillet or large sauté pan (with straight sides)

tongs

ESSENTIAL TECHNIQUES

mise en place

frying

MAKES 6 SERVINGS.

Panfried Chicken Fingers with Three Dipping Sauces

1   First, prepare the sauces. To make the barbecue sauce, combine all the ingredients in a small saucepan and cook over a medium-low heat for 15 minutes. To make the chili orange sauce, thin the marmalade with the orange juice in a small saucepan over medium heat and stir in the red pepper flakes. To make the honey mustard sauce, combine all the ingredients in a small bowl.

2   Slice each chicken breast diagonally into 6 strips, making a total of 24 strips. Place the strips on a dish and set aside.

3   Combine the flour, salt, and pepper in a wide shallow bowl and set aside. Then beat the egg (and buttermilk, if using) with a fork in a wide shallow bowl and set aside. Put the breadcrumbs in a wide shallow bowl and set aside. From left to right, line up the seasoned flour, egg mixture, and breadcrumbs, respectively.

4   Dredge one chicken strip in the seasoned flour and shake off excess. Then dip the coated chicken into the egg mixture, then directly into the breadcrumbs. With a dry hand, toss well to coat and set aside. Repeat with the remaining chicken strips.

5   Heat 1 inch of vegetable oil in a cast iron skillet or large sauté pan over medium-high heat until the surface begins to shimmer. To test if the oil is hot, carefully lower the tip of one chicken finger into the oil. If the chicken finger sizzles and begins to brown, the oil is ready. If nothing happens, the oil is not yet hot, so remove the meat immediately.

6   Depending on the size of your pan, fry 6 to 8 chicken fingers at a time in 3 or 4 batches. Fry on one side for 2 to 3 minutes, or until the bottom and edges are golden brown. Turn each chicken finger carefully with tongs in the order in which they entered the pan, and fry for another 2 to 3 minutes, or until the chicken is fully cooked.

7   Remove the chicken fingers to a large platter or cutting board lined with paper towels to drain the fat. The chicken fingers can be warmed in a 400°F oven in a single layer on a sheet pan for 2 minutes. ✳

BREADING IS AS EASY AS 1-2-3

Breading is very procedural. It can be a messy proposition if you don't follow the method. You need three bowls: one shallow bowl with flour and seasonings, a second shallow bowl with eggs and other wet ingredients, and a third shallow bowl with breadcrumbs. Moving from left to right is key, and so is keeping one hand dry and one hand wet. Directions are given for a right-handed person; reverse the procedures if you're left-handed. That is, flour the food with your left hand (dry), but dip it in egg with your right hand (wet). Move the food from the egg, shaking off excess, to the breadcrumbs using your wet, right hand. Dredge the food in the breadcrumbs with your dry, left hand and move it to a pan or plate. Never put your dry hand in the eggs, or your wet hand in the flour or breadcrumbs.

BAKED, NOT FRIED

If you don't want to splurge on fried chicken fingers, bake them instead. The preparation is the same, but the cooking is different. Preheat the oven to 425°F. Spray a sheet pan lightly and evenly with oil, and place the chicken fingers on the pan in a single layer, spraying them lightly with oil, too. Bake for 10 to 12 minutes, or until cooked and golden brown.

Chicken Potpie

Comfort food has made a permanent comeback. Chicken potpie is still the essential one-dish cold-weather meal, packed with tender chicken, loads of colorful vegetables, and savory herbs. Throw anything in a potpie to make it fit your palate. You can even substitute the chicken with some salmon or cod for a spin on an English fish pie.

1½ pounds cooked boneless chicken breast, cubed

6 tablespoons butter, divided

½ cup all-purpose flour

2 cups chicken stock

1½ cups whole milk

½ teaspoon ground nutmeg

1 cup pearl onions, peeled

3 carrots, sliced crosswise into coins

2 celery ribs, diced

1 sweet potato, diced

2 cups cubed butternut squash

1 cup frozen peas, thawed

leaves from 4 sprigs of thyme

¼ cup finely chopped parsley

kosher salt and freshly ground black pepper to taste

Basic Pie Dough (page 162)

1 egg beaten with 1 tablespoon cold water

ESSENTIAL EQUIPMENT

dry and wet measuring cups

measuring spoons

cutting board

chef's knife

fork

large saucepan or small stockpot

wooden spoon

whisk

large sauté pan

rolling pin

casserole

pastry brush

ESSENTIAL TECHNIQUES

mise en place

knife skills

sautéing

baking

thickening sauces (with a roux)

MAKES 8 SERVINGS.

Chicken Potpie

1   Heat 4 tablespoons of the butter in a large saucepan over medium heat. Once melted, add the flour and whisk until smooth, stirring constantly for one minute. Add the chicken stock and whisk until smooth. Then add the milk and bring the mixture to a simmer, increasing the heat to medium-high. Continue to whisk the mixture until it thickens to a creamy consistency. Remove the pot from the heat and add the cubed cooked chicken and nutmeg. Season to taste with kosher salt and freshly ground black pepper. Set aside.

2   Preheat the oven to 400°F and position the rack to the upper third of the oven. Heat the remaining 2 tablespoons butter in a large sauté pan over medium-high heat. Add the pearl onions, carrots, celery, sweet potato, and butternut squash. Cook, stirring often, for 5 to 7 minutes. Add the vegetables to the chicken mixture, along with the peas, thyme, and parsley. Season again with kosher salt and freshly ground pepper to taste.

3   Roll the pie dough to the shape of the dish you are using to bake the pie. Fill this vessel with the creamed chicken and vegetables and place the dough on top. Tuck in the edges down against the sides and brush the top with the egg and water mixture.

4   Bake uncovered for 30 to 40 minutes, or until the crust is golden and the filling is bubbling. ✳

STRIP HERBS FROM HEAD TO TOE

Herbs like rosemary and thyme flower on woody stems that can be as thick and stiff as tiny twigs. Hold the stem in one hand and pull the herbs downward with the other hand, opposite to the direction in which they grow. They'll come right off the stem in just one motion.

CHAPTER

14

Side Dishes

* Applesauce
* Festive Coleslaw
* Shrimp Fried Rice
* Creamy Mashed Potatoes
* Butternut Squash Gratin
* Braised Fennel
* Cold Sesame Peanut Noodles
* Spinach and Pignoli Orzo
* String Beans Almandine
* Roasted Root Vegetables

Applesauce

pplesauce is basically cooked apples. A touch of lemon, a sprinkling of sugar, and a few drops of water help the apples along as they release their juices and break down. It's so easy to do, that there is no sense in buying the jarred variety. Fresh apple taste comes through when applesauce is homemade. The flavor and moisture content of the applesauce change depending on the apple used. Granny Smith apples, for example, lend a full, dense flavor with a chunky texture, if desired. Cortland apples, on the other hand, have more water and therefore make a lighter, thinner, and finer applesauce.

> 6 tart apples, peeled and cored
>
> 1 lemon
>
> ¼ cup granulated sugar
>
> ¼ cup water
>
> dash of cinnamon or nutmeg, fresh ginger, horseradish (optional)

1   Peel and core the apples, then cut them in half. Cut the lemon in half and use one half for rubbing the apples. Cut the apples into small chunks and place them into a medium saucepan. Add the sugar, water, and a squeeze of lemon juice from the remaining lemon half. Cook, covered, over low heat until the apples begin to break down and release their juices, about 15 to 20 minutes.

2   Remove the lid and continue cooking, stirring frequently until you reach the desired consistency. For chunky applesauce, cook for approximately 3 to 5 more minutes. For a smoother applesauce, cook for approximately 5 to 10 more minutes. Stir in desired seasoning and serve. ✱

Applesauce may be served warm or cold and can be stored in the refrigerator for up to two weeks.

ESSENTIAL EQUIPMENT

dry and wet measuring cups

cutting board

peeler

chef's knife

saucepan

wooden spoon

ESSENTIAL TECHNIQUES

mise en place

knife skills

MAKES APPROXIMATELY 4 CUPS.

Festive Coleslaw

Color is what makes this coleslaw festive. Bright purple cabbage, flecks of orange carrots, and strips of green pepper jump off the plate. The combination of mayonnaise with sour cream makes this coleslaw truly creamy. The celery seed adds that unidentifiable but distinctive flavor every competent cook seeks to impart. Top this slaw on your favorite sandwich or bring it to a barbecue. Throw in some grated apple or chopped pecans for another dimension.

½ cup mayonnaise

¼ cup sour cream

2 teaspoons sugar

2 teaspoons lemon juice or cider vinegar

½ teaspoon celery seed

kosher salt and freshly ground black pepper to taste

1 small head of red cabbage, chiffonade or finely shredded

1 carrot, shredded

1 small green pepper, julienned

1　In a large bowl, mix the mayonnaise, sour cream, sugar, lemon juice, and celery seed. Season with kosher salt and freshly ground pepper to taste. Add the shredded cabbage, carrot, and green pepper. Toss well to coat.

2　Cover and refrigerate until ready to serve. ✳

This dish is best if made one day in advance, which allows the dressing to slightly wilt and tenderize the cabbage.

ESSENTIAL EQUIPMENT

dry measuring cups

measuring spoons

cutting board

chef's knife

peeler

box grater or food processor

large mixing bowl

rubber spatula

ESSENTIAL TECHNIQUES

mise en place

knife skills

GET RIGHT TO THE CORE

Cabbage has a woody, tough core. Before you begin shredding or cutting the cabbage, split it down the middle, stand it up on its base, and slice a triangle around the core. Remove the cut chunk from the base and discard. Repeat the process with the second half.

MAKES 8–10 SERVINGS.

Shrimp Fried Rice

Preparing fried rice at home turns a greasy take-out standby into a healthful, delicious dish. Using day-old rice not only saves time, but prevents the fried rice from being soggy and mushy (freshly cooked rice is too moist to stir-fry). Add roasted cashews or diced pineapple for extra punch. This dish is easily made vegetarian by eliminating the shrimp and egg.

4 tablespoons vegetable oil, divided in half

½ pound small raw shrimp (approximately 20)

2 eggs, lightly beaten

4 garlic cloves, minced

1 tablespoon minced fresh ginger

4 scallions, trimmed and chopped, or ½ red onion finely diced

⅔ cup frozen peas and carrots, thawed

4 cups cooked long-grain white rice (cold)

¼ cup soy sauce

1 tablespoon toasted sesame oil

1 Heat a large nonstick sauté pan or wok over medium high heat. Add 2 tablespoons vegetable oil and swirl to coat the pan. Place the shrimps along perimeter of the pan. Add the beaten egg in the center and allow it to set for several seconds before pushing the eggs to the center of the pan. Using a spatula, flip the egg mass and allow it to cook another several seconds before lifting it onto a plate to break into pieces. Stir the shrimp with a wooden spoon to finish cooking and place them next to the scrambled egg.

2 Add the remaining 2 tablespoons of oil to the pan. Add the garlic and ginger and sauté until fragrant and soft, about 2 minutes. Add the scallion or onion and continue cooking for another 2 minutes. Add the rice, peas and carrots, soy sauce, and sesame oil, stirring constantly to evenly distribute and heat the ingredients. Use the back of a fork to break up the rice if it's sticking in chunks. Add the shrimp and egg, and mix well. ⌗

ESSENTIAL EQUIPMENT

dry and wet measuring cups

measuring spoons

cutting board

chef's knife

large nonstick sauté pan or wok

wooden spoon

spatula

tongs

ESSENTIAL TECHNIQUES

mise en place

knife skills

sautéing

RICE: THE LONG AND SHORT OF IT

There is so much to learn about rice. But for any competent cook, there are just a few things you really need to know. Rice is classified by its grain. Long-grain rice, such as basmati or jasmine, is about four times as long as it is wide. When cooked properly, it is fluffy and each grain separates from the others. Short-grain rice, like Arborio rice used in paella or Koshihikari rice used for sushi, is nearly round in shape and has a far greater starch content than long-grain rice. Short grain rice, then, tends to stick to itself.

MAKES 4 SERVINGS.

Creamy Mashed Potatoes

Mashed potatoes are usually satisfying no matter how they are made. Poaching them in half and half (equal parts milk and heavy cream) instead of water makes for a thoroughly creamy side dish. Idaho potatoes are always appropriate for mashed potatoes, but using Yukon Golds instead gives them a richer look and flavor.

> 2 pounds Yukon Gold potatoes, peeled and cut into 1-inch cubes
>
> 3 cups half and half
>
> 2 tablespoons butter
>
> kosher salt and freshly ground black pepper to taste

1 Place potatoes in a large saucepan and cover with the half and half. Bring to a boil over medium high heat, then reduce to a simmer and continue cooking until the potatoes are tender, about 12 minutes.

2 Remove the potatoes from the pot to a large mixing bowl using a strainer or slotted spoon. Reserve the half and half.

3 Add the butter to the potatoes, along with some of the half and half. Mash with a fork (or put the potatoes through a food mill or ricer, for completely smooth mashed potatoes). Add more half and half until the potatoes reach the desired consistency. Season with kosher salt and freshly ground black pepper to taste. ✳

ESSENTIAL EQUIPMENT

wet measuring cup

cutting board

chef's knife

peeler

large saucepan or small stockpot

strainer or slotted spoon

mixing bowls

wooden spoon

fork, food mill, or ricer

ESSENTIAL TECHNIQUES

mise en place

poaching

MAKES 6 SERVINGS.

Butternut Squash Gratin

Very similar to a potato gratin, this recipe requires evenly thin slices of squash in order for the dish to bake successfully so that every bit is equally tender and delightful. Serve this dish with Roast Duck with Glazed Bing Cherries (page 193) or as an alternative to sweet potatoes for your Thanksgiving feast.

> 1 large butternut squash (about 3 pounds)
>
> 1 tablespoon butter
>
> 1 tablespoon chopped thyme
>
> 2 teaspoons kosher salt
>
> 1 teaspoon ground black pepper
>
> 1 cup heavy cream
>
> 1 cup shredded Gruyère
>
> 3 tablespoons grated Parmesan

1   Preheat the oven to 400°F.

2   Trim the squash by removing the stem and then cut the squash crosswise into two pieces: the neck and the bottom. Peel the skin of the neck so that the orange flesh comes through (remove the layer of green, like with a melon). Peel the round, bottom part of the squash, then cut in half lengthwise. Using a spoon, scoop out the seeds and stringy pulp. Cut both the neck and the bottom halves into ⅛- to ¼-inch slices with a knife, mandoline, or food processor's slicing blade.

3   Butter a baking or gratin dish with the tablespoon of butter. Place enough squash slices in the dish to form a single layer and sprinkle with some of the kosher salt, freshly ground black pepper, chopped thyme, and Gruyère. Repeat until all the squash slices have been used.

4   Pour the cream evenly over the top of the squash. Cover with the Parmesan, and bake for about 35 to 45 minutes. You can brown the top of the gratin by placing it under a hot broiler for 4 to 5 minutes. Serve immediately. ❊

You can make this dish in advance, but do not place it under the broiler to brown the cheese until you are ready to serve.

ESSENTIAL EQUIPMENT:

dry and wet measuring cups

measuring spoons

cutting board

chef's knife

peeler

spoon

mandoline or food processor (optional)

casserole or baking pan

ESSENTIAL TECHNIQUES

mise en place

knife skills

baking

broiling

IN SEASON

Winter squash varieties (butternut, acorn, turban, spaghetti, kabocha, and the like) are available from August to March, but they peak in October and November. So why not be called autumn squash? Squash are either categorized as "summer" or "winter." Summer squash are thin-skinned with delicate, soft flesh, such as zucchini and pattypan. Winter squash, on the other hand, have thick rinds that protect the hard flesh, making them last much longer than summer squash.

MAKES 6–8 SERVINGS.

Braised Fennel

Braising meat might take hours in the oven, but braising vegetables is quick and easy on the stovetop. The subtle licorice flavor of fennel and the competent cooking technique of braising makes this recipe an elegant vegetable dish. When fennel is halved or quartered, it takes on the contours of a pear with an onion-like interior. With just a few ingredients, you can develop a depth of flavor that is unmistakably sophisticated.

> 2 fennel bulbs with fronds
>
> 2 tablespoons extra-virgin olive oil
>
> ¼ teaspoon salt
>
> ⅛ teaspoon black pepper
>
> ¾ cup chicken stock

1 Cut off and discard the stalks from fennel bulbs, reserving the fronds. Chop one tablespoon of the fronds and discard the remainder. Cut bulbs lengthwise into quarters, or sixths if necessary, leaving the core intact.

2 Heat a large sauté pan over moderately high heat and add the oil. Brown the fennel slices, turning over once, 3 to 4 minutes total.

3 Reduce the heat to low. Sprinkle the fennel with salt and pepper, then add the stock. Cook, covered, until the fennel is tender, 10 to 12 minutes. Sprinkle with the chopped fennel fronds and serve. ⌗

ESSENTIAL EQUIPMENT

wet measuring cups

measuring spoons

cutting board

chef's knife

large sauté pan with a lid

wooden spoon

tongs

ESSENTIAL TECHNIQUES

mise en place

braising

MAKES 4–6 SERVINGS.

Cold Sesame Peanut Noodles

Tender pasta soaks up a spicy sesame peanut sauce to create a chewy noodle dish with a crunchy peanut finish. The noodles will be sitting in what might appear to be excess liquid at first. Be patient because they will soak up a lot of it within a half-hour. Serve the noodles immediately if you like them "wet" and do not mind if they are warm. Ideally, make them a few hours ahead of time and refrigerate them if you like them to be a bit drier and cold.

1 pound noodles, such as soba, spaghetti, or linguine

2 tablespoons sesame oil

½ cup canola oil

½ cup creamy peanut butter

½ cup strong brewed tea

4 garlic cloves, peeled and trimmed

½ cup soy sauce

¼ cup dry sherry

¼ cup white wine vinegar

3 tablespoons sugar

1 teaspoon black pepper

1 bunch scallions, chopped (white and green)

1 cup coarsely ground peanuts

1 In a large pot, bring salted water to a boil and cook pasta. Strain the noodles, rinse with cold water, and transfer to a large mixing bowl. Toss with sesame oil and set aside.

2 In a blender, combine the canola oil, peanut butter, and tea. Then add in the remaining ingredients, except for the scallions and peanuts.

3 Pour the mixture over the noodles and toss well to coat. Allow the noodles to absorb the peanut sauce for at least a half-hour before garnishing with the chopped scallions and peanuts. ✳

ESSENTIAL EQUIPMENT

wet and dry measuring cups

measuring spoons

cutting board

chef's knife

stockpot

colander

blender or food processor

large mixing bowl

tongs

ESSENTIAL TECHNIQUES

mise en place

MAKES 8 SERVINGS.

Spinach and Pignoli Orzo

Warm or cold, this dish is delicious. You can use fresh spinach, but the pre-chopped frozen variety is perfectly appropriate here. Toasted pine nuts are a welcome textural contrast to the chewy orzo coated in Parmesan cheese. Stuff the mixture in scooped and seeded tomato halves for pretty, individually portioned servings.

> 1 pound orzo
>
> 1, 10-ounce package frozen spinach, thawed and well drained
>
> ½ cup finely grated Parmesan cheese
>
> ¼ cup pignoli nuts, toasted
>
> ¼ cup basil, chiffonade
>
> 3 tablespoons extra virgin olive oil
>
> kosher salt and freshly ground black pepper to taste

1   Bring a large pot of salted water to a rolling boil. Add orzo and stir gently. Cook 4 to 7 minutes, checking occasionally. The pasta should be firm but cooked through. Strain the orzo through a large mesh strainer shaking off as much excess water as possible.

2   Toss the orzo with the drained chopped spinach, grated cheese, toasted pignoli nuts, and basil chiffonade. Add the olive oil and season to taste with kosher salt and freshly ground black pepper. Stir well to coat and serve immediately. ✳

ESSENTIAL EQUIPMENT

dry measuring cup

measuring spoons

cutting board

chef's knife

large saucepan

mesh strainer

large mixing bowl

rubber spatula or wooden spoon

ESSENTIAL TECHNIQUE

mise en place

TOASTING NUTS

Toasting nuts brings out the essential oils and therefore all the flavors. Add nuts to a dry and cold sauté pan over medium heat, shaking the pan every 30 seconds or so to move the nuts, and cook until fragrant and golden brown. Alternatively, toast almost any nut in an even layer on a sheet pan in a 375°F oven for about 8 to 10 minutes. Let your nose do as much work as the timer: once you smell the nuts, they are likely done. Pignolis are best toasted in a sauté pan because the moment they turn golden brown, if they are not removed from both the heat source and the pan, they'll burn.

MAKES 6–8 SERVINGS.

String Beans Almandine

This timeless side dish pairs well with almost anything. The best part is that it's made using two techniques: blanching and sautéing. That means you can blanch the beans the day before your dinner, and then sauté them just before serving. Add some crumbled goat cheese, chopped bacon, or dried cranberries for that extra touch any time of year. Add all three for truly scrumptious holiday fare.

> 1 pound haricots verts (French string beans), cleaned and trimmed
>
> kosher salt
>
> ¼ cup sliced almonds
>
> 2 tablespoons unsalted butter
>
> 1 teaspoon chopped fresh dill
>
> kosher salt and freshly ground black pepper to taste

1   Fill a large pot with water and add 1 to 2 tablespoons salt so the water tastes like the sea. Bring to a rolling boil over high heat, then add the haricots verts. Once the water returns to a boil, blanch them uncovered until cooked crisp-tender (no longer crunchy, but with a little resistance), about 5 minutes.

2   Strain the haricots verts and then immediately plunge them into a bowl of ice water to shock the vegetables. Alternatively, strain beans in a colander and immediately run cold water over them until cool. Drain any excess water and set them aside.

3   In a large sauté pan without any fat, toast the almonds over medium high heat, stirring occasionally with a wooden spoon, until they become a pale golden hue. Add the butter, and continue stirring until melted. Add the string beans, and toss well to warm them and distribute the almonds. Remove the pan from the heat, add the chopped dill and toss well to coat. Serve immediately. ✳

ESSENTIAL EQUIPMENT

dry measuring cup

measuring spoons

cutting board

chef's knife

large saucepan or small stockpot

colander

large sauté pan

wooden spoon

tongs

ESSENTIAL TECHNIQUES

mise en place

blanching

sautéing

COLD BEANS KILL BOILING WATER

Remove the beans from the refrigerator at least an hour before you plan to blanch them. If the beans are room temperature the water will return to a boil quickly, which makes for brighter, better beans.

MAKES 6–8 SERVINGS.

Roasted Root Vegetables

oasted root vegetables are colorful and have hearty, rustic, and slightly sweet flavors, a perfect match for rich, savory dishes like Beer-Braised Beef Short Ribs (page 144). This recipe uses the autumn colors as inspiration with red beets, purple shallots, orange carrots, yellow fingerling potatoes, and cream-colored parsnips. Any seasonal vegetable you like can go in the pan, including butternut squash, turnips, and Brussels sprouts. Drizzle with some fig vinegar, or top with a sprinkling of chopped toasted hazelnuts. It's important to keep the beets apart from the other vegetables until the last moment when you serve them so they don't stain everything red.

ESSENTIAL EQUIPMENT

measuring spoons

cutting board

peeler

chef's knife

paring knife

rubber gloves

small and large mixing bowls

sheet pan

wooden spoon

tongs

ESSENTIAL TECHNIQUES

mise en place

knife skills

roasting

MAKES 6–8 SERVINGS.

6 small beets, peeled and quartered (or 2 large beets, peeled and cut in eighths)

1 tablespoon olive oil

a pinch of kosher salt and freshly ground black pepper

12 small whole shallots, trimmed and peeled

6 slender carrots, peeled and cut in 3-inch pieces

10 fingerling potatoes, cut in half lengthwise

3 large parsnips, peeled and cut in quarters at the top, in 3-inch pieces

1 tablespoon, freshly chopped thyme (or sage or rosemary)

3 tablespoons olive oil

2 teaspoons kosher salt

1 teaspoon freshly ground black pepper

1   Preheat the oven to 400°F.

2   Wearing rubber gloves, peel and quarter the beets. In a small bowl, toss them with 1 tablespoon olive oil, and sprinkle with salt and pepper. Set aside and discard the gloves.

3   Combine all the other vegetables in a large mixing bowl and toss with the chopped thyme, olive oil, kosher salt, and freshly ground black pepper. Spread the vegetables in one layer on the sheet pan, leaving a little room at one end for the beets. Add the beets to the pan using tongs.

4   Roast in the preheated oven for 45 minutes, stirring occasionally (stir the beets separately from the other vegetables). Once the vegetables are tender and golden brown, remove them from the oven, quickly toss the beets with the other vegetables, and serve. ✳

CHAPTER
15

Desserts

* Basic Pie Dough
* Classic Apple Pie
* Vanilla Poached Pears
* Triple Chocolate Brownies
* Chewy Chocolate Chunk and Walnut Cookies
* Chocolate White Chocolate Chunk Cookies
* Chocolate Mousse
* Key Lime Pie with Cashew Graham Cracker Crust
* New York Cheesecake
* Linzer Tarts
* Apple Turnovers
* Apricot and Almond Tart
* Winter Citrus Salad with Pomegranate and Mint
* Berry Peach Cobbler
* Strawberry Shortcakes with Chantilly Cream

Basic Pie Dough

There is nothing quite as good as homemade piecrust. Tender and flaky, buttery and golden, the right dough makes a pie truly great. It is so easy to make, there really is no reason to buy it. The following recipe can be used for desserts as well as savory dishes, like Chicken Potpie (page 148). Make the dough with your hands, or use a food processor if you have one. Instructions are provided for both.

ESSENTIAL EQUIPMENT

dry and wet measuring cups

measuring spoons

cutting board

large mixing bowl

paring or chef's knife

food processor (optional)

ESSENTIAL TECHNIQUES

mise en place

"spoon and sweep" flour

MAKES 2 PIE CRUSTS.

2½ cups all-purpose flour

1 tablespoon powdered sugar

1 teaspoon kosher salt

1¼ cup (2½ sticks) cold unsalted butter

⅓ cup ice water

---

1 **By hand:** Combine the flour, kosher salt, and sugar in a large mixing bowl. Cut the butter into tablespoon chunks, then cut each tablespoon into quarters. Scatter the butter pieces over the flour mixture and squeeze the butter with the tips of your fingers, working it into the flour, until the fat is the size of peas.

2 Drizzle the water over the mixture and continue working the dough with your fingers until all that fat and flour is incorporated and the dough comes together in a large ball.

3 Gather the dough, form it into two discs, wrap each in plastic and refrigerate.

1 **In the food processor:** Combine the flour, kosher salt, and sugar in a food processor for 10 seconds. Cut the butter into tablespoon chunks and scatter over the flour mixture (while the machine is off). Very carefully pulse in 2-second intervals until the fat is the size of peas.

2 With the machine turned off, drizzle the water over the mixture. Pulse until the dough begins to form into small balls. If the dough comes together when pressed with your fingers, gather the dough, form it into two discs, wrap each in plastic, and refrigerate. If it doesn't, drizzle a bit more ice water over the dough and pulse again. ✳

Classic Apple Pie

The familiar flavors of apple pie are always pleasing. The size you cut your apples determines the body and texture of the filling once the pie is baked. The smaller you cut the apples, the less chunky and more mushy the filling will be.

3 tablespoons all-purpose flour

1 teaspoon lemon zest

½ teaspoon ground cinnamon

⅛ teaspoon kosher salt

⅔ cup granulated sugar

6 apples, peeled, cored and cut into eights

1 tablespoon fresh lemon juice

Basic Pie Dough (page 162)

1 egg, lightly beaten

1 tablespoon sugar

Basic Pie Dough (page 162)

ESSENTIAL EQUIPMENT

dry measuring cup

measuring spoons

cutting board

chef's knife

grater or Microplane

fork

mixing bowl

rolling pin

pie dish

pastry brush

paring knife

ESSENTIAL TECHNIQUES

mise en place

baking

MAKES 8 SERVINGS.

1   Preheat the oven to 425°F and position the rack in the middle.

2   In a large bowl, whisk together the flour, lemon zest, cinnamon, kosher salt, and sugar. Toss with apples and lemon juice. Set aside.

3   Roll out one piece of dough into a 12-inch round. Press it into a 9-inch pie pan. Trim the edge leaving ½-inch excess. Refrigerate while rolling out another piece of dough into an 11-inch round for the top crust.

4   Remove the pie shell from the refrigerator and spoon in the apple filling. Cover the pie with the second pastry crust and trim, leaving just ¼-inch excess. Press the edges together of the bottom and top crusts, then crimp with your thumb or a dinner fork.

5   Lightly brush the top with the beaten egg and sprinkle with one tablespoon of sugar. Cut three small slits in the center of the crust with a paring knife to make steam vents.

6   Bake the pie for 20 minutes, then reduce the oven temperature to 375°F and continue to bake for about 40 minutes, or until the top crust is golden and the filling is bubbling.

7   Cool for 2 to 3 hours before serving to allow the juices to settle and thicken. ✻

Vanilla Poached Pears

Poached pears, like poached salmon, can be served warm or cold. They are a superb choice for dinner parties because they can be made in advance, are naturally single-serving items, and require no fuss. The red-hued pears are striking and sculptural on their own without any embellishment . . . except perhaps for a scoop of vanilla ice cream.

> 4 firm pears, Bosc or Comice
>
> 1 bottle of red wine
>
> 1 cup sugar
>
> 1 cup water
>
> 1 vanilla pod, split open and beans removed
>
> zest of one orange

1   Peel the pears, core them from the bottom (using a paring knife or melon baller, if you have one), leaving on the stems. Split the vanilla pod lengthwise and then scrape each half with the back of the paring knife to remove the beans.

2   In a large saucepan, add all of the ingredients except the pears, including the vanilla pod and beans, and bring to a low boil. Reduce the heat and add the pears. Place a parchment lid or two full sheets of paper towel stacked and fully moistened with the poaching liquid on the pears (this keeps the pears moist with, and immersed in, the poaching liquid). Simmer until the pears are tender, yet slightly firm in the center, about 30 minutes.

3   Remove the pears and set aside. Discard the vanilla pod. Bring the mixture to a boil and cook over medium heat until the liquid is reduced by half.

4   Serve the pears in individual bowls or coupes with some poaching liquid. ✳

ESSENTIAL EQUIPMENT

wet measuring cup

cutting board

peeler

paring knife

grater or Microplane

large saucepan

parchment or paper towels

ladle or slotted spoon

ESSENTIAL TECHNIQUES

mise en place

poaching

DOUBLE THE SERVINGS BUT NOT THE RECIPE

If you want to poach 8 pears, double the pears but not the poaching liquid ingredients. Multiply the recipe by 1½ instead of 2, and you'll have plenty of poaching liquid to get the job done.

MAKES 4 SERVINGS.

Triple Chocolate Brownies

Chocoholics, look no further. These brownies are moist, rich and packed with chocolate at every turn. Just remember to let the brownies cool completely before you cut them.

> 1 cup (2 sticks) unsalted butter, cut into pieces
>
> 2 cups semisweet chocolate chips
>
> 1 cup sugar
>
> ½ cup sifted unsweetened cocoa powder
>
> ⅓ cup flour
>
> 6 large eggs
>
> ½ teaspoon kosher salt
>
> 1 teaspoon vanilla extract
>
> 8 ounces dark chocolate
>
> 1 tablespoon vegetable shortening

ESSENTIAL EQUIPMENT

dry measuring cups

measuring spoons

baking pan

aluminum foil

saucepans

rubber spatula

mixing bowls

whisk

sheet pan

wax paper

cutting board

chef's knife

ESSENTIAL TECHNIQUES

mise en place

"spoon and sweep" flour

baking

MAKES 20 BROWNIES.

1 Preheat the oven to 350°F. Line the brownie pan with aluminum foil hanging 2 inches over two of its sides. Grease well with butter and set aside.

2 Stir the butter and chocolate in a large saucepan over low heat until melted, then set it aside. Mix the sugar, cocoa, and flour in a large bowl. Add the eggs and whisk until well blended. Then add the vanilla extract and kosher salt.

3 Whisk the chocolate-butter mixture into the cocoa-sugar-egg mixture until thoroughly combined. Pour the batter into the prepared pan. Bake for about 45 minutes, or until a toothpick inserted into the center comes out clean. Remove the pan to a rack to cool (the brownies might have puffed and cracked a bit; they will settle while they cool).

4 Once the brownies have cooled completely, lift them from the pan using the foil and place them in the freezer for about an hour. Line a sheet pan with wax paper and set it aside.

5 After an hour, remove the brownies from the freezer and peel away the foil. Slice the brownies into 2-inch squares on a cutting board using a sharp chef's knife.

6 Melt the dark chocolate and vegetable shortening in a saucepan over medium low heat, or in a microwave-safe bowl. Drizzle the chocolate over the brownies with a spoon. Place them on a sheet pan lined with wax paper. Remove to store in an airtight container when set. ✱

Chewy Chocolate Chunk and Walnut Cookies

Everybody seems to have an opinion about chocolate chip cookies. There is no right or wrong way—it's just a matter of preference. If you underbake your cookies by a few minutes so that the edges are golden and crisp, but the centers appear still slightly raw, you will have a chewy cookie. To make crispy chocolate chip cookies, bake them for a few minutes longer than the recipe calls for, and remove them from the sheet pan immediately to cool. The best way to achieve your ideal chocolate chip cookie is to experiment with ingredients and techniques. Try using different fats and sugars, as well as baking times.

> 3 cups all purpose flour
>
> 1 teaspoon baking soda
>
> ½ teaspoon salt
>
> 1 cup (2 sticks) unsalted butter
>
> 1 cup light brown sugar
>
> ½ cup granulated white sugar
>
> 2 large eggs
>
> 2 teaspoons pure vanilla extract
>
> 16 ounces bittersweet or semisweet chocolate, coarsely chopped
>
> 1 cup chopped walnuts

1   Preheat the oven to 350°F. Line two baking sheets with parchment paper or silicone baking liners.

2   Combine the first three ingredients in a medium bowl and set aside.

3   In a large bowl, cream together the butter and both sugars with an electric mixer until fluffy. Add eggs one at a time and beat well. Mix in vanilla. Add dry ingredients and combine well. Fold in chocolate chunks and walnuts with a wooden spoon or rubber spatula.

4   Form dough into 1½-inch balls. Place each ball two inches apart on the baking sheets, and flatten with the bottom of a cup. Bake 8 to 10 minutes, or until lightly golden brown on the edges but appearing a bit underbaked in the center. Cool cookies on the sheet for 5 minutes and then transfer to wire racks to cool completely. ✳

ESSENTIAL EQUIPMENT

dry measuring cup

measuring spoons

medium mixing bowl

large mixing bowl

hand or standing mixer

wooden spoon or rubber spatula

parchment paper or silicone baking liners

cookie sheets or sheet pans

spatula

ESSENTIAL TECHNIQUES

mise en place

"spoon and sweep" flour

creaming butter and sugar

combine dry and wet ingredients separately

baking

CRACKING THE COOKIE CODE

Cookies made with butter spread out as they bake because butter melts at a lower temperature than, say, margarine or shortening. Cookies made with margarine, shortening, or even oil hold their shape better. The degree to which the cookies spread out in the baking process plays a role in whether they are flat and potentially crispy, or puffy and chewy.

MAKES 5 DOZEN COOKIES.

Chocolate White Chocolate Chunk Cookies

These cookies are so good, you'll want to make a double batch. Bake one half right away and enjoy the rich chocolate dough with oozing, creamy white chocolate chunks. Roll the other half in a log in tightly sealed plastic wrap, cover with another layer of aluminum foil, and freeze for up to three months.

2 cups flour

¾ cup cocoa powder

1 teaspoon baking soda

1 teaspoon kosher salt

1 cup (2 sticks) unsalted butter, room temperature

⅔ cup light brown sugar

⅔ cup white sugar

1 teaspoon vanilla extract

2 eggs

4, 4-ounce white chocolate bars, cut into small chunks

1   Preheat oven to 350°F. Line two cookie sheets with silicone liners or parchment paper. Set aside.

2   In a small bowl, combine the flour, cocoa, baking soda, and kosher salt. Set aside.

3   In a large bowl, beat the butter, both sugars, and vanilla extract until smooth, creamy, and fluffy. Add the eggs, one at a time, and beat until fully incorporated. Add the flour and cocoa mixture, and beat until smooth and incorporated. Add the white chocolate pieces and mix until evenly dispersed.

4   Drop the cookie dough by the tablespoon onto the lined cookie sheet at least one inch apart. Bake for 8 to 10 minutes. Allow the cookies to rest on the cookie sheet for 5 to 10 minutes before removing them to a rack to cool. Alternatively, roll the cookie dough into two logs, each wrapped in plastic wrap, then in aluminum foil. Refrigerate until firm. When ready to bake, slice the dough into ½-inch slices using a sharp knife and place them on a cookie sheet at least 1 inch apart. Bake for 8 to 10 minutes. Allow the cookies to rest on the cookie sheet for 5 to 10 minutes before removing them to a rack to cool. ✳

ESSENTIAL EQUIPMENT

dry measuring cup

measuring spoons

small mixing bowl

large mixing bowl

hand or standing mixer

wooden spoon or rubber spatula

parchment paper or silicone baking liners

cookie sheets or sheet pans

spatula

tablespoon

cooling rack

ESSENTIAL TECHNIQUES

mise en place

"spoon and sweep" flour

creaming butter and sugar

combine dry and wet ingredients separately

baking

CHOCOLATE CAN'T BE WHITE

The truth about white chocolate is short and sweet. This super-sweet confection does not contain any chocolate. That's right. No chocolate. It's derived from cocoa butter (the fat from the cocoa bean), which gives it the trace of a faint chocolate flavor. The cocoa butter is then blended with sugar and milk solids, hence white chocolate's creamy white color.

MAKES 5 DOZEN COOKIES.

Chocolate Mousse

Meringue (beaten egg whites) gives chocolate mousse the spongy, fluffy quality that makes it so distinct from its cousin, chocolate pudding. Whipped cream and meringue are gently folded into melted dark chocolate. Plan to make this dessert well in advance of serving it, since it requires chilling to hold its shape. Serve with fresh berries or toasted almonds for that extra special touch.

8 ounces dark chocolate, chopped

1½ cups heavy cream

whites from 3 large eggs

1 tablespoon sugar

1   Place a saucepan filled two-thirds with water over high heat and bring to a simmer. Add the chopped chocolate to a large metal or glass bowl, and place it on top of the saucepan. Reduce the heat to low, and stir constantly with a rubber spatula until the chocolate is thoroughly melted. Turn off the heat and leave the bowl in place.

2   Meanwhile, beat 1½ cups heavy cream in a large mixing bowl, using either a balloon whisk, or hand or standing mixer, until stiff peaks form. Set aside in the refrigerator.

3   In another bowl, beat the egg whites, using either a balloon whisk, or hand or standing mixer, until soft peaks form. Gradually add the sugar while beating continuously until stiff peaks form (meringue).

4   Remove the bowl of melted chocolate from the saucepan and gently fold the meringue into the chocolate mixture. Be careful not to stir or beat the mixture, otherwise you will lose a lot of air in the meringue. Now gently fold in the whipped cream until well blended.

5   Cover the bowl with plastic wrap and refrigerate the mousse for at least 2 hours before serving. ✻

ESSENTIAL EQUIPMENT

wet measuring cup

measuring spoon

cutting board

chef's knife

saucepan

rubber spatula

mixing bowls

balloon whisk, or hand or standing mixer

ESSENTIAL TECHNIQUES

mise en place

MERINGUE MAGIC

When egg whites are room temperature, they can be beaten up to seven times their volume. Remove eggs from the refrigerator at least 30 minutes prior to preparing a meringue. Be very careful when separating the yolk from the white. Pass the eggs through your hands instead of between shells to avoid a jagged edge from piercing the delicate yolk. Any presence of yolk in separated egg whites is considered contaminated, and will compromise the result of the meringue.

MAKES 6–8 SERVINGS.

Key Lime Pie with Cashew Graham Cracker Crust

The salty, roasted accent of cashew nuts in the crust is optimally paired with the sweet yet tangy citrus flavor of the creamy key lime custard. Key limes are more acidic and have a yellow, tarter juice than the large, seedless, green citrus fruits we find in virtually every grocery store. They are round and about the size of golf balls, often with a pale yellow-green skin. The key lime season is summer, from about June to August. Key lime juice is now sold bottled year-round. But fresh key lime juice is far superior, and the perfect ingredient for any competent cook's no-bake dessert.

1 cup graham cracker crumbs

½ cup ground cashews

¼ cup sugar

5 tablespoons unsalted butter, melted

14 ounces sweetened condensed milk

½ cup key lime juice

1   To make the crust, combine the graham cracker crumbs, cashews, sugar, and butter. Using the back of a large spoon, press the crumb mixture firmly on the bottom and sides of an 8- or 9-inch pie dish. Chill or freeze the crust for 10 minutes before filling.

2   To make the filling, combine the sweetened condensed milk and key lime juice using a whisk.

3   Pour the filling into the pie shell and refrigerate overnight (or freeze for one hour and return to the refrigerator if you need to serve it before then). ❋

The filling may be made with four egg yolks to give added color to the pie. Combine the yolks and sweetened condensed milk before slowly adding key lime juice. Follow the same procedure as above.

ESSENTIAL EQUIPMENT

dry and wet measuring cups

measuring spoon

cutting board

chef's knife

mixing bowl

whisk

pie pan

wooden spoon

ESSENTIAL TECHNIQUES

mise en place

MAKES 8 SERVINGS.

New York Cheesecake

New York cheesecake is distinct from Italian cheesecake because it's made with cream cheese instead of ricotta. The cream cheese is sweetened with some sugar, beaten with eggs, and baked to a dense, rich, creamy finish. The crust is traditionally made with graham cracker crumbs, but ground Oreo cookies please any chocolate lover. Remove the cream cheese from the refrigerator an hour before you plan to bake the cake to help it soften (this will make beating it easier). Let the cake cool completely before slicing, giving it time to set.

For the crust:

2 cups graham cracker crumbs, or 2 cups ground Oreo cookies (about 30 cookies)

3 tablespoons unsalted butter, melted

3 tablespoons sugar (only if using graham cracker crumbs)

For the filling:

2 pounds cream cheese, softened

1 cup sugar

3 tablespoons all-purpose flour

1 tablespoon vanilla

⅓ cup heavy cream

4 large eggs

For the topping:

8 ounces sour cream

1 teaspoon vanilla

1 tablespoon superfine sugar

1 pint strawberries

ESSENTIAL EQUIPMENT

dry and wet measuring cups

measuring spoons

mixing bowls

rubber spatula

springform pan

hand or standing mixer

ESSENTIAL TECHNIQUES

mise en place

baking

MAKES 12 SERVINGS.

New York Cheesecake

1 Preheat the oven to 325°F.

2 To make the crust, combine the graham cracker or Oreo crumbs, sugar, and melted butter. Press the crumb mixture firmly on the bottom and sides of springform pan. Bake for 10 minutes.

3 Meanwhile, prepare the filling. Beat the cream cheese, sugar, flour, and vanilla with an electric mixer on medium speed until blended and creamy. Blend in the heavy cream, then lower the speed to low and add the eggs, one at a time, so that each egg is fully blended before the next one is added. Pour the filling in the pan.

4 Bake for one hour, or until the center is almost set. The cheesecake might rise like a soufflé and crack at the top. This is okay. Remove the cheesecake from the oven, and let it rest for an hour until it has cooled and settled to be more or less level with the top of the pan.

5 Prepare the topping. Combine the sour cream, sugar, and vanilla and spread over the top of the cheesecake. Refrigerate the cheesecake overnight.

6 Line the border of the sour cream top with strawberries. Run a paring knife around the edge of the pan before removing the springform rim. ✳

Linzer Tarts

Dating back to the 1700s, the linzertorte was an almond crust tart with a black currant filling named after its hometown of Linz, Austria. Over time, a sandwich cookie evolved with a middle layer of raspberry preserves. The top cookie, dusted with confectioners' sugar, has a cutout to make the preserves visible.

1 cup granulated sugar

¾ cup (1½ sticks) unsalted butter, softened

2 large eggs

1 teaspoon vanilla extract

2½ cups flour

¾ cup almonds or hazelnuts, finely ground

1 teaspoon baking powder

1 teaspoon kosher salt

2 cups raspberry jam

confectioners' sugar for dusting

1 Beat the sugar, butter, eggs, and vanilla in a large mixing bowl until creamy.

2 In a smaller bowl, sift flour, ground nuts, baking powder, and kosher salt. Add the flour mixture to the butter mixture and stir until well incorporated. Gather into a ball and press into a disc. Cover with plastic wrap, and put it in the refrigerator for at least one hour or overnight.

3 Preheat the oven to 350°F. Roll out the dough to ⅛-inch thickness on a floured surface. Cut the cookies into rounds or flowers using cookie cutters. Cut a small circle or smaller flower on half the cut cookies to be the tops of the linzer tarts. Gather the scraps and repeat the process until all the dough is used.

4 Bake the cookies on a cookie sheet for 7 to 10 minutes, or until golden brown. Cool on a cooling rack. The cookies must be completely cool before the tarts can be assembled.

5 Spread a generous amount of raspberry jam on the cookie bottoms. Dust powdered sugar over the cutout cookie tops. Place the sugared cookie tops on the raspberry jam cookie bottoms and serve immediately or store in an airtight container. ✽

ESSENTIAL EQUIPMENT

dry measuring cups

measuring spoons

mixing bowls

hand or standing mixer

rubber spatula

wooden spoon

rolling pin

cookie cutters

silicone baking liners

cookie sheets

cooling rack

butter knife

sifter

ESSENTIAL TECHNIQUES

mise en place

"spoon and sweep" flour

beating sugar and eggs (blanchir)

combining wet and dry ingredients separately

baking

MAKES 18 4-INCH SANDWICHES.

Apple Turnovers

It's "easy as pie" to make apple turnovers, pastry pockets filled with sweet and tender apples. You can use puff pastry or pie dough to make a turnover. But be sure not to overstuff the pastry. It might literally burst at the seams.

> grated zest of 1 orange
>
> 2 tablespoons freshly squeezed orange juice
>
> 4 Granny Smith (tart) apples
>
> 3 tablespoons sugar, plus extra to sprinkle on top
>
> 1 tablespoon all-purpose flour
>
> ¼ teaspoon ground cinnamon
>
> 1 package (17.3 ounces, 2 sheets) frozen puff pastry, defrosted
>
> 1 egg beaten with 1 tablespoon water, for egg wash

1   Preheat the oven to 400°F.

2   Combine the orange zest and orange juice in a bowl. Peel, quarter, and core the apples and then cut them into large dice. Immediately toss the apples with the zest and juice to prevent them from turning brown. Add the sugar, flour, and cinnamon.

3   Flour a board and lightly roll each sheet of puff pastry to a 12" × 12" square. Cut each sheet into 4 smaller squares (8 squares total) and keep chilled until ready to use.

4   Brush the edges of each square with the egg wash and neatly place about ⅓ cup of the apple mixture on half of the square. Fold the pastry diagonally over the apple mixture and seal by pressing the edges with a fork. Transfer to a sheet pan lined with parchment paper or silicone baking liner. Brush the tops with egg wash, sprinkle with sugar, make 2 small slits, and bake for 20 minutes, until browned and puffed.

5   Serve warm or at room temperature. ✵

ESSENTIAL EQUIPMENT

cutting board

chef's knife

grater or Microplane

measuring spoons

mixing bowls

fork

rolling pin

pastry brush

sheet pan

parchment paper or silicone baking liner

ESSENTIAL TECHNIQUES

mise en place

knife skills

baking

MAKES 8 SERVINGS.

Apricot and Almond Tart

This is a sophisticated tart that is incredibly easy to make. The base is store-bought puff pastry. The filling between the fruit and the pastry is frangipane, a creamy and buttery almond paste. This tart tastes best when served at room temperature.

For the frangipane:

⅓ cup sugar

⅔ cup slivered almonds

6 tablespoons unsalted butter

1 egg

¼ teaspoon vanilla extract

¼ teaspoon almond extract

1½ tablespoons flour

For the tart:

1 sheet frozen puff pastry, thawed

12 fresh or canned apricot halves, pits removed

¼ cup sliced almonds, toasted

confectioners' sugar for dusting (optional)

1   Preheat the oven to 425°F.

2   To make the frangipane, place the almonds and sugar in a food processor and grind until sandy. Add the butter and continue mixing. Then add the egg, vanilla, almond extract, and the flour and process until smooth.

3   To make the tart, on a floured work surface pass your rolling pin over the pastry just to flatten any ridges. Place it on a sheet pan lined with parchment paper or a silicone baking liner and cut out a 9-inch disc, discarding the scraps. Spread the almond paste in the center of the tart leaving a 1-inch border. Firmly place the apricot halves into the frangipane.

4   Bake the tart until the crust is puffy and golden brown, about 30 to 40 minutes. Let the tart cool for 20 minutes before sprinkling with the toasted almonds, and dusting with the confectioners' sugar. **#**

ESSENTIAL EQUIPMENT

dry measuring cups

measuring spoons

cutting board

chef's knife

food processor

rubber spatula

rolling pin

parchment paper or silicone baking liner

sheet pan

sifter (optional)

ESSENTIAL TECHNIQUES

mise en place

baking

MAKES 8 SERVINGS.

Winter Citrus Salad with Pomegranate and Mint

Juicy, sweet citrus fruits peak in winter months. This fruit salad entices with the jewel-like colors of several varieties of grapefruit and orange. The pomegranate seeds offer a pleasing textural contrast. When you section the citrus fruit into suprêmes, be sure to do it over a large mixing bowl so you catch all the juice. The combination of juices at the bottom of the bowl is the most delicious nectar you'll ever taste!

> 2 pink grapefruits, suprême
>
> 1 white grapefruit, suprême
>
> 2 navel oranges, suprême
>
> 2 blood oranges, suprême
>
> 1 pomegranate, seeded
>
> 10 mint leaves, chiffonade

1 Suprême all the grapefruits and oranges over a large bowl, being sure not to waste any juice. Squeeze juice from the membrane of each fruit into the bowl. Be sure not to include any pith or seeds.

2 Break the pomegranate with a fork. Peel back the rind to expose the seeds in a large bowl with cool water. The seeds will sink to the bottom and the pith will float to the top. Remove the floating waste with a slotted spoon, then strain the seeds. Combine the pomegranate seeds with the citrus salad (juices and suprêmes).

3 Stack, roll, then chiffonade the mint leaves. Divide the salad among four shallow bowls and sprinkle with the mint chiffonade. ❊

This salad may be made ahead and stored in the refrigerator for up to 3 days. Do not add mint until service.

ESSENTIAL EQUIPMENT

large mixing bowls

fork

slotted spoon

strainer

cutting board

chef's knife

ESSENTIAL TECHNIQUES

mise en place

knife skills

AN UNDERWATER EFFORT

Getting the seeds from the pomegranate fruit can be a challenge. Break the pomegranate open with a regular dinner fork. Then submerge the halves in a bowl of cold water and pull away the seeds with your fingers. The undesirable pith will float to the top, and the seeds will sink to the bottom. This way, you can discard what you don't want and strain exactly what you need. Also, you'll avoid splattering hot pink pomegranate juice all over your counter and walls.

MAKES 4 SERVINGS.

Berry Peach Cobbler

Berries and peaches are a natural summer pair. Their flavors and colors blend beautifully in this unfussy dessert. Cobbler is a sort of fruit pie with a crumb topping and no pastry base. It can be made in a single vessel to be served tableside, or it can be prepared in small, individual ramekins. Don't forget a dollop of yogurt, sour cream, frozen yogurt, or ice cream to top it off.

For the filling:

1 cup blueberries

1 cup raspberries

1 cup blackberries

3 peaches, cut into chunks

juice of one lemon

¼ cup sugar

2 tablespoons flour

For the topping:

½ cup light brown sugar

½ cup all purpose flour

½ cup oats

¼ cup butter (half stick), cut into small pieces

½ teaspoon ground cinnamon

ESSENTIAL EQUIPMENT

dry measuring cups

measuring spoons

cutting board

chef's knife

large mixing bowls: wooden spoon

baking pan, or ramekins (with a sheet pan)

ESSENTIAL TECHNIQUES

mise en place

baking

PEACH AND THE FAMILY STONE

Stone fruits are those with a large pit in the center, such as peaches, plums, apricots, nectarines, cherries, dates, mangoes, and even coconuts.

MAKES 6 SERVINGS.

1 Preheat the oven to 375°F. Grease the baking pan or ramekins and set aside.

2 To make the topping, stir together the sugar and the flour in a large bowl. With your fingers, work the butter into the flour mixture to the texture of coarse crumbs. Add in oats and cinnamon. Set aside.

3 To make the berry and peach mixture, toss the fruit in lemon juice and sugar. Sprinkle with flour, then gently toss. Put the filling in a small baking pan, or evenly distribute the filling between the four ramekins. Top with some of the oat mixture, packing it down.

4 If using ramekins, place them on a sheet pan. Place the cobbler in the oven and bake for 15 to 20 minutes, or until the topping is browned and the berries are bubbling.

5 Serve warm or at room temperature. ✳

Strawberry Shortcakes with Chantilly Cream

Strawberries macerated in sugar and orange juice are a vibrant and luscious topping to this classic American dessert. Sweetened whipped cream and a buttery cream biscuit give this strawberry shortcake recipe "essential" status. Use any component for other favorite dishes: top a bowl of vanilla yogurt with the strawberries and some Decadent Granola (page 110); cover the Chicken Potpie (page 148) with the biscuit dough instead of pie dough; and use the Chantilly cream to garnish the Key Lime Pie with Cashew Graham Cracker Crust (page 169).

For the biscuits:

2 cups all-purpose flour

1 tablespoon baking powder

2 teaspoons sugar

1 teaspoon kosher salt

¼ cup cold unsalted butter

1 cup heavy cream

2 tablespoons melted butter

For the filling:

2 pints strawberries, hulled and quartered

3 tablespoons sugar

¼ cup freshly squeezed orange juice

For the Chantilly cream:

2 cups heavy cream

2 tablespoons confectioners' sugar

1 teaspoon vanilla extract

ESSENTIAL EQUIPMENT

dry and wet measuring cups

measuring spoons

cutting board

chef's knife

large mixing bowls

wooden spoon

spatula

rolling pin

cookie or biscuit cutter

pastry brush

parchment paper or silicone baking liner

sheet pan

cooling rack

balloon whisk

ESSENTIAL TECHNIQUES

mise en place

knife skills

baking

MAKES 8–10 SERVINGS.

Strawberry Shortcakes with Chantilly Cream

1   Preheat the oven to 425°F.

2   To make the biscuits, thoroughly combine the flour, baking powder, sugar, and kosher salt in a large bowl. With your fingers, work the butter into the flour mixture to the texture of coarse crumbs. Add in the cream, and stir the mixture with a rubber spatula until it forms dough. Gather the dough into a ball and roll it on a floured work surface to a ½-inch-thick disc. Cut as many biscuits as possible using a floured biscuit or cookie cutter. Collect the scraps, roll to a ½-inch-thick piece again, and cut more. Place the rounds on a sheet pan lined with parchment paper or a silicone baking sheet. Brush the tops with the melted butter and bake for 15 minutes. Remove the biscuits from the oven and cool on a rack for 10 minutes.

3   Meanwhile, prepare the berries. Combine the berries, sugar, and orange juice in a bowl and cover with plastic wrap. Set aside while the biscuits bake.

4   Now prepare the Chantilly cream. Beat the cream with a balloon whisk in a large mixing bowl until it begins to foam and thicken slightly. Add the confectioners' sugar and vanilla extract and continue beating until soft peaks form.

5   To assemble the shortcakes, split open each biscuit horizontally. Spoon some of the strawberries on each biscuit bottom, then dollop with some Chantilly cream. Top with the biscuit tops, and add more strawberries and cream. Serve immediately. ❈

The biscuits can be made a day in advance. Do not assemble the dessert until you are ready to serve it.

chapter 16

For the Baker

French Lemon Tart

Beautifully bright yellow lemon curd in a lemon-scented shortbread crust is a refreshing finish to any meal. The shortbread crust is blind baked before the filling is added, since the whole tart only bakes for 5 minutes. Raspberries and mint are the ideal garnish for a slender slice of this classic dessert.

For the crust:

1 cup (2 sticks) unsalted butter

½ cup confectioners' sugar

2 cups all-purpose flour

1 tablespoon grated lemon zest

For the filling:

⅔ cup fresh lemon juice (about 5–6 lemons)

10 tablespoons unsalted butter, cut into pieces

1 cup granulated sugar, divided

3 large eggs

2 large egg yolks

1   Preheat the oven to 375°F.

2   For the crust, mix all the ingredients in a food processor, pulsing every few seconds, until well combined. Alternatively, use your fingers or a pastry cutter to mix the butter into the flour and sugar. Form the dough into a disc and refrigerate until chilled enough to roll. Roll a flat disc large enough to fit in an 8- or 9-inch tart pan. Press the dough into the pan.

3   Once the tart pan is lined in dough, cover with parchment paper or foil and fill with pie weights or dried beans. Blind bake the tart shell for 20 to 30 minutes, or until golden brown. Remove the parchment paper and beans, and set the tart pan aside.

4   For the filling, heat the lemon juice, butter, and ¾ cup sugar over low heat in a pot until the butter has melted and the mixture comes to a gentle simmer, about 2 minutes.

ESSENTIAL EQUIPMENT

dry and wet measuring cups

measuring spoons

cutting board

paring or chef's knife

grater or Microplane

large mixing bowls

rubber spatula

wooden spoon

food processor (optional)

rolling pin

pie weights or dried beans

parchment paper or aluminum foil

saucepan

whisk

strainer or chinois

ESSENTIAL TECHNIQUES

mise en place

beating sugar and eggs (blanchir)

baking

GET THE BALL ROLLING

Before you cut a citrus fruit in half crosswise to juice it, roll it back and forth on the cutting board applying a bit of pressure with the palm of your hand. This action helps to loosen pulp and release the juice. You'll get much more from the lime, lemon, or orange this way.

MAKES 8 SERVINGS.

French Lemon Tart

5   Using a whisk, beat the eggs, egg yolk, and remaining ¼ cup sugar until the mixture is pale and light yellow, about 3 to 4 minutes. Slowly pour some of the hot lemon mixture into the egg yolk mixture to temper. Beat until blended and fluffy. Return this mixture to the pot with the remaining lemon juice mixture. Cook over a medium-low heat, stirring constantly with a wooden spoon, until the mixture is thickened, about 3 minutes.

6   Pass the lemon curd through a fine mesh strainer or chinois to collect any undesirable scrambled egg pieces. Transfer the strained mixture to a bowl and chill immediately (either over an ice bath or in the refrigerator). When cool, spoon the curd into the pastry shell.

7   Return the tart to the 375°F oven and bake for about 5 minutes to set the filling without coloring it. Remove the tart from the oven and let it cool. Then refrigerate the tart until the filling is firm.

8   Remove the tart from the refrigerator 10 to 15 minutes before serving. ✴

Chocolate Soufflés with Mocha Crème Anglaise

Like omelets and risotto, a soufflé must be served the moment it leaves the oven. The hot air of the oven gets trapped in the air bubbles of the meringue-based batter, making the soufflé puff and rise. Once the soufflé hits the relatively colder air of the kitchen, it is only a matter of time before it deflates. Break the soufflé open with a fork, pour in the mocha sauce, and indulge!

For the soufflés:

½ cup whole milk

2 teaspoons cornstarch

⅓ cup sugar

5 ounces bittersweet chocolate, chopped

3 large egg yolks

6 large egg whites

pinch of kosher salt

butter and extra sugar for the ramekins

For the mocha crème anglaise:

¾ cup whole milk

¾ cup heavy cream

3 ounces bittersweet chocolate, chopped

⅓ cup sugar

3 large egg yolks

1½ cups crushed coffee beans

1 First, set up the mise en place for the soufflés to give the egg whites time to come to room temperature. Then prepare the crème anglaise. Heat the milk, heavy cream, and crushed coffee beans in a saucepan over medium high heat and bring to a boil. Turn off the heat and allow the mixture to infuse for 20 minutes.

2 After 20 minutes, strain the mixture through a fine mesh sieve lined in cheesecloth, or through a chinois. Place the chopped chocolate in the pan and return the infused milk and cream to the pan. Let the chocolate and milk mixture rest for one minute, then combine with a whisk. Turn the heat to medium.

ESSENTIAL EQUIPMENT

dry and wet measuring cups

measuring spoons

cutting board

paring or chef's knife

saucepans

wooden spoon

strainer or chinois

large mixing bowls

whisk

rubber spatula

hand or standing mixer

ramekins

baking sheet

ESSENTIAL TECHNIQUES

mise en place

beating sugar and eggs (blanchir)

baking

MAKES 6 SERVINGS.

Chocolate Soufflés with Mocha Crème Anglaise

3   In a large mixing bowl, beat the yolks and sugar with a clean whisk until the mixture is pale yellow and light.

4   Temper the egg mixture with one third of the hot mocha mixture. Return this tempered egg mixture to the remaining hot mocha mixture in the pan and cook gently, over medium heat, stirring constantly with a wooden spoon, until the mixture has thickened enough to coat the back of a spoon and leaves a track when you run your fingertip through it.

5   Strain the sauce immediately into a large bowl through a sieve lined with cheesecloth, or a chinois, to rid of any remaining crushed coffee beans, as well as any potentially scrambled egg. Cover with plastic wrap and set aside.

6   To prepare the soufflés, place an oven rack in the middle of the oven and preheat to 375°F. Lightly grease six small ramekins with butter and coat each with ½ tablespoon sugar, shaking out any excess.

7   Whisk together the milk, cornstarch, and half the ⅓ cup sugar in a saucepan until smooth. Cook, whisking over moderate heat until the mixture boils and thickens, about 1 to 2 minutes. Melt the chocolate in a bowl over a pot of simmering water, over low heat, until smooth. Remove the bowl from the heat and stir in the yolks, then beat in the thickened milk mixture. Set aside.

8   Beat all six egg whites with a pinch of salt in a large bowl with an electric mixer at medium speed until the whites hold soft peaks. Gradually add the remaining sugar, then beat until the whites hold stiff peaks. Stir one quarter of the whites into the chocolate/yolk/milk mixture to lighten it, then gently but thoroughly fold in the remaining whites.

9   Spoon the mixture into ramekins. Make sure the rim of each ramekin is clean to allow the soufflés to rise (use your thumb to wipe away any excess butter, sugar, or batter). Place the ramekins on a baking sheet and bake until soufflés are puffed and golden brown, about 15 minutes.

10   Serve immediately with the mocha crème anglaise. ✳

Pumpkin Bread

There is a lot of sugar in this bread, it's true. But it's by far the best tasting pumpkin bread there is. The batter is very dense before the pumpkin and milk are added, so use an electric mixer if you have one. Canned pumpkin works best with this recipe because of its smooth consistency. If you are carving a jack-o'-lantern and want to make use of the flesh, you can cook and purèe the pumpkin, and experiment with it in this recipe.

3 cups sugar

1 cup vegetable oil

4 eggs

2 teaspoons vanilla

3½ cups flour

1½ teaspoons kosher salt

1½ teaspoons cinnamon

1½ teaspoons nutmeg

2 teaspoons baking soda

⅔ cup whole milk

1, 15-ounce can pumpkin (1¾ cups)

1   Preheat the oven to 350°F. Grease two loaf pans with oil or butter and set aside.

2   Mix the sugar, oil, eggs, and vanilla in a large bowl. Combine the flour, salt, cinnamon, nutmeg, and baking soda in a small bowl. Add the dry ingredients to the wet ingredients and blend.

3   Alternately combine portions of the pumpkin and milk with other ingredients, mixing well after each addition.

4   Pour the batter into two greased loaf pans. Bake for one hour or until a toothpick inserted into the center comes out dry. Be careful not to overbake or the bread inside the pans might burn.

5   Let the loaves rest for 10 minutes before turning out onto a cooling rack. ✳

ESSENTIAL EQUIPMENT

dry and wet measuring cups

measuring spoons

mixing bowls

rubber spatula

loaf pans

hand mixer or standing mixer

cooling rack

ESSENTIAL TECHNIQUES

mise en place

"spoon and sweep" flour

combine dry and wet ingredients separately

baking

THE NOT-SO-MESSY BUSINESS OF GREASING PANS

So many quick bread, cake, and muffin recipes call for a greased pan. Whatever fat you use in the batter is the fat you should use to grease the pan. Use your fingers or a paper towel. Do not use excessive fat; you need only enough to coat the pan lightly and evenly.

MAKES 2 LARGE LOAVES.

Toasted Coconut Cookies

Delicious as an afternoon pick-me-up with a cup of tea, these cookies also make a lovely garnish to a bowl of coconut sorbet.

1, 7-ounce package sweetened shredded coconut

2¼ cups flour

1 teaspoon baking powder

½ teaspoon cinnamon

½ teaspoon kosher salt

¾ cup light brown sugar

¾ cup (1½ sticks) unsalted butter, softened

2 large eggs

1 teaspoon vanilla extract

1 Preheat the oven to 325°F.

2 Spread the coconut in an even layer on a baking sheet. Toast in the oven until golden brown, about 10 minutes. Set aside.

3 In a small bowl, combine the flour, baking powder, cinnamon, and kosher salt. Set aside.

4 Using a mixer, cream the sugar and butter until light and fluffy. Add the eggs, one at a time, beating well after each addition. Then add the vanilla.

5 Add the flour mixture to the butter mixture and blend just until well incorporated. Stir in the toasted coconut with a wooden spoon.

6 Gather the dough and divide in half. Place each half on a piece of plastic wrap and roll into a tightly sealed log. Put the two logs in the refrigerator for at least 2 hours or overnight.

7 Once the dough has chilled, preheat the oven to 350°F. Unwrap one of the logs and cut into ¼-inch slices using a chef's knife. Place one inch apart on a lined cookie sheet and bake until the edges turn golden brown, about 12 minutes. Remove from the oven and place the cookies on a cooling rack for 5 minutes. ✸

ESSENTIAL EQUIPMENT

dry measuring cups

measuring spoons

sheet pan

mixing bowls

wooden spoon

hand or standing mixer

rubber spatula

silicone baking liners

cookie sheets

cooling rack

ESSENTIAL TECHNIQUES

mise en place

"spoon and sweep" flour

combine wet and dry ingredients separately

beating sugar and eggs (blanchir)

baking

MAKES 3 DOZEN COOKIES.

Birthday Cake with Buttercream Frosting

If you are a competent cook and a baker at heart, you probably enjoy making birthday cakes for your loved ones. Cake from the box and frosting from the jar is fine, but a homemade layer cake is a most special birthday gift. The frosting in this recipe is a basic vanilla that can be dyed any color you like. If you want winter white icing, go to a specialty cake supply store to purchase colorless vanilla extract, and use only vegetable shortening.

For the cake:

2¾ cups self-rising (cake) flour

1 teaspoon kosher salt

1 cup (2 sticks) unsalted butter, softened

2¼ cups sugar

4 large eggs

1 tablespoon vanilla extract

1¼ cups whole milk

For the buttercream frosting:

1 cup (2 sticks) unsalted butter, softened

¼ cup vegetable shortening

8 cups confectioners' sugar

½ cup whole milk

1 teaspoon vanilla extract

1   Preheat the oven to 350°F. Grease and lightly flour two round cake pans, then line the bottom with parchment paper (see Parchment Lid Lesson, page 187).

2   In a small mixing bowl, sift the self-rising flour with the kosher salt and set aside.

3   In a large mixing bowl, cream the butter with an electric mixer until smooth. Gradually beat in the sugar and beat until light and fluffy. Add the eggs, one at a time, beating well to incorporate after each addition. Beat in the vanilla. Add the flour mixture and milk in thirds, beating well after each addition.

ESSENTIAL EQUIPMENT

dry and wet measuring cups

measuring spoons

cake pans

parchment paper

mixing bowls

sifter

hand or standing mixer

rubber spatula

cooling rack

cutting board

bread knife

wax paper

offset spatula

ESSENTIAL TECHNIQUES

mise en place

"spoon and sweep" flour

beating sugar and eggs

baking

FLOUR POWER

The difference between cake flour and all-purpose flour is the percentage of gluten, a protein that provides structure and texture. Cake flour is about 4 percent gluten, whereas all-purpose flour is 10 to 11 percent gluten.

MAKES 12–16 SERVINGS.

Birthday Cake with Buttercream Frosting

4 Pour half the batter in each cake pan and bake for 25 minutes, or until a toothpick comes out clean when inserted in the cake.

5 Let the cakes cool for 15 minutes before turning out onto a cooling rack to cool completely.

6 To make the icing, beat the butter and shortening in large mixing bowl. Add half the confectioners' sugar, plus all the milk and vanilla. Beat until creamy and smooth. Then add the sugar, ½ cup at a time, until the frosting is thick enough to be spreadable. If you want to dye the icing, now is the time to add a few drops of food coloring.

7 To assemble the layer cake, be sure the cakes have cooled completely. If they have rounded tops, and are not perfectly flat, trim them. Using a bread knife, move the knife back and forth as you slice across the top of the cake to make a perfectly flat layer.

8 Put several small pieces of wax paper around the edge of a plate or cake stand to protect the plate from getting messy and smudged while you frost the cake. Place one cake in the center, the trimmed top facing up. Using an offset spatula, frost the sides and top of the cake. Then add the second cake to the frosted cake, but this time with the trimmed top down, touching the frosted cake. Frost the cake, paying close attention to blending the sides well so you do not see the layers.

9 Carefully remove the wax paper before serving. ✳

THE PARCHMENT LID LESSON

Sometimes a lid made of paper does a better job than one that came with the pan. A hole in the center allows some steam to escape, while the lid itself keeps ingredients covered and moist.

Take a sheet of parchment paper and fold it half, then fold it in half again (you should have a square). Fold that square in half again diagonally, and then fold it one more time. Place the point of the folded parchment paper over the center of the pot to measure its radius. Trim the excess parchment paper just inside the edge of the pan, and then snip the tip to create a small opening in the center of the lid. When you unfold the paper, you will have a perfect lid for your pot with a steam hole.

Follow the same technique for making a cake pan liner, but do not snip the tip of the parchment since you don't need a center hole.

For the Serious Cook

✳ Red Wine Risotto
✳ Salmon Purses in Puff Pastry with Shitake Cream Sauce
✳ Braised Lamb Shanks
✳ Roast Duck with Glazed Bing Cherries
✳ Sweet Potato Gnocchi with Fried Sage

Red Wine Risotto

Risotto is both a method and a finished dish: short-grain rice is sautéed in fat and "toasted" before hot liquid is added as the rice cooks. It is usually cream colored. This recipe is fit for a serious cook because it celebrates, through the use of red wine, the joy of experimentation.

5 ounces dried porcini mushrooms

2 cups hot water

4 cups vegetable or chicken stock, hot

3 tablespoons olive oil

¼ pound shitake mushrooms, sliced

¼ pound crimini mushrooms, sliced

kosher salt and freshly ground black pepper

¼ cup extra-virgin olive oil

1 medium onion, cut into ¼ -inch dice

2 cups Arborio rice

½ cup red wine

4 tablespoons (½ stick) unsalted butter

½ cup freshly grated Parmigiano-Reggiano, plus more for garnish

ESSENTIAL EQUIPMENT

dry and wet measuring cups

measuring spoons

cutting board

chef's knife

box grater or Microplane

saucepans

wooden spoon

strainer (with cheesecloth)

sauté pan

ladle

ESSENTIAL TECHNIQUES

mise en place

sautéing

MAKES 4 SERVINGS.

1   Soak the porcini mushrooms in 2 cups of hot water. Let them soak for 20 minutes, then drain, reserving the liquid. Pour the liquid through a fine sieve lined with cheesecloth or paper towels to catch any grit. Add the clean mushroom liquid to warm stock. Keep stock warm over medium-low heat. Dry the reconstituted porcinis with paper towels and set aside.

2   In a large sauté pan, heat the 3 tablespoons olive oil. Sauté the shitakes and criminis over medium-high heat just to soften, about 3 to 4 minutes. Season with kosher salt and freshly ground pepper and set aside.

3   Heat a medium-sized heavy saucepan over medium heat, and add the ¼ cup olive oil. Add the onion and cook until softened and translucent but not browned, 8 to 10 minutes. Once the onions are translucent, add the rice and stir with a wooden spoon until toasted and opaque, 3 to 4 minutes.

4   Add the wine to the toasting rice, and then add four 6-ounce ladles of stock and cook, stirring, until it is absorbed. Continue adding the stock a ladle at a time, waiting until the liquid is absorbed before adding more. Cook until the rice is tender and creamy, yet still a little al dente, about 20 minutes. Stir in the sautéed mushrooms, butter, and cheese until well mixed.

5   Portion the risotto into four serving plates, topping with extra cheese. #

Salmon Purses in Puffed Pastry with Shitake Cream Sauce

This dish looks like a beautifully wrapped gift, and that's exactly what it is: a moist and tender pavé of salmon covered in puff pastry, tied with a chive "ribbon." The shitake cream sauce takes mere minutes to make but tastes like a fine restaurant prepared it. Assemble the purses a few hours ahead of time for convenience, store them in the refrigerator, and bake just before serving.

For the fish:

1 pound salmon, cut into 4 square pieces, skin removed

kosher salt and freshly ground black pepper

1 sheet puff pastry

1 egg beaten with 1 tablespoon water, for the egg wash

4 chives

For the sauce:

1½ cups heavy cream

1 tablespoon butter

1 large shallot, minced

2 cups sliced shitake mushrooms

½ cup white wine

½ cup fumet (fish stock) or chicken stock

1 tablespoon lemon juice

1 tablespoon chopped parsley

kosher salt and freshly ground black pepper to taste

ESSENTIAL EQUIPMENT

wet measuring cup

measuring spoons

cutting board

chef's knife

small bowl

fork

parchment paper or silicone baking liner

sheet pan

rolling pin

pastry brush

small saucepan

spatula

sauté pan

ESSENTIAL TECHNIQUES

mise en place

knife skills

baking

blanching

sautéing

deglazing

reducing sauce

FUMET, S'IL VOUS PLAIT

Fumet is the French word for fish stock. It's made with the heads and tails of white-fleshed fish, plus some onions and leeks. It takes less than an hour to make and freezes well.

MAKES 4 SERVINGS.

Salmon Purses in Puffed Pastry with Shitake Cream Sauce

1   Preheat the oven to 400°F.

2   Line a sheet pan with a piece of parchment paper or a silicone baking liner and set aside.

3   Cut the puff pastry sheet into quarters. Roll out each piece of pastry to fit around a piece of salmon. Place a piece of salmon in each puff pastry square. Season the tops of the fish generously with kosher salt and freshly ground black pepper. Gather together the edges of the dough and twist and pinch to form a purse. Set each purse on the sheet pan and brush lightly with the egg mixture. Place the pan in the oven and bake for 25 to 30 minutes, or until the pastry is golden brown.

4   While the purses are baking, blanch the chives. Bring a small saucepan of water to a boil and plunge the chives for 10 seconds. Remove the chives to a paper towel and set aside. Discard the boiling water and reserve the saucepan.

5   Now prepare the sauce. Reduce the heavy cream in a saucepan by about half and set it aside. Heat the butter in a sauté pan. When the foam subsides, add the shallot and sweat until tender, about 2 minutes. Add the mushroom slices and sauté until tender and wilted. Add the white wine and fish fumet to the mushroom mixture to deglaze the pan. Cook until the wine and fumet is reduced by at least half. Add the reduced cream to the mushrooms and continue to reduce the sauce until it has thickened enough to coat the back of a spoon.

6   Remove the sauce from the heat and add the lemon juice, chopped parsley, kosher salt, and freshly ground pepper to taste.

7   Remove the salmon purses from the oven, and tie each with a chive ribbon. Spoon the sauce evenly onto four plates and top with the garnished salmon purses. Serve immediately. ✳

Braised Lamb Shanks

Shanks are legs, which means they are walking muscle. Any part of the animal that gets a lot of exercise is going to yield tougher meat, which is perfect for the tenderizing effect of braising. A red wine and tomato base produces a deeply colored and flavored gravy. By cutting the meat off the bone and returning it to the sauce, you have almost a stew.

4 lamb shanks

3 tablespoons olive oil

1 large onion, cut into chunks

4 carrots, cut into chunks

2 celery stalks, cut into chunks

6 garlic cloves, peeled and crushed

4 sprigs thyme

2 sprigs rosemary

1 bay leaf

2 cups red wine

3 cups brown chicken or veal stock

2 cups diced canned tomatoes, drained

kosher salt and freshly ground black pepper

ESSENTIAL EQUIPMENT

wet measuring cups

measuring spoons

cutting board

chef's knife

Dutch oven or large saucepan with lid

wooden spoon

tongs

ESSENTIAL TECHNIQUES

mise en place

knife skills

braising

MAKES 4–6 SERVINGS.

1   Preheat the oven to 300°F.

2   Trim the shanks, if necessary, of excess fat. Season with kosher salt and freshly ground pepper. Heat a small Dutch oven or large saucepan with olive oil. Sauté the lamb shanks, in batches, until well browned on all sides. Remove and set aside.

3   Add the onions, carrots, celery, and garlic to the same pot and cook for a few minutes, until softened. Add the thyme, rosemary, and bay leaf. Then add the wine to deglaze the pan. Add the stock and tomatoes. Season lightly with kosher salt and freshly ground pepper, then return the shanks to the pot.

4   Cover the pot with a tight-fitting lid and place it in the oven for about 2½ hours. When the shanks are tender, remove the pot from the oven and let the shanks rest for about 10 minutes. After resting, serve the shanks whole with the sauce, or cut the meat from the bone and return it to the sauce. Season with additional kosher salt and freshly ground pepper before serving. ✳

Roast Duck with Glazed Bing Cherries

It's almost unthinkable that a dinner this impressive could come together in under an hour, if you are willing to tackle the first part of the recipe in advance. Duck is notoriously fatty. Boiling it first and then roasting it renders a lot of the fat so that most bites are the best bites—tender, gamey duck with thin, crispy skin. Glazed Bing cherries provide a pleasantly sweet note to this classic melody.

For the duck:

1,5-pound Long Island or Peking duckling (fully defrosted, if frozen)

1 teaspoon kosher salt

½ teaspoon finely ground black pepper

For the cherries:

1 cup pitted fresh Bing cherries

⅓ cup balsamic vinegar

2 tablespoons honey

1 sprig of thyme

kosher salt and freshly ground black pepper to taste

1 Fill a tall stockpot with enough cold water to cover the duck (make sure there is enough room left in the pot for the duck). Cover the pot and bring to a boil over high heat.

2 Meanwhile, using the tines of a fork at an angle, prick the skin of the duck all over, especially the fattiest areas, such as the breast and thighs. Do not pierce the meat.

3 Once the water is vigorously boiling, carefully lower the duck into the stockpot, neck end first, allowing the cavity to fill with water so the duck sinks to the bottom of the pot. Place a heavy dinner plate over the duck to weigh it down so it is always submerged. When the water returns to a boil, reduce the heat and simmer gently for 40 minutes.

4 When the duck has finished simmering, remove the plate and carefully lift out the duck, using two wooden spoons, one in each hand, through the cavity. Carefully hold the duck over the stockpot to drain any liquid from the cavity.

ESSENTIAL EQUIPMENT

dry and wet measuring cups

measuring spoons

cutting board

chef's knife

large stockpot with lid

fork

plate

wooden spoons

roasting or heavy-bottomed sheet pan

small saucepan

spatula

ESSENTIAL TECHNIQUES

mise en place

roasting

poaching

MAKES 2 SERVINGS.

Roast Duck with Glazed Bing Cherries

5   Place the duck on a cutting board lined with a few paper towels. Pat the duck dry thoroughly and coat the skin on all sides with the kosher salt and freshly ground pepper. Transfer the duck to a roasting pan, breast-side up.

6   Now preheat the oven to 500°F and move the rack to the bottom third of the oven. In the time it takes the oven to come to temperature, the duck will have time to dry its skin prior to roasting, which makes for the crispiest skin.

7   As the oven preheats and the duck air-dries, prepare the glazed cherries. In a small saucepan, combine the cherries, vinegar, honey, and thyme and bring to strong simmer. Cook for 10 to 15 minutes until the liquid has thickened to a syrup and the cherries have softened. Season with kosher salt and freshly ground black pepper. Set aside.

8   Place the duck in the oven legs first. Roast for 30 minutes. After the first 15 minutes, remove the pan from the oven and shut the door. Spoon out the fat that accumulates in the roasting pan to prevent the fat from smoking. To prevent the back of the duck from sticking to the pan, move the duck around with a spatula.

9   Return the duck to the oven for the remaining 15 minutes. Before carving, let the duck rest for 10 minutes. Serve one breast and one leg with the thigh attached per person, drizzled with the glazed cherries. ✳

BALANCING ACT

If you are ever stuck with a less-than-desirable quality vinegar, simply add a little honey or sugar to the mix. The sweetness removes the intense acidity of the vinegar, smoothing out the flavor.

Sweet Potato Gnocchi with Fried Sage

Gnocchi are potato-based dumplings, named for their shape (gnocco means "lump" in Italian). The dough in this recipe is made with sweet potato instead, which provides a lovely orange color and unique taste. Fried sage offers both a fragrant finish to the dish, as well as a textural highlight thanks to its paper-thin crunch. Toasted chopped hazelnuts or crumbled Italian almond cookies also make beguiling garnishes for this versatile from-scratch appetizer, main course, or side dish.

For the gnocchi:

3 large sweet potatoes (about ¾ pound each), baked, cooled, and peeled

12 ounces ricotta cheese

1 cup freshly grated Parmesan, plus extra for garnish

1 tablespoon dark brown sugar

1 tablespoon maple syrup

1½ teaspoons kosher salt

¼ teaspoon freshly ground nutmeg

¼ teaspoon ground cardamom

3 cups all-purpose flour

For the sage:

1 bunch fresh sage, leaves only

½ cup olive oil

½ cup (1 stick) butter

ESSENTIAL EQUIPMENT

dry and wet measuring cups

measuring spoons

cutting boards

chef's knife

box grater

grater or Microplane

fork

large mixing bowl

rubber spatula

large saucepans or stockpot

strainer or slotted spoon

sheet pan (lined with parchment paper)

small and large sauté pans

tongs

wooden spoon

ESSENTIAL TECHNIQUES

mise en place

"spoon and sweep" flour

frying

sautéing

MAKES 8 SERVINGS.

Sweet Potato Gnocchi with Fried Sage

1   In a large bowl, mash the sweet potato flesh with a fork. Fold in the ricotta, Parmesan, brown sugar, maple syrup, salt, nutmeg, and cardamom. Mix well to blend, then sprinkle in the flour, ½ cup at a time, and gather the dough into a ball.

2   Divide the dough into quarters. On a floured surface, roll each piece of dough with the palms of your lightly floured hands into a long rope, about ¾-inch wide. Cut each rope into 1-inch pieces. Roll gnocchi over the tines of a fork to make a patterned surface. Transfer the gnocchi to another cutting board.

3   In a large saucepan or stockpot, bring salted water to a boil over high heat. Cook the gnocchi in batches until tender, about 5 minutes. Strain with a slotted spoon on a sheet pan lined with parchment paper.

4   Once all the gnocchi are cooked, fry the sage. Heat the olive oil in a small sauté pan over medium heat until it shimmers. Add a few sage leaves at a time and fry until the surface of the sage bubbles and crisps, about 10 seconds (turn if necessary). Transfer the fried sage to a paper towel to drain. Repeat until all the sage leaves have been fried.

5   In a large sauté pan, melt the butter and cook until it begins to turn golden brown. Add the gnocchi, and heat through, tossing well to coat in the brown butter. Transfer to a serving bowl or individual dishes, sprinkle with freshly grated Parmesan, and garnish with the fried sage. ✳

For the Health-Conscious Cook

* Carrot Ginger Soup
* Fish Tacos with Watermelon and Jicama Slaw
* Mango Curry Chicken Salad
* Baked Lemon Potatoes
* Steamed Asparagus with Red Pepper Coulis

Carrot Ginger Soup

There are dozens of recipes for carrot soup, but this recipe uses carrot juice instead of the more typical chicken or vegetable stock as its base. The result is an intensely carrot-flavored soup that can be served hot or chilled. If you do not care for ginger, consider using a teaspoon of cumin or curry powder instead. Use fresh carrot juice—not from the can—even if you do not juice your own.

For the soup:

6 cups carrot juice, divided

3 cups chopped carrots

1 small onion, chopped

1-inch piece of ginger, peeled and thinly sliced

kosher salt and freshly ground black pepper to taste

Optional garnishes:

dollop of plain nonfat yogurt

toasted sunflower seeds

chopped chives

shelled pistachios

1   In a large saucepan, add 4 cups of carrot juice, the chopped carrots, chopped onions, and sliced ginger. Bring to a simmer over medium heat, cover, and reduce heat to low. Cook until the carrots are tender, about 10 minutes.

2   Transfer the contents of the saucepan to a blender and purée in batches. Add some of the additional 2 cups carrot juice to help blend, if necessary. Return the puréed mixture to the saucepan with the remaining carrot juice, stirring gently until thickened and thoroughly heated through.

3   Season with kosher salt and freshly ground black pepper to taste. Garnish as desired. ✳

ESSENTIAL EQUIPMENT

wet and dry measuring cups

cutting board

chef's knife

electric juicer

large saucepan with lid

wooden spoon

blender

ESSENTIAL TECHNIQUES

mise en place

juicing

poaching

MAKES 4 SERVINGS.

Fish Tacos with Watermelon and Jicama Slaw

These fish tacos are filled with flavor, but low in fat and calories. A firm white fish, like tilapia or snapper, packs a powerful punch with a coating of spices.

For the slaw:

1 cup watermelon, julienne

1 small jicama, julienne

¼ cup chopped cilantro

juice of two limes

kosher salt and freshly ground black pepper to taste

For the tacos:

2 teaspoons ground coriander

2 teaspoons ground cumin

2 teaspoons chili powder

2 teaspoons black pepper

2 teaspoons kosher salt

2 pounds tilapia, red snapper, or fluke

3 tablespoons olive oil

8 flour tortillas

Garnish:

1 avocado, sliced

½ cup nonfat sour cream

ESSENTIAL EQUIPMENT

dry measuring cup

measuring spoons

cutting board

chef's knife

large mixing bowl

rubber spatula

shallow bowl

pastry brush

nonstick sauté pan

spatula

ESSENTIAL TECHNIQUES

mise en place

knife skills

sautéing

MAKES 4 SERVINGS.

1 Prepare the slaw by gently tossing the watermelon, jicama, chopped cilantro, and lime juice in a large bowl. Season with kosher salt and freshly ground black pepper to taste. Set aside.

2 Stir together the coriander, cumin, chili powder, black pepper, and kosher salt in a shallow bowl. Brush the fish on all sides with the olive oil, then coat both sides evenly with the spice mixture. Heat a nonstick skillet over medium heat, and add the fish. Cook for about 3 to 4 minutes per side.

3 Divide the fish into eight portions. Place two tortillas on each of four plates. Top each tortilla with a portion of fish, some slaw, a few slices of avocado, and a tablespoon of nonfat sour cream. ✤

Mango Curry Chicken Salad

Even people who swear they don't like curry love this chicken salad. Made with yogurt instead of mayonnaise, packed with unpeeled crisp green apple and sweet golden raisins, and finished with a touch of mango chutney, this recipe makes a satisfying and healthy lunch. Serve this colorful dish over greens or on a toasted whole-wheat pita. Chop the chicken and apples into a small dice, and serve the salad in endive spears for an elegant hors d'oeuvre. The recipe doubles easily to feed a larger crowd.

> 1 pound boneless chicken breast
>
> ⅓ cup plain yogurt
>
> 1 tablespoon curry powder
>
> 2 tablespoons mango chutney
>
> ¼ cup golden raisins
>
> ½ Granny Smith apple, diced
>
> kosher salt and freshly ground black pepper to taste

1 To poach the chicken, place the breasts in a medium saucepan. Cover with cold water, and bring to a simmer over medium heat. Lower the heat and cover. Poach the chicken for 15 minutes or until firm to the touch. Remove the chicken from the liquid and cool for 20 minutes on a cutting board. Then cut the chicken into ½-inch dice.

2 In a mixing bowl, combine the plain yogurt, curry powder, and chutney. Add the chicken, raisins, and apple. Season to taste with kosher salt and freshly ground black pepper. Mix gently until combined. Cover and refrigerate until ready to serve. ✳

The chicken can be poached up to several days in advance. Alternatively, use leftover chicken from a roasted whole bird, chicken soup, etc.

ESSENTIAL EQUIPMENT

dry measuring cups

measuring spoons

cutting board

chef's knife

saucepan

tongs

large mixing bowl

rubber spatula

ESSENTIAL TECHNIQUES

mise en place

poaching

knife skills

MAKES 4 SERVINGS.

Baked Lemon Potatoes

This recipe is inspired by *potates lemonates*, a Greek dish of potatoes baked in lemon juice and olive oil. Greece has an ancient and rich culture, but the appeal of its cuisine is rooted in simplicity and honesty. Any authentic Greek kitchen boasts a pantry of healthful foods: sea salt, black pepper, olive oil, lemons, oregano, paprika, onions, and garlic. Seasoned with traditional Mediterranean flavors and baked until tender, this recipe is as delicious as it is guilt-free. Best of all, it can be paired with virtually anything.

---

2 pounds waxy potatoes, peeled and cut into evenly sized chunks

2 tablespoons dried oregano

¼ cup olive oil

juice of two lemons

sea salt to taste

water

---

1   Preheat the oven to 400°F.

2   Place the potatoes in one layer in a shallow baking pan or casserole. Sprinkle with the oregano, then drizzle with the olive oil and the juice of two lemons. Sprinkle with sea salt, then pour enough water into the pan so that the potatoes are almost covered.

3   Bake uncovered for 30 to 40 minutes until the liquid has almost completely evaporated and the potatoes are tender to the touch and light golden brown on top. ✳

ESSENTIAL EQUIPMENT

wet measuring cup

measuring spoon

cutting board

chef's knife

baking pan or casserole

ESSENTIAL TECHNIQUES

mise en place

baking

WHY WAXY POTATOES?

Waxy potatoes are low-starch potatoes, also called boiling potatoes. The most typical varieties are white or red round potatoes. Such potatoes hold their shape best after cooking, but other types are preferred for baking, frying, or mashing. Waxy potatoes work best in the Baked Lemon Potatoes recipe because this preparation technique falls somewhere between baking, roasting, and braising. The potatoes are placed in a baking pan, but the 400°F temperature is more typical of roasting. The process is akin to braising because the potatoes are partially submerged in water and lemon juice. Since the liquid ultimately evaporates, and the tops of the potatoes crisp and brown while the bottoms stay moist and tender, it is ultimately a baked dish.

MAKES 6–8 SERVINGS.

Steamed Asparagus with Red Pepper Coulis

Steamed asparagus spears are wonderfully paired with a bright red pepper sauce in this recipe. In fact, the red pepper coulis is so easy and so delicious, you'll find yourself serving it with chicken, drizzling it over fish, and using it as a sandwich spread or vegetable dip. Season the asparagus spears with a little sea salt before you serve them so they taste as vibrant as they look.

For the red pepper coulis:

4 red bell peppers

4 tablespoons olive oil, divided

2 tablespoons red wine vinegar

2–3 tablespoons water

kosher salt and freshly ground black pepper

For the asparagus:

2 bunches asparagus

olive oil

kosher salt and freshly ground black pepper

ESSENTIAL EQUIPMENT

measuring spoons

cutting board

chef's knife

sheet pan

tongs

large mixing bowl

blender or food processor

peeler

saucepan or stockpot

steamer basket

strainer or colander

ESSENTIAL TECHNIQUES

mise en place

roasting

steaming

MAKES 6–8 SERVINGS.

1   Preheat the oven to 400°F.

2   Slice the peppers in half, removing stems, seeds, and white ribs. Rub the peppers with 2 tablespoons olive oil and place them on a sheet pan, skin-side up. Roast in the oven for about half an hour, or until they become charred and soft. Remove the sheet pan from the oven and place the peppers in a bowl. Cover the bowl with plastic wrap for about 5 minutes to allow the peppers to steam and soften further. Uncover and let them cool before handling them to peel.

3   Once cool, remove and discard the skins. Place the peppers in a blender or food processor. Purée with the vinegar, remaining olive oil, and water. Season to taste with kosher salt and freshly ground black pepper. Set aside.

4   To make the asparagus, trim the spears of their tough, dry bottoms and discard. One by one, peel each asparagus from about an inch below the tip to the bottom to get rid of the tough and fibrous outer skin.

5   Place a steamer basket in a deep saucepan or shallow stockpot, and fill with water to the surface of the basket. Bring to a boil. Once the water comes to a boil, lower the asparagus spears in the pot and cook for about 1 to 2 minutes, or until bright green, but tender when pierced with a paring knife.

6   Serve steamed asparagus drizzled with red pepper coulis. ✳

CHAPTER

19

For the Grill Master

* Pork Teriyaki Skewers with Peppers and Pineapple
* Ahi Tuna Steaks with Toasted Mustard Seeds and Yogurt Sauce
* Grilled Chicken Satay Skewers with Coconut Lemongrass Sauce
* Grilled Eggplant with Mint and Feta
* Grilled Corn on the Cob with Chili Lime Butter

Pork Teriyaki Skewers with Peppers and Pineapple

The marinade in this recipe is not a traditional teriyaki sauce (reduced soy sauce and sugar) because it has oil, ginger, dry mustard, and garlic. It can be used for virtually any meat or fish dish, whether grilled, broiled, or sautéed. Make this recipe with chicken, steak, or swordfish.

For the marinade:

½ cup soy sauce

¼ cup vegetable oil

2 tablespoons dark brown sugar

2 teaspoons dry mustard

1 teaspoon powdered ginger

4 cloves garlic, mashed into paste

For the kebabs:

2 pounds pork (loin or boneless chops), cut into 1-inch chunks

1 red bell pepper, cut into chunks

1 yellow bell pepper, cut into chunks

1 green bell pepper, cut into chunks

1 Vidalia onion, cut into chunks

1 small pineapple, cut into chunks

ESSENTIAL EQUIPMENT

wet measuring cups

measuring spoons

cutting board

paring or chef's knife

large mixing bowls

whisk

rubber spatula

metal (or bamboo) skewers

outdoor or indoor electric grill

pastry brush

ESSENTIAL TECHNIQUES

mise en place

knife skills

marinating

grilling

MAKES 4 SERVINGS.

1   To make the marinade, combine all the ingredients in a large bowl and blend with a whisk. Add the pork, vegetables, and pineapple. Gently toss with a rubber spatula and mix well to coat. Cover the bowl with plastic wrap and marinate for 2 to 4 hours in the refrigerator.

2   Place a piece of pork on a skewer, threading down to the bottom, leaving enough room to handle the skewer. Add a piece of onion, red pepper, yellow pepper, green pepper, another piece of onion, and a piece of pineapple. Repeat this pattern until you reach the tip of the skewer.

3   Once all the skewers have been assembled, preheat the grill. Save any remaining marinade to baste the kebabs as they cook. Place the kebabs on the grill and cook for 3 minutes per side for a total of about 12 minutes. Baste as necessary with the excess marinade while grilling.

4   Serve immediately either on the skewers, or removed from the skewers on a large platter. ✳

If you make the marinade in advance, store it in a tightly sealed container in the refrigerator for up to one week.

Ahi Tuna Steaks with Toasted Mustard Seeds and Yogurt Sauce

Ahi tuna is yellow-fin or "big eye" tuna, called by its Hawaiian name. When sliced into steaks and grilled, the tuna takes on a meat-like flavor and texture. Preference prevails, but the best way to enjoy the fish fully is to cook it rare so that it retains its supple and moist interior flesh. The yogurt sauce provides a pleasing contrast in temperature and texture. When the toasted and warm mustard seeds are added to the yogurt, they instantly infuse the sauce.

For the yogurt sauce:

1 cup plain yogurt

2 tablespoons yellow mustard seeds

2 tablespoons black mustard seeds

1 tablespoon freshly grated ginger

juice of one lime

1 tablespoon chopped cilantro

For the tuna:

4, 6-ounce 1-inch thick tuna steaks

2 tablespoons canola oil

1 teaspoon ground coriander

1 teaspoon ground cumin

½ teaspoon kosher salt

½ teaspoon freshly ground black pepper

1 To make the yogurt sauce, place the yogurt in a medium bowl. Then toast the yellow and black mustard seeds in a sauté pan until toasted and fragrant (they will begin to pop and jump). Pour the warm, toasted seeds into the yogurt. Then add the ginger, lime, and cilantro. Stir and set aside.

2 For the tuna, combine the oil, coriander, cumin, kosher salt, and freshly ground black pepper in a small bowl, then brush evenly over the four fish steaks on both sides. Grill the tuna steaks to taste (rare to medium). After 2 minutes, turn the steaks 90 degrees to "mark" them.

3 To serve, place each tuna steak on a plate and drizzle with yogurt sauce and chopped herbs. ⚹

ESSENTIAL EQUIPMENT

dry measuring cup

measuring spoons

cutting board

chef's knife

box grater or Microplane

large and small mixing bowls

sauté pan

rubber spatula

pastry brush

outdoor or indoor electric grill

ESSENTIAL TECHNIQUES

mise en place

mark your meat (quadrillage)

grilling

MAKES 4 SERVINGS.

Grilled Chicken Satay Skewers with Coconut Lemongrass Sauce

Satay, a dish found all over Southeast Asia, is made of sliced, skewered meat grilled over a fire. Peanut sauce is likely what makes satay so popular—the perfect blend of sweet and spicy to accompany grilled chicken, pork, beef, lamb, or even fish. This recipe uses coconut milk and lemongrass to punctuate the creamy texture and fragrant tone of the dipping sauce. Replacing the chicken with any meat you like makes this recipe even more versatile. Look for the nam pla (fish sauce) and curry paste in the Asian section of your local grocery store.

For the chicken:

1 pound skinless, boneless chicken breasts

½ teaspoon freshly ground black pepper

1 teaspoon ground coriander

1 teaspoon ground cumin

¾ teaspoon turmeric

2 garlic cloves, minced

¼ cup canola oil

juice of half a lemon

1 tablespoon soy sauce

2 teaspoons sugar

1 teaspoon nam pla (fish sauce)

For the peanut sauce:

1 cup unsalted peanuts

1 tablespoon canola oil

2 tablespoons finely chopped fresh lemongrass

2, 13.5-ounce cans unsweetened coconut milk (about 3½ cups)

2 tablespoons red (or green) curry paste

2 tablespoons sugar

juice of half a lemon

1 tablespoon nam pla (fish sauce)

ESSENTIAL EQUIPMENT

wet and dry measuring cups

measuring spoons

cutting board

chef's knife

large mixing bowl

rubber spatula

food processor

large saucepan

wooden spoon

bamboo skewers

pastry brush

outdoor or indoor electric grill

ESSENTIAL TECHNIQUES

mise en place

marinating

grilling

MAKES 4–6 SERVINGS.

Grilled Chicken Satay Skewers with Coconut Lemongrass Sauce

1   To make the chicken, cut thin, ¼-inch slices that run the length of the chicken breasts. Add all the remaining ingredients in a large bowl and combine. Toss the chicken in the marinade. Cover and refrigerate for at least 2 hours or overnight.

2   Meanwhile, prepare the dipping sauce. In a food processor, grind the peanuts as fine as possible without making paste. Heat a saucepan over medium heat, and add the canola oil and chopped lemongrass. Sauté until softened, about 3 minutes. Add 2 cups of the coconut milk and the curry paste. Raise the heat to high, stir to dissolve the curry paste, and cook for about 10 minutes, until the oil from the coconut milk separates and rises to the surface.

3   Add the ground peanuts and the remaining coconut milk, and stir. Bring the sauce to a vigorous boil, then lower the heat to medium. Add the sugar, lemon juice, and nam pla (fish sauce). Cook for about 15 minutes, until the sauce has thickened slightly and the oil separates and rises to the top again. Remove the sauce from the heat and set aside.

4   Preheat the grill to medium-high. Remove the chicken from the refrigerator. Thread each slice of chicken on a bamboo skewer, down the middle of the meat. Lightly brush each piece of meat with canola oil and place on the grill. Cook for 2 minutes per side.

5   Remove about half the oil from the top of the dipping sauce, then stir in the remaining oil and mix well to incorporate. Serve the skewers with a bowl of dipping sauce. ✳

The sauce can be served hot or lukewarm. Leftover sauce should be stored in the refrigerator or freezer where it will solidify. It can be reheated in the microwave, and thinned with a bit of water or additional coconut milk if it's too thick.

Grilled Eggplant with Mint and Feta

Fresh mint sprigs and salty feta crumbled over thick slices of eggplant hot off the grill is a dish hard to resist. The cheese melts a little from the heat of the eggplant, which helps to marry the flavors. Serve this as a side dish with grilled lamb, steak, chicken, or fish. Any leftovers can be enjoyed cold the next day.

> 2 large Italian eggplants, cut crosswise into 1-inch thick slices
>
> 1 cup olive oil for brushing
>
> kosher salt and freshly ground black pepper
>
> 1 cup crumbled feta cheese
>
> 12 fresh mint leaves
>
> extra olive oil for drizzling

1 Preheat the grill to medium-high. Brush one side of the eggplant slices with olive oil and place the oiled side on the hot grill. Meanwhile, brush the top of each slice with olive oil and season with kosher salt and freshly ground black pepper. Cook for 5 minutes on the first side, then turn the eggplant over, cover the grill, and cook for another 5 minutes, or until the eggplant is cooked and tender. Depending on the size of your grill, you might need to cook in batches.

2 Remove the eggplant slices to a platter, neatly overlapping, and tent with aluminum foil.

3 Cut the mint leaves in chiffonade. Sprinkle the feta over the eggplant, and then drizzle lightly with olive oil. Sprinkle with mint and serve. ✳

ESSENTIAL EQUIPMENT

wet and dry measuring cups

cutting board

chef's knife

pastry brush

outdoor or indoor electric grill

tongs

ESSENTIAL TECHNIQUES

mise en place

knife skills

grilling

MAKES 8–10 SERVINGS.

Grilled Corn on the Cob with Chili Lime Butter

Fresh summer corn . . . the flesh is so good and the taste is so sweet than many people run their teeth across these ears raw, relishing the juicy corn milk inside each bursting kernel. Grilled corn is equally delicious, especially when the kernels char and every bite screams "barbecue!" There are two ways to grill corn on the cob: in the husk, or out of the husk. Either way is far better than boiling beautiful corn to death in a pot inside when the best of the meal is grilled outdoors. Serve the compound butter made with chili and lime with either version.

4 tablespoons unsalted butter, softened

zest of 1 lime

½ jalapeno, seeded and finely minced

½ teaspoon kosher salt

6 ears of corn

1 To make the compound butter, combine the butter, lime zest, minced jalapeno, and kosher salt in a small bowl. Place in plastic wrap and roll into a log. Refrigerate for at least one hour. Slice into discs to serve.

2 **In the husk:** Pull the husks of the corn back, but do not remove them. Trim the excess silk from the end of the corn. Soak the corn in a bowl of cold water for 30 minutes to 1 hour. Preheat the grill to a medium temperature.

3 Remove the corn from the water and shake to remove any excess water. Place the husks over the kernels and tie each ear with twine. Place cobs on the heated grill (or in a grill basket first) and cook for approximately 15 to 30 minutes, turning frequently. Remove the husk and any remaining silk after grilling. Be careful, as the corn will be extremely hot when it comes off the grill.

1 **No husk:** Preheat the grill to a medium temperature. Remove the husk and corn silk from each ear. Place the corn on the grill, and cook for approximately 10 minutes, turning frequently. Corn is done when the kernels have browned. ✲

ESSENTIAL EQUIPMENT

cutting board

chef's knife

grater or Microplane

large and small mixing bowls

kitchen twine

grill basket (optional)

outdoor grill

tongs

ESSENTIAL TECHNIQUES

mise en place

grilling

THE ETIQUETTE OF SHOPPING FOR CORN

There are a few things to keep in mind when selecting and storing fresh sweet corn. Corn husks should be bright green, and the kernels should be colorful, plump, and moist. The size of the ears themselves varies and is not in itself an indicator of quality. Once the husk and silk are removed, corn should be prepared and eaten immediately. For this reason, it is best to buy corn in the husk, and only take just a peek, if at all. Do not fully peel back the husk whether or not you plan to take the ear home; it will not stay as fresh for you or the next buyer.

MAKES 6 SERVINGS.

chapter 20

For the Holidays

* Herbed Roast Turkey
* Perfect Pan Gravy
* Chestnut Cornbread Dressing
* Maple Pecan Sweet Potatoes
* Champagne Cranberry Sauce
* Roasted Brussels Sprouts with Pancetta
* Holiday Gingerbread

Herbed Roast Turkey

Bathed in butter on the outside and infused with fresh herbs on the inside, this turkey is golden brown, moist, and savory. When it comes to salt and pepper, the inside of the bird must be seasoned just as much as the outside. The flavors infuse from within during cooking. Rub the cavity with lots of kosher salt and freshly ground black pepper before filling it with herbs.

12- to 14-pound whole turkey

kosher salt and freshly ground pepper

½ cup unsalted butter, melted

½ bunch each fresh sage, thyme, and savory

1 medium carrot, cut in chunks

1 medium celery stalk, cut in chunks

2 onions, cut in chunks

1   Preheat the oven to 450°F.

2   Wash the turkey well under cold running water. Pat it thoroughly dry. Remove any excess fat from cavity. Tuck the wings underneath body.

3   Season the outside and inside of the turkey heavily with kosher salt and freshly ground black pepper. Stuff the turkey cavity with several sprigs each of sage, thyme, and savory. Tie the legs together with twine.

4   Place the chopped carrots, celery, and onions in the bottom of a roasting pan. Place the rack on top of the vegetables. Then put the turkey, breast side up, on the rack. Brush the butter over the top and sides of the turkey.

5   Put the turkey in the oven and immediately lower the heat to 325°F. Roast the turkey for one hour undisturbed. After an hour, remove the turkey from the oven (shut the oven door), and baste the turkey with the fat in the bottom of the pan. Continue roasting for approximately 2½ hours more (15 minutes per pound), until the internal temperature in the thickest part of the thigh measures 180°F or the breast measures 170°F. ❊

Allow the turkey to rest for at least 20 minutes before carving.

ESSENTIAL EQUIPMENT

wet measuring cup

cutting board

chef's knife

kitchen twine

roasting pan with rack

pastry brush

ESSENTIAL TECHNIQUES

mise en place

roasting

TO BRINE OR NOT TO BRINE

Brining is a process in which food is placed in a strong solution of water and salt (a brine) in order to season, pickle, or preserve it. Other ingredients, such as sugar or molasses, can be added to this solution for flavor or color. Specifically, brining a turkey helps the bird to retain moisture and impart flavor throughout the meat. Brining can take anywhere from 4 hours to overnight, depending on your schedule and needs. The longer you plan on brining the turkey, however, the less salt you should use. When the bird is removed from the brine to be put in the oven, it first must be rinsed thoroughly inside and out, and then patted dry inside and out. These are two critical steps to ensure that the turkey is neither unpleasantly salty nor damp before being cooked.

MAKES 8 SERVINGS.

Perfect Pan Gravy

Once the turkey is done and spends at least 20 minutes resting, it's time to make the gravy. Perfect timing, just the way the culinary gods intended. While the turkey rests, you have plenty of time to prepare fresh pan gravy—and gather all the wonderful flavors from the drippings. Use chicken broth from the can if you have not made your own stock.

> ¼ cup fat from the pan drippings
>
> ¼ cup all-purpose flour
>
> 1 quart chicken stock
>
> kosher salt and freshly ground black pepper to taste

1   Remove the turkey and the rack from the roasting pan. Carefully pour off all the liquid fat in the roasting pan. Measure ¼ cup of fat and set the rest aside.

2   Place the roasting pan over two burners on a medium flame. Add the chicken stock to the pan, and scrape up all the drippings (sucs) using a wooden spoon. Continue scraping until the pan is fully deglazed. Transfer the liquid back to a large measuring cup or other pouring vessel.

3   Using a whisk, combine the flour and ¼ cup pan drippings in a large saucepan over medium heat, whisking constantly for 2 minutes. While whisking and in a steady stream, pour in the chicken stock from deglazing the roasting pan. Continue whisking until the mixture comes to a boil and begins to thicken. Add more chicken stock or water, if the mixture becomes too thick too quickly. Lower the heat and cook for a few minutes more, then season with kosher salt and freshly ground black pepper to taste.

4   Once the turkey is carved, pour some of the juices into the gravy, season again, and serve. ✳

ESSENTIAL EQUIPMENT

dry and wet measuring cups

measuring spoons

wooden spoon

large saucepan

whisk

ESSENTIAL TECHNIQUES

mise en place

thickening sauces (with a roux)

MAKES APPROXIMATELY 3 CUPS.

Chestnut Cornbread Dressing

This recipe is made with white bread to balance the density of the corn bread. The celery is cooked only briefly before being added to the mix to provide a delightful crunch once baked. The chestnuts are a welcome and hearty accent, but any of the following items could be added in their place: 1 pound sausage; 1 cup chopped dried apples; 1 cup dried cranberries; 1 cup toasted pecans.

8 tablespoons (1 stick) unsalted butter

1 large onion, diced

3 medium celery ribs with leaves, finely diced

10 slices white sandwich bread, cut into ½-inch cubes and dried overnight or in the oven

6 small or 3 jumbo corn muffins, crumbled

2 eggs, lightly beaten

1 teaspoon fresh thyme, chopped

6 large sage leaves, chopped

1 quart chicken stock

1, 15-ounce jar whole chestnuts

kosher salt and freshly ground black pepper to taste

1   Preheat the oven to 350°F.

2   In a large sauté pan, melt the butter over medium heat. Add the onion and cook, stirring often, until the onion is golden, about 10 minutes. Add the celery and cook for an additional 2 minutes.

3   Scrape the vegetables and butter into a large bowl. Allow the vegetables to cool, then add the beaten eggs, dried white bread, cornbread, and chestnuts. Stir in enough of the stock to moisten the stuffing, about 3½ cups or the full 4 cups. Season with thyme, sage, kosher salt, and freshly ground black pepper.

4   Place the mixture in a buttered baking dish, cover with aluminum foil, and bake for 30 minutes. Remove the foil and bake for an additional 15 to 20 minutes, or until the top browns. ✳

ESSENTIAL EQUIPMENT

wet measuring cup

measuring spoons

cutting board

chef's knife

fork

sauté pan

wooden spoon

large mixing bowl

baking pan or casserole

ESSENTIAL TECHNIQUES

mise en place

sautéing

baking

MAKES 6–8 SERVINGS.

Maple Pecan Sweet Potatoes

If marshmallow-topped sweet potatoes aren't really your thing, give this recipe a try. Maple syrup and pecans, both indigenous to North America, are a natural pair. The sweet and nutty accent transforms sweet potatoes into a splendid holiday side dish. Add your own personal touch with a pinch of ginger, nutmeg, cinnamon, or orange zest.

> 6 sweet potatoes, peeled and cut into large chunks
>
> 4 tablespoons butter, melted
>
> ¼ cup maple syrup
>
> 3 tablespoons dark brown sugar
>
> ½ cup chopped pecans

1   Preheat oven to 400°F.

2   In a large mixing bowl combine the sweet potatoes, melted butter, maple syrup, and brown sugar.

3   Butter a baking dish and add the sweet potato mixture. Top with pecans and bake uncovered 30 to 40 minutes, until the sweet potatoes are tender and the top is lightly browned. ⌗

ESSENTIAL EQUIPMENT

dry and wet measuring cups

measuring spoons

cutting board

chef's knife

mixing bowls

wooden spoon or rubber spatula

baking pan

ESSENTIAL TECHNIQUES

mise en place

baking

YOU SAY SWEET POTATO, AND I SAY YAM

Only one of us is right (it's you!). Sweet potatoes are the sweet orange-fleshed roots we sometimes cover in marshmallows and bake into pies. Yams are not actually sweet, and they don't have orange flesh. Cultivated in Latin America and Africa, yams have brown skin and yellow flesh. There are other varieties, some with pink skin, some with purple flesh. Since some sweet potatoes in the U.S. have white flesh, producers used the African word for the tuber "nyami" to inspire "yam." It's kind of like Chilean sea bass . . . neither Chilean nor bass, it's actually Arctic tooth fish, so named for marketing purposes.

MAKES 6–8 SERVINGS.

Champagne Cranberry Sauce

A festive time of year calls for a little bubbly, even in the holiday cranberry sauce. And with all the toasting and roasting around the family table, there is likely a cup of champagne to spare. Reduce the sauce as little or as much as you like, keeping in mind that it naturally thickens as it cools. Add chopped pecans or currants for a meatier sauce. Go ahead ... splurge!

> 1, 12-ounce package fresh cranberries
>
> 1 cup champagne or sparkling wine
>
> 1 cup granulated sugar
>
> zest of one orange
>
> freshly squeezed juice of one orange

1 Mix the sugar and champagne in a large and deep sauté pan over low heat until the sugar is dissolved. Bring the mixture to a boil on high heat, and add the cranberries.

2 Return to a boil and reduce the heat. Add the orange zest and juice. Simmer gently for 10 minutes. The cranberries will pop and break down. Stir occasionally, until the sauce has reduced and thickened.

3 Remove the sauce from the heat and cool completely before refrigerating. The sauce may be served warm or chilled (it will congeal when chilled). ✳

Water may be substituted for the champagne.

ESSENTIAL EQUIPMENT

dry and wet measuring cups

grater or Microplane

large sauté pan

wooden spoon

ESSENTIAL TECHNIQUES

mise en place

reducing sauce

MAKES 8–12 SERVINGS.

Roasted Brussels Sprouts with Pancetta

Brussels sprouts are bite-sized cabbages. When roasted, they caramelize and take on a wonderfully savory flavor. By slicing them in half, double the surface area becomes caramelized and the outer leaves crisp. Prepared this way, they can be as addictive as potato chips, but much better for you. Cooking them with a little pancetta, an Italian bacon, adds a smoky accent. Toss in some dried cranberries before serving this side dish for a sweet touch and some complementary color.

2 pounds Brussels sprouts, halved

6 ounces pancetta, chopped

¼ cup olive oil

kosher salt and freshly ground pepper to taste

1   Preheat the oven to 425°F.

2   In a large mixing bowl, combine the Brussels sprouts, pancetta, and olive oil. Toss well to coat, then season with kosher salt and freshly ground black pepper.

3   Spread the mixture in one even layer on a rimmed sheet pan. Roast in the oven for 25 to 30 minutes, or until the Brussels sprouts are fork-tender. ✸

ESSENTIAL EQUIPMENT

wet measuring cup

cutting board

chef's knife

large mixing bowl

wooden spoon

rimmed sheet pan

ESSENTIAL TECHNIQUES

mise en place

roasting

MAKES 8 SERVINGS.

Holiday Gingerbread

The following is a recipe for rolled cookie dough from which shapes can be cut. Molasses and dark brown sugar give the dough an intensely dark color and rich flavor. The spices are basic: ginger, cinnamon, and cloves. The result is a crispy "snap" that is sweet with a medium spice. Other spices certainly could be added within the framework of this recipe, such as cardamom, allspice, nutmeg, or mace. The gingerbread cookies stay crisp for weeks if stored properly in an airtight container. Once iced, however, these cookies soften and become chewy within a few days. Use the buttercream frosting from the Birthday Cake recipe (page 186).

2¼ cups all purpose flour, divided

2 tablespoons ground ginger

1 teaspoon baking soda

1 teaspoon ground cinnamon

½ teaspoon ground cloves

1 cup brown sugar

¾ cup (1½ sticks) butter

¼ cup molasses

1 large egg

1 Combine the first five ingredients, but just half the flour, in a mixing bowl. Then whisk in the brown sugar.

2 In a small saucepan, melt the butter and whisk it into the flour mixture with the molasses and egg. With a wooden spoon, stir in the remaining flour.

3 Form the dough into four small balls and wrap each one in plastic. Chill the dough until firm, for at least 1 hour or up to 2 days.

4 Line two baking sheets with silicone baking liners or parchment paper, and preheat the oven to 350°F.

5 Roll one ball of dough with a rolling pin on a floured surface. Use cookie cutters to create fun holiday shapes, and place the cookies two inches apart on the lined sheet.

6 Place the sheet on the middle oven rack and bake for 10 to 12 minutes. Cool on a cooling rack before decorating. ✳

ESSENTIAL EQUIPMENT

dry and wet measuring cups

measuring spoons

cutting board

large mixing bowl

wooden spoon

whisk

saucepan

rubber spatula

hand or standing mixer (optional)

rolling pin

cookie cutters

silicone baking liners or parchment paper

sheet pans

cooling rack

ESSENTIAL TECHNIQUES

mise en place

"spoon and sweep" flour

baking

LEAVE SOMEONE HANGING

Use this recipe to make gingerbread men ornaments by adding an additional cup of flour to the recipe. Second, decorate the dough with hard candies, dried fruits, and nuts. Finally, make holes at the top of each cookie before baking.

MAKES 8 DOZEN COOKIES.

APPENDIX

A

Equipment Materials

MATERIAL	USED FOR	PROS	CONS
Aluminum	Stockpots, sauté pans, roasting pans, cake pans, muffin and loaf pans	Conducts heat well if heavy gauge, inexpensive, and lightweight	Warps easily if thin, can pit and discolor, can react with some foods and impart metallic flavor
Anodized aluminum	Stockpots, sauté pans, roasting pans, cake pans, muffin and loaf pans	Stain-resistant material is harder than steel, conducts heat well, durable, does not chip or peel, nonporous, smooth surface	Must be washed by hand to avoid color fading
Cast iron, enameled cast iron	Sauté pans, Dutch ovens, griddles, baking pans	Retains heat evenly, durable, strong, nonstick, and easy to clean when coated in enamel	Heavy, slow to heat, breakable, rusts and requires seasoning if uncoated, enamel coating may chip or scratch
Ceramic (for knives)	Chef and paring knives	Second hardest material next to diamonds, holds an extremely sharp long-lasting edge	Can chip, requires a special sharpening process (through the manufacturer)
Copper	All pots and pans, mixing bowls, cookie cutters	Durable, conducts heat uniformly and quickly	Reactive, discolors, demanding to clean, expensive
Earthenware (ceramic)	Casserole, baking pans, pie dishes	Porous (good for "slow and low" cooking), nonreactive, retains heat well	Not flameproof, does not handle sudden temperature changes (must cool before being cleaned)
Glass (tempered)	Pie dishes, baking pans, bowls, measuring cups	Nonreactive, retains heat well	Ovenproof glass can crack at high temperatures, flameproof glass conducts heat unevenly
High-carbon steel	Knives	Holds an extremely sharp edge, rustproof, stainless, doesn't discolor itself or the food	Unless stainless, it rusts and discolors over time

MATERIAL	USED FOR	PROS	CONS
Low-carbon steel	Knives	Holds an extremely sharp edge	Discolors, imparts metallic flavor and possibly color to food, reacts with acidic foods
Nonstick coating (polytetrafluoroethylene, or PTFT)	Pots, pans, roasting pans, electric grills, bakeware, casseroles, utensils	Nonreactive, stick-resistant, easy to clean	Scratches easily, can peel, some materials can be toxic above a certain heat
Plastic	Colanders, bowls, measuring spoons and cups, utensils	Lightweight, dishwasher-safe	Melts on contact with heat (unless heatproof)
Porcelain (ceramic)	Casseroles, baking pans, pie dishes, ramekins, bowls	Nonreactive, nonporous, conducts and retains heat evenly	Breakable, does not handle sudden temperature changes (must cool before cleaning)
Silicone	Bakeware, utensils	Heatproof, flexible, dishwasher-safe	Soft material is easily punctured
Stainless steel	Pots, pans, roasting pans, bowls, colanders, racks, knives, utensils	Stainless, nonreactive, rust-proof, durable	Conducts heat unevenly (on its own), can stain from salt, hard water, acids, and detergent if not dried after washing
Stoneware (ceramic)	Casseroles, bowls	Durable, nonporous	Heavy, does not handle sudden temperature changes (must cool before cleaning)
Titanium	Knives	Holds a sharp long-lasting edge, flexible	Expensive
Wood	Spoons, rolling pins, cutting boards, bowls	Does not conduct heat, inexpensive	Absorbs food flavors, stains, must be hand washed, and can splinter, split, or warp

APPENDIX

B

Measurement Conversions

Volume Measurements

1 gallon = 4 quarts = 8 pints = 16 cups = 128 fluid ounces

4 cups = 1 quart = 2 pints = 32 fluid ounces = 64 tablespoons = 1 liter

2 cups = 1 pint = 16 fluid ounces = 32 tablespoons = 500 milliliters

1 cup = ½ pint = 8 fluid ounces = 16 tablespoons = 250 milliliters

¾ cup = 6 fluid ounces = 12 tablespoons = 175 milliliters

⅔ cup = 5⅓ ounces = 10 tablespoons + 2 teaspoons = 150 milliliters

½ cup = 4 fluid ounces = 8 tablespoons = 125 milliliters

⅓ cup = 2⅔ ounces = 5 tablespoons + 1 teaspoon = 75 milliliters

¼ cup = 2 fluid ounces = 4 tablespoons = 60 milliliters

⅛ cup = 1 fluid ounce = 2 tablespoons = 30 milliliters

1 tablespoon = 3 teaspoons = 15 milliliters

1 teaspoon = 5 milliliters

½ teaspoon = 2 milliliters

¼ teaspoon = 1 milliliter

⅛ teaspoon = a pinch

Weight Measurements

16 ounces = 455 grams = 1 pound

8 ounces = 225 grams = ½ pound

4 ounces = 115 grams = ¼ pound

3 ounces = 85 grams

2 ounces = 55 grams

1 ounce = 30 grams

Linear Measurements

1 inch = 2.54 centimeters

1 centimeter = 0.394 inch

Glossary

al forno:

an Italian phrase for baked foods, meaning "from the oven"

aromatics:

any herbs, spices, or vegetables used in a recipe expressly to flavor food

arugula:

also known as rocket, lettuce that is dark green with a bitter, peppery flavor

au gratin:

from the French *gratter* meaning "to scrape," a dish made in a casse-role with grated cheese or breadrcrumbs that is browned in the oven, baked, or roasted

beurre manié:

meaning "kneaded butter" in French, equal parts flour and softened butter used to thicken sauces

beurre noir:

meaning "black butter" in French, butter cooked over low heat until the milk solids turn dark brown (not black)

beurre noisette:

meaning "brown butter" in French, butter cooked over low heat until the milk solids turn a golden, hazelnut (noisette) color

Bibb:

a type of lettuce also known as Boston or Butter for its light green, tender, and mildly flavored leaves

Bing cherries:

a variety of cherry, large and ranging in color from dark red to almost black

blanchir:

meaning "to whiten" in French, a method of beating sugar and eggs (or egg yolks) until the mixture becomes fluffy and lighter in color

blind bake:

to bake an empty pie shell for the purpose of adding a filling that requires no cooking (as in chocolate cream)

boiling:

heating something (usually water) until it reaches 212°F (at sea level)

brioche:

a French yeast bread made with lots of eggs and butter, somewhat similar in color, taste, and texture to challah

buffalo mozzarella:

known as *mozzarella di bufala* in Italian, this is the most revered of the fresh mozzarella cheeses, made from water buffalo and cow milks

buttercream:

a creamy frosting made with confectioners' sugar, softened butter, and cream or milk, used as both a filling and a topping for cakes

butterfly:

to split food down the center, usually meat, for the purpose of opening it up to flatten it

caramelize:

to roast, sauté, sear, or grill something so that its natural sugars release, browning the surface and often imparting a touch of sweet flavor

casserole:

both a vessel and a completed dish, baked in the oven

ceviche:

a Latin American dish of raw fish cooked in citrus juice

chanterelles:

trumpet-shaped wild mushrooms, also known as *girolles*, that range in color from yellow to deep orange

cheesecloth:

a kind of porous cotton muslin used to strain sauces or makes sachets to hold herb bundles in stocks

china cap:

a conical metal sieve with perforated holes used to strain stocks and sauces

chinois:

a conical metal sieve with exceptionally fine mesh used to strain sauces and custards, producing a very fine, smooth texture

compound butter:

a flavored butter (butter mixed with other ingredients)

concentration:

a cooking method, such as grilling, broiling, sautéing, and roasting, used to lock in, or concentrate, juices by coagulating the surface protein

confectioners' sugar:

powdered or dusting sugar, also referred to as 10X sugar because it is ten times finer than granulated sugar (standard sugar crystals)

coulis:

a thick purée or sauce, typically made from vegetables or fruit

coupe:

a footed dish for serving dessert, such as ice cream or poached pears, that requires a bowl

cream:

to beat and combine ingredients, such as butter and sugar, until they form a smooth, uniform, "creamy" mixture

crimini:

miniature Portobello mushrooms

crimp:

to press or pinch pastry edges together for the purpose of both sealing and decorating the seam

crostini:

Italian for "little toasts," thin slices of toasted bread, often brushed with olive oil

curd:

a mixture made from juice, sugar, eggs, and butter that thickens when cooked

deglaze:

to remove the crusty bits (sucs) on the bottom of a pan by adding wine, stock, or water and scraping for the purpose of making a pan sauce to accompany the food originally cooked in that pan

dressing:

both a sauce for salads (as in vinaigrette), and a dish of what would otherwise be called "stuffing" baked in a casserole (not stuffed in meat or fish)

egg wash:

a combination of egg and either water or cream used to brush over pastries or breads before they bake, giving them added sheen and golden color

en papillote:

French for "in parchment," a sealed package made of parchment paper used to steam foods in the oven

extraction:

a method, such as poaching, to draw juices out of food during cooking

flapjacks:

pancakes

frenched:

a piece of meat with an exposed bone, trimmed of fat and flesh

frisée:

a chicory-like lettuce with frizzy leaves that ranges in color from yellow-white to light green

fumet:

French for "fish stock"

galangal:

a member of the ginger family found in Southeast Asia, with a hot, peppery flavor

gluten:

a starch protein found in rye, wheat, oats, and barley

Gorgonzola:

an Italian blue cheese with a pungent flavor made from cow's milk

green curry paste:

a Southeast Asian blend of fat and spices used to flavor sauces and soups

Gruyère:

a Swiss, aged cow's-milk cheese with a sweet and nutty taste, used in cheese fondue

haricots verts:

French string beans, marked by their particularly slender and elegant shape

hone:

to smooth a newly sharpened edge of a knife

hothouse cucumbers:

also known as English cucumbers, these are considerably longer than standard cucumbers, have thinner skins, and fewer seeds

hull:

to remove the outer skin or leafy top, as with strawberries

ice bath:

a bowl of ice water used to cool foods quickly either by plunging them directly in, or setting them in another vessel over the bath

Japanese eggplant:

smaller and more slender than the Italian variety, with white or bright purple skin

jicama:

a Mexican root vegetable with a brown skin and white flesh, somewhat similar in flavor and texture to a radish but much more mild

latkes:

potato pancakes made, in particular, to celebrate Chanukah, the Jewish Festival of Lights

legume:

a pod with multiple seeds, such as peas and beans

liaison:

an ingredient used in an emulsion to bind, or to thicken a sauce, by suspending itself in the liquid

macerate:

to soak food in a liquid to flavor and perhaps tenderize it

meringue:

egg whites stiffly beaten multiple times their volume, usually with sugar, to form white peaks

mesclun:

a salad mix of young, small greens, including arugula and frisée

mirepoix:

aromatic vegetables composed traditionally of 50 percent onions, 25 percent carrots, and 25 percent celery used to flavor roasts, stocks, and sauces

Mission fig:

a particular type of fig with small seeds introduced into Northern California by the Franciscan missionaries

mustard seed:

either white, brown, or black, used to make mustard as well as pickling spice

orzo:

a rice-shaped pasta

paillard:

the French word for thinly pounded cutlets of meat, typically chicken; the Italians call this *scaloppini*

pan sauce:

a sauce for meat or fish made in the same pan in which the main dish was cooked by deglazing the sucs

pancetta:

an Italian cured bacon that comes in a roll

panfried:

cooked in a sauté pan (frying pan or skillet) with a small amount of fat

panko:

Japanese breadcrumbs, coarse and crunchy

parboil:

to blanch, or to partially cook briefly in boiling water

parchment paper:

a nonstick, heat-, moisture-, and grease-resistant paper used in baking to line pans; also used to make cooking pouches as in *en papillote*

pare:

to trim, after something is peeled but before it is cut

patty melt:

a thin hamburger topped with cheese and caramelized onions, served between two slices of buttery, toasted rye bread

pavé:

meaning "square paving stone" in French, this refers to a square-shaped food

pearl onions:

baby onions about the size of a gumball

peel:

to remove the outer skin of a fruit or vegetable

pie weights:

little metal or clay balls used to weigh down an empty piecrust in blind baking

pignoli:

the Italian word for pine nut, a high-fat nut that comes from pine cones

porcini:

also called *cèpes*, these wild mushrooms are usually sold dried in the United States

quadrillage:

criss-cross marks branded on grilled meat

quail:

a small game bird

quick bread:

as opposed to yeast bread, a cake-like batter (as in banana bread)

rotisserie:

a device that cooks meat slowly over a turning spit

roux:

a liaison of equal parts flour and fat (usually butter) cooked over heat to which hot liquid is added and then subsequently thickened

rump roast:

a triangular cut of beef, taken from the upper part of the hind leg

San Marzano tomatoes:

a variety of plum tomatoes, considered to be the best sauce tomatoes

satay:

a Southeast Asian dish of skewered marinated meats or fish, typically grilled and served with peanut sauce

savory:

the opposite of sweet, as in piquant

scallopini:

the Italian word for thinly pounded cutlets of meat, typically veal and chicken; the French call this *paillard*

sear:

to cook over or under direct heat (as in sautéing, grilling, or broiling) to lock in juices and provide a browned surface to the food

sheath:

a case to store knife blades safely

shitake:

an Asian mushroom, now cultivated, with a meaty flesh and tough stems

shock:

to chill abruptly by plunging in an ice bath or running under a heavy stream of very cold water

sift:

to pass ingredients through a mesh apparatus to remove unwanted matter, and to aerate and lighten

simmer:

to cook food gently in water, just below the boiling point, indicated by a constant presence of little bubbles

simple syrup:

liquefied sugar (dissolved in water) used to flavor drinks, glaze foods, and moisten cakes

skim:

to remove fat or impurities from the top layer of a soup, sauce, or stock

slurry:

a liaison made of starch (arrowroot, corn starch, potato starch, or rice flour) and liquid (water, wine, or stock) to thicken sauces

smokepoint:

also known as the flashpoint, the temperature at which fat begins to decompose and visible fumes (smoke) are given off

smoker:

a heated apparatus filled with burning wood that gives off smoke to flavor food

soufflé:

meaning "to blow up" in French, a puffed, airy, flavored egg yolk-based dish lightened with a meringue, prepared in a ramekin, usually sweet but sometimes savory

steel:

a honing tool used to smooth and polish a knife's edge

stone:

as in a whetstone, a rectangular block made of fine-grain carborundum, used to sharpen the edge of a blade

sucs:

the savory crusted bits and juice left in the pan from searing meat and fish; used to make pan sauce by deglazing with water, wine, or stock

superfine sugar:

also known as castor sugar, has finer granules than standard granulated sugar, but larger than confectioners' sugar

sweat:

to soften vegetables without browning, cooking them slowly over low heat, perhaps covered, so they release their own juices

temper:

(1) a process of heating and cooling chocolate, (2) a technique to prevent eggs from curdling when making a custard by adding a bit of hot liquid to the eggs before putting the eggs in the hot liquid

tikka:

a baked Punjabi (Pakistani) dish of skewered chunks of chicken that have been marinated in yogurt and spices, baked in the tandoor (oven)

tilapia:

also called St Peter's fish, this pink- and white-fleshed fish is mild and sweet

toque:

a chef's tall white hat, either soft and poufy or stiff and pleated

truss:

to tie together, as in the legs of a bird or the length of a roast, for the purpose of maintaining uniform shape and sealing in juices during cooking

twine:

kitchen string made of cotton or nylon used to truss

utility knife:

a straight-edged knife larger than a paring knife, smaller than a chef's knife

Vidalia onion:

the sweetest and juiciest onions, which come from Vidalia, Georgia, and peak in late spring

vinaigrette:

an emulsified salad dressing classically composed of one part vinegar to three parts oil with a liaison of Dijon mustard

viscous:

being resistant to flow (viscosity), as in a liquid that is thicker than water

zest:

to extract the surface skin of citrus fruit—also called zest—by finely grating

APPENDIX

D

Cooking with Eggs

EGGS ARE SO ESSENTIAL TO THE ART OF COOKING and baking that without them we might as well all throw in our whisks and give up. Eggs are often used to thicken, bind, and coat, but they are equally multipurposeful on their own. Think of all the different ways we eat just eggs, anywhere from breakfast to dessert, savory to sweet: omelets, quiches, frittatas, custards, meringues, sponge cakes, and soufflés, to name a few. Both versatile and nutritious, eggs are an excellent source of protein; iron; and vitamins A, D, and E. There are many kinds of eggs to cook with, such as quail and ostrich, but the following advice focuses on the ubiquitous chicken egg.

What's in an Egg?

An egg is made of the following components:

1. The shell

2. The yolk (the yellow part)

3. The chalaza (the rope-like white strand)

4. An air cell

5. Shell membranes

6. Albumen (the egg white)

The albumen, making up about 70 percent of the liquid weight of the egg, is opalescent in the raw state and turns white when cooked. When beaten to a foam (meringue), the volume is increased up to 8 times. The egg yolk, about 30 percent of the egg, contains all the egg's fat and about half the protein. It also contains a higher proportion of the egg's vitamins. The chalaza is what anchors the yolk in place in the thick white. Contrary to popular misconception, the chalaza is not an embryo or an imperfection.

Egg Chemistry

The chemistry of eggs is too complex to cover in detail in this format. However, there are some points worth discussing that are helpful for the home cook. Eggs serve many purposes in recipes, ranging from emulsification to aeration. When eggs whites are whisked, they trap many millions of air bubbles, holding air and therefore lightening mixtures to which they are added. When cooked, this microscopic lattice structure sets, which stabilizes and increases the volume of the food. Many recipes are based on this unique trait, such as meringues and soufflés.

Eggs are sticky and moist, which makes them excellent binders. Ground meat is often combined with eggs (e.g., meatballs and hamburgers). Croquettes, griddle cakes, and fish cakes all call for whole eggs to bind the remaining ingredients. Omitting an egg from a crab mixture, for example, would be problematic if you are making crab cakes. Without the egg, the lean crab mixture would not hold together when the cakes are formed. A hamburger, on the other hand, may have enough fat and stickiness, in which case an egg would be superfluous. The egg's sticky property also makes it the universal undercoating onto which an outer coating can adhere, such as bread crumbs.

Whole eggs are excellent thickening agents when beaten and added to soups and sauces. The combination of the egg's protein content and textural properties thickens liquids when heated. As eggs heat, they disperse and suspend themselves in the liquid. This is the foundation of a custard or crème anglaise. If the mixture is overheated, however, the eggs will curdle, which is a scrambling of sorts. A double boiler can be helpful in this respect.

The emulsifying power of eggs is best exemplified by the miracle of mayonnaise (perhaps the inspiration for one famous brand's name?). Without eggs, mayonnaise would be oil, seasoning, and some form of acid, such as vinegar or lemon juice. When oil is slowly added to the egg while being beaten, the egg grabs and suspends the oil, changing the color, texture, and taste of the product. The acid aids in maintaining the emulsification and balances the flavors.

Color Me Brown

So many people want to know whether the color of the egg's outer shell makes a difference in the taste, quality, nutrients, or ultimate cooking properties. The answer is no. The shell color is determined by the breed of hen. Breeds with white feathers and white earlobes lay white eggs; breeds with red feathers and red earlobes lay brown eggs. Brown eggs tend to be more expensive than white eggs because they are often laid by larger birds that require more food.

Size Matters

Several factors influence egg size, including environment, hen size, hen age, and hen weight. There are six sizes in total, from big to small: jumbo, extra large, large, medium, small, and pee wee. Most of us have access, at the very least, to large or extra large eggs.

The bigger the egg does not mean the better. But size does matter when it comes to cooking and baking. Most recipes—baking in particular—call for large eggs. The minimum weight for a large egg is 2 ounces, whereas the minimum weight for an extra large egg is 2.25 ounces. So, if you casually use extra large eggs, and the recipe calls for half a dozen large eggs, you are increasing your egg quantity by almost another whole egg. When a recipe does not specify the egg size, it is best to use large eggs.

The Freshness Factor

Eggs are an appealing food for so many reasons, one of which is staying power. They last a long time without losing much of anything in quality or flavor. The packing date on the egg carton is some indicator of freshness. It usually takes about four to five days for eggs to get from the chicken to the store. If refrigerated after being purchased from a refrigerated case, eggs can be stored for up to four to five weeks. Ideally, eggs should be stored in their carton in order to insulate the eggs, maintain moisture, and avoid odor absorption. Eggs age more in one day at room temperature than in one week in the refrigerator. Fresh eggs tend to stand tall and firm in the frying pan, while older eggs tend to spread out. The more prominent the chalaza, the fresher the egg.

The Scramble Preamble

Scrambling eggs is so simple—perhaps too simple, and therefore often overlooked as an invaluable skill to master. In fact, a traditional test of a cook is whether he can roast a chicken or scramble an egg.

To scramble two eggs, break two eggs in a bowl and season with salt and pepper. Add 1 tablespoon of heavy cream or milk to make the eggs more tender (adding this dairy dilutes the protein). Mix with a fork, but do not overbeat the eggs; the goal is to combine them thoroughly, not to incorporate air. Heat 1 teaspoon of butter in a nonstick pan over medium heat. Once the pan is hot and the butter begins to bubble, pour the eggs into the pan and lower the heat. Cook the eggs, stirring constantly, until the eggs are soft, thick, and creamy. Do not overcook the eggs so they are dry and tough. Scrambled eggs should be moist, even when well done.

Scrambled Eggs Are Omelets Too

Many people have trouble making omelets. "I put the mixed eggs in the pan. The bottom cooks, but I can't get the top to ever cook." Classic mistake. An omelet is made from scrambled eggs. Yes, you scrambled the eggs, then set the omelet.

The French prefer their omelets rolled, as opposed to flat, and generally should have a completely smooth, unbrowned surface while being slightly runny in the middle. In my opinion, this is the very best way to make an omelet. Unlike scrambled eggs, the egg mixture for an omelet generally has no added dairy. But you certainly may add cream or milk, if you like. Just remember to cook omelets to order; they cannot be held successfully.

To make a rolled omelet, break three eggs into a bowl, season with salt and pepper, and mix well with a fork. Heat a nonstick 8-inch skillet over medium heat and add 1 tablespoon of butter. When the butter foams, add the eggs and let the mixture set for about 30 seconds. Then stir continuously with a fork (ideally wooden, if you have one) until the eggs are at a runny scramble stage. Spread the eggs out evenly over the surface of the pan, stop stirring, and let them set over low heat. (The point at which you stop stirring is the key to having a smooth omelet without any brown coloring.)

Place ¼ cup of filling—cheese, tomatoes, mushrooms, ham, caramelized onions—in the middle of the omelet. Fold the edge of the omelet over into itself, tilt the pan from the handle, and lightly tap the handle so that the omelet moves up from the pan. Form the omelet with a fork. Roll the omelet onto a warm plate seam-side down.

Hard Boiling Made Easy

Every cloud may have a silver lining, but no hard-boiled egg yolk should have a green ring. This common problem is easy to avoid as long as you are attentive and precise about the boiling point and cooking time. Also, remember the importance of egg size. Use older eggs, as they are much easier to peel. For large eggs, follow one of two methods.

1 Cover the egg(s) with cold water in a small pot. Bring to a rapid boil, and immediately reduce to a simmer and cook uncovered for exactly 10 minutes.

2 Cover the egg(s) with cold water in a small pot. Bring to a boil, and then immediately cover the pot with a tight-fitting lid and remove entirely from the heat. Let the eggs sit for exactly 15 minutes, then remove from the water.

In both cases, rinse the eggs in cold water before peeling to stop the eggs from cooking further and to avoid burning your hands when peeling. You will have perfect hard-boiled eggs without any trace of a green ring. The yolks will be tender and bright yellow. If soft-boiled eggs are more your taste, simply reduce the cooking time in the first method from 10 minutes to 3 minutes (medium-boiled eggs would be 5 minutes).

A fun fact: if you prick the egg shell with a sewing needle prior to cooking, it will release the air from the air cell that normally traps the egg white (albumen), which forms that flat surface during cooking.

Coddling

What is a coddled egg? Basically boiled eggs are coddled eggs—soft, medium, or hard. But many of us consider a coddled egg one that is gently cooked (the word itself implies as much) so that it remains soft and runny. In this case, you gently lower the egg into boiling water for a mere two minutes. So what in the world do you do with the egg once it's coddled? Good question.

The most common application today of coddled eggs is for caesar salad dressing. A raw egg yolk is used in this classic recipe to emulsify and add a creamy texture and flavor. Since the consumption of raw eggs is considered both dangerous and unhealthy due to salmonella, the egg is coddled to kill off such hazardous bacteria. Other than that, coddled eggs are eaten on their own, very similar to a soft-boiled egg. The difference is that the egg is cooked outside the shell in an "egg coddler," a porcelain ramekin with a tight-fitting lid that is immersed into heated water and then removed when the eggs are done for serving.

Sunny Side Up, Over Easy, Over Hard . . .

Fried eggs come many ways, but the common characteristic should be tender and tasty. Ultimately, frying eggs is easy. But it is important to remember a few key steps to ensure desirable results. First, use a non-stick skillet, or a very well-seasoned cast-iron pan or griddle. Second, make sure that the pan and the fat are hot. If the pan is not hot enough, the egg will not seize immediately and this causes sticking and prolonged cooking, which can toughen the egg white. Last, but not least, always use fresher eggs when frying. Older eggs will spread out in the pan and not hold their shape, becoming thin and loose.

Fried eggs are cooked in stages: sunny side up, over easy (runny yolk), over medium (soft yolk), and over hard (firm yolk). Once the butter (or any other fat that appeals to you . . . bacon drippings are delicious) is melted over a medium heat and the pan is hot, crack the egg directly into the pan, holding it as close to the bottom of the pan as possible so that the egg does not spread out too much. Once the egg hits the hot pan, the white seizes and its shape sets. Season with salt and pepper, then lower the heat to medium-low so that the eggs are cooked more gently to ensure tenderness.

A sunny-side-up egg is cooked on one side until the whites are firm and the yolk is runny, about 4 to 6 minutes. The whites can be basted with the hot fat, or the egg can be steamed by adding a few drops of water to the pan and then covered with a lid (a technique often used at diners on the griddle); this will also contribute to cooking the yolk without touching the cooking surface.

If you want to turn the eggs, carefully flip them using a spatula once the whites have set. For over-easy eggs, cook for a mere 30 seconds or so, just long enough for a thin film to form over the yolk without coloration. For over-medium eggs, cook for about 1 minute, or until the yolk develops a thick skin. For over-hard eggs, cook for 1 to 2 minutes, or until the yolk is firm and golden brown.

The Poaching Coach

Poaching is probably one of the more difficult ways to prepare eggs, but also one of the more delicate and elegant. Unlike hard-boiled eggs, fresh eggs make the best poached eggs because the eggs whites hold their shape better (so does adding vinegar to the water, which is a standard technique in poaching eggs).

To poach eggs, combine 2 quarts water with ¼ cup distilled white vinegar in a large saucepan and bring to a boil. Keep the eggs very cold, until you are ready to drop them into the water, since cold raw albumen will contract when it hits the hot water, allowing it to hold its shape better. Eggs should be poached in simmering water, but the first egg can go into boiling water because its cold temperature will help to cool the poaching liquid.

You can poach many eggs at once, but is easiest to poach one egg at a time. Crack an egg into a small ramekin. Using a spatula or wooden spoon, briskly swirl the inside of the pan to make a vortex in the center of the hot water. As the vortex is at full speed, drop the cracked egg into the water positioning the ramekin as close to the water as possible. Continue stirring the keep the vortex going until the egg's shape has formed. The vortex will force the egg white to encase the yolk, forming a spherical shape. Also, once the outer egg white has formed and hardened a bit, the egg will not stick to the bottom of the pan.

Cook the egg for about 3 minutes. Monitor the water temperature to ensure that the egg poaches at a bare simmer and adjust the heat accordingly. Boiling water will make tough and rubbery whites. Remove the egg with a slotted spoon and gently press the egg with your finger to test its doneness. Poached eggs should have set whites and runny yolks.

When the egg is cooked to your liking, gently plunge into a bowl of ice water, which rinses off the vinegar and stops the eggs from cooking further, much like shocking vegetables. Once the egg is cold, trim off any excess with a paring knife and place it in a bowl of fresh water in the refrigerator.

Repeat the process for each egg until you have all the eggs you need for service. When you are ready to serve the poached eggs (think Eggs Benedict for six at an elegant brunch!), simply lower them with a slotted spoon into salted simmering water for about 1 minute to make them hot and seasoned. Once they have been reheated, drain them on paper towels before serving.

More Tips for Cooking with Eggs

Here are a few more fun facts so that you get what you expect when cooking or baking with eggs:

- Hard-cook eggs that are at least one week old; you will find them easier to peel after cooking and cooling them than fresher eggs.

- Egg whites beat to a higher volume when left at room temperature for at least 15 minutes.

- Eggs are easier to separate when they are cold.

- To tell if an egg is raw or hard-cooked, spin it. If the egg spins easily, it is hard-cooked. If it wobbles, it is raw.

- If you accidentally drop an egg on the floor, sprinkle it heavily with salt for easy cleanup.

Index

F

About the Author

LAUREN BRAUN COSTELLO developed her craft in the kitchens and classrooms of some of the world's most renowned chefs, and as the owner and Executive Chef of Gotham Caterers in New York City.

Today, Lauren is an author, food stylist, and culinary instructor who has gained both local and national media exposure. Her recipes and party-planning advice have appeared in the *Los Angeles Times*, and she has made several television appearances over the years on WNBC's *Today* in New York and *News 4 You*. Lauren's food styling has been featured in various national and local television broadcasts, including segments for ABC's *The View*, *The Early Show* on CBS, and Fox & Friends.

Laura is also the author of *Notes on Cooking: A Short Guide to an Essential Craft* (June 2009, RCR Creative Press). Chef Daniel Boulud says that in *Notes on Cooking*, Lauren and her coauthor "bring you indispensable advice, experience, and know-how of many great chefs." He hails the book as "both inspirational and practical, and a superb addition to the library of any passionate cook." *Today* show health expert and nutritionist Joy Bauer says, "I've always been blown away by Lauren's culinary creations. In *The Competent Cook*, she teaches basic cooking methods that will maximize nutrition and flavor."

Lauren was also the author of a weekly cooking column entitled "The Competent Cook," which appeared on CDKitchen.com. She has served as a recipe tester, most notably for the 75th anniversary edition of the *Joy of Cooking* cookbook, working with a team of chefs to test and develop recipes. Prior to her culinary pursuits, she enjoyed a successful career on Wall Street in corporate communications, managing the employee newsletters and intranet sites of Prudential Securities, Goldman Sachs, and Société Générale.

Lauren holds a BA from Colgate University and earned a Grand Diploma in Culinary Arts with distinction from the French Culinary Institute (FCI). While studying at FCI, she was named a recipient of the Les Dames d'Escoffier scholarship.

She lives in New York City with her husband Sean, son Jonathan, and Portuguese Water Dog Bogart.

Praise for "Notes on Cooking"

"Concise, focused, and sensible . . . full of useful advice."
   —Jacques Pépin, Chef, Cookbook Author, and PBS-TV Cooking
      Series Host

"Every cookbook should have this short book as a preface. The message and guidance of this book is invaluable to all who dare to enter the delicious world of food preparation."
   —Lidia Matticchio Bastianich, Host, *Lidia's Italy*

"I wish *Notes on Cooking* had been written about 35 years ago, when I started cooking professionally. It is an excellent source of level-headed, practical, and essential advice; indispensable and wonderfully succinct."
   —Michael Romano, Chef, Union Square Hospitality Group

"An abundance of tips, ideas, and caveats. The list of food adjectives is one I'll refer to myself and the list of recommendations is indispensable. The food pairings are the most insightful I've ever seen. Work well done."
   —James Peterson, Five-Time James Beard Award Winner

"I love the short statements that lead to long reflections. They bring me back to basics that pare away the 'nonsense' in the kitchen . . . Listen to the common sense of *Notes on Cooking* and you will find yourself a happier cook."
   —Dorothy Hamilton, Founder & CEO, The French Culinary Institute

"This practical guide is an easy, amusing read for home cooks and professionals."
   —*New York Times*

"Beginning home cooks: This is your lucky day. Old kitchen dogs: We all can learn new tricks—or stand for some brushing up. This is one book we all can chew on for the rest of our cooking lives."
   —*Washington Post*

Praise for "Notes on Cooking"

"This little book is perfect for leafing through at random or zeroing in on any subject you might have questions about. In either case, it is very likely to accomplish two goals devoutly to be wished: to improve the food you cook, and to make cooking it more fun. Even if you think you know it all, *Notes on Cooking* is likely to have some ideas that will make you a better cook."
    —*Gourmet Magazine*

"My favorite new book on cooking has no recipes . . . concise . . . witty . . . brilliant."
    —*Food & Wine Magazine*

"This is a unique book that will be appreciated by any foodie and would make a lovely host or hostess gift . . . a very useful, highly enjoyable collection of tips for any cook."
    —About.com

"This small primer delivers both practical and philosophical advice beyond what one will find in a cookbook. Useful and valuable . . . a delightful culinary resource."
    —*Library Journal*, Starred Review

Anyone who's ever wielded a whisk or screwed up a sauté will find this book both tantalizing and indispensable."
    —*Booklist*

"In all ways to-the-point, Costello and Reich . . . lay down the major rules of cooking and kitchen conduct in as few as a couple of lines . . . Strong declarations that, once learned by heart, make cooking easier and end with better food."
    —*Publishers Weekly*